CLEVELAND SPORTS LEGENDS

THE 20 MOST GLORIOUS AND GUT-WRENCHING MOMENTS OF ALL TIME

BOB DYER

GRAY & COMPANY, PUBLISHERS • CLEVELAND

Gray & Company, Publishers
1588 E. 40th St.
Cleveland, OH 44103

Library of Congress Cataloging-in-Publication Data
Dyer, Bob.
Cleveland sports legends : the 20 most glorious and
gut-wrenching moments of all time / Bob Dyer.
1. Sports—Ohio—Cleveland—History. I. Title.
GV584.5.C58D94 2003
796'.09771'32—dc22   2003022507

ISBN 1-886228-73-6

Printed in the United States of America

First Printing

To the memory of Grandpa Dyer, who led me into that massive horseshoe down by the lake, bought me a hot dog and a program, and pointed out the guy in the orange helmet wearing Number 32.

To the memory of Grandpa Schellentrager, whose obsession with golf I could not initially understand, but whose dedication to the game taught me that excellence isn't free.

To Dad and my late Mom, who drove me all over Northeast Ohio to play and watch sports—and who loved me enough to provide childhood discipline. One of their most painful punishments was doled out the day after the Browns' 1964 title game, when I was not allowed to watch a television replay of the victory because of some now-forgotten childhood indiscretion. They knew the punishment would hurt me deeply, but only temporarily. In the long run, they knew, it would make me a stronger person.

Maybe even strong enough to become a lifelong Cleveland sports fan.

THE TOP 20 MOMENTS
IN CLEVELAND SPORTS HISTORY

#20 **Apr. 7, 1946**: Little-known Akron golfer Herman Keiser beats legend Ben Hogan to win Masters despite Augusta National's dirty tricks.

#19 **June 4, 1974**: Indians stage "Beer Night" promotion that tanks.

#18 **May 15, 1981**: Len Barker pitches perfect game for the Tribe.

#17 **Feb. 22, 1912**: Johnny Kilbane wins World Featherweight Championship and is welcomed home by 200,000 ecstatic Clevelanders.

#16 **Oct. 3, 1993**: Last baseball game at Cleveland Stadium draws sell-out crowd that celebrates its shared history with tearful farewell.

#15 **Sep. 5, 1949**: Hugely popular National Air Races halted after plane crashes into house in Berea.

#14 **Sept. 29, 1954**: "The Catch" by Willie Mays stuns Indians and sets tone for World Series defeat.

#13 **Apr. 17, 1960**: Indians trade Rocky Colavito, biggest box-office star in their history.

#12 **Apr. 8, 1975**: Frank Robinson homers in his first at-bat as the first African-American manager in baseball history.

#11 **Jan. 17, 1988**: Browns appear ready to even score with Denver until "The Fumble."

#10 **Oct. 12, 1920**: Indians win World Series in spite of late-season death of their shortstop.

#9 **Oct. 17, 1995**: Kenny Lofton's dash home from second base on a passed ball propels Indians to their first World Series in four decades.

#8 **May 7, 1989**: Michael Jordan knocks out Cavs with "The Shot."

#7 **Jan. 11, 1987**: Browns are five minutes from Super Bowl when John Elway engineers "The Drive."

#6 **Jan. 4, 1981**: Browns drop playoff game on "Red Right 88."

#5 **Oct. 26, 1997**: Indians are two outs from winning first World Series in 49 years but blow Game Seven.

#4 **Apr. 29, 1976**: Cavaliers stage "the Miracle of Richfield."

#3 **Nov. 6, 1995**: Art Modell moves the Browns to Baltimore.

#2 **Oct. 4, 1948**: Indians win first one-game playoff in American League history; go on to take World Series.

#1 **Dec. 27, 1964**: Browns upset heavily favored Baltimore Colts to win NFL title.

CONTENTS

"Cleveland sports fans are 90 percent scar tissue."

— Chris Rose, Fox Sports Television

INTRODUCTION

THE QUOTE ON THE previous page was uttered in January 2003 at a big sports fundraiser at the Renaissance Cleveland Hotel on Public Square. More than 1,100 fans heard the remark after venturing out on a frigid Thursday night to mingle with famous sports figures in the Grand Ballroom.

The minimum ticket price was $250. Nearly half the crowd paid $500, the amount required to upgrade to the roster of "Heavy Hitters," enabling a donor to schmooze at an open-bar cocktail party with wall-to-wall celebrities. Such is the drawing power of athletes.

Among those in attendance were millionaires and even a billionaire—Randy Lerner, son of the late Browns owner, Al Lerner. The senior Lerner had ranked 67th on *Forbes* magazine's list of the richest people in the world. But in this crowd, the Lerner name was almost a footnote.

Jim Brown, the biggest icon in the history of Cleveland sports, was in the house. So was Bob Feller, the Hall of Fame pitcher. So was an active Cleveland quarterback, Tim Couch, accompanied by a former Playmate of the Year, Heather Kozar. Ohio State running back Maurice Clarett, from Youngstown, and coach Jim Tressel, from Berea, came to talk about winning the national championship. Don King, he of the electric hairdo, the machine-gun prattle, and the Cleveland roots, was off on his usual rants. Also milling about were folks like Austin Carr and Brian Brennan and Wayne Embry and Campy Russell and Joe Charboneau and Dick Schafrath and Bobby Mitchell and LeBron James.

When the moderator, Chris Rose, stood up and delivered his quip about scar tissue, the crowd roared. Little wonder. It's a great line, the almost-perfect summation of sports on the North Coast, where championships have been scarcer than palm trees.

Just ask Brian Sipe. Sipe, one of the best quarterbacks in a half-century of Cleveland football, told me five years after retiring to his hometown of San Diego that when he thinks of his days in Cleveland, his first thoughts are of failure. This from a guy who held—and still holds—most of the team's all-time passing records, a guy whose house contains the NFL's 1980 MVP trophy. It's a sad commentary.

But let's not forget about the other 10 percent of the Cleveland sports fan, the part that is free of scar tissue. That small, unblemished surface is a powerful force, indeed. It can keep us up late into the night, honking our horns in parking garages and exchanging high-fives with total strangers on East Ninth Street. It can induce us to trudge down to the edge of Lake Erie when the wind chill matches the IQ of a dead carp. That same 10 percent tricks us into putting on dog masks and drawing elaborate banners on bedsheets and spending ridiculous amounts of money on souvenirs. That amazing 10 percent is even strong enough to make us want to pass along to our offspring tales of long-ago players and games.

The vibe at the banquet had little to do with scar tissue. It had everything to do with celebrating our shared experience, of reveling in our communal sports history. It is a history that helps us define who we are, that differentiates us not only from the people in places like San Diego but from those in other Midwest cities our size. And that's the real story of Cleveland sports.

To grow up in Northeast Ohio is to have a unique vocabulary. Even if you weren't alive in 1981—and 35 percent of today's sports fans were not—you still know the term "Red Right 88," just as you know "The Drive," "The Fumble," and "The Shot." In Northeast Ohio, the phrase "diminishing skills" is a secret code that eludes outsiders. We also know exactly what someone means when he or she says "1948" or "1954" or "1995" or "1997" or—Hallelujah!—"1964."

For the purposes of this book, those particular years were no-brainers. But after the first dozen selections, things got a little dicey. In compiling the list, I was forced to reject a bundle of highly significant events. Compelling arguments could be mounted for half a dozen that do not appear.

So how did I come up with this particular list? I asked a number of fans what moments lingered in their memories, what moments they continued to talk about. But in the end, the final decisions came down to sheer personal taste.

This could have been done scientifically, perhaps by setting up a computer model and assigning various weightings to factors such as attendance, the size of newspaper archives, or the amount of time spent on a subject on talk shows. But what fun would that be? We don't need no stinkin' computers. That would be like doing away with baseball umpires and substituting some sort of laser contraption to call balls and strikes. A true sports fan wouldn't stand for it.

Therefore, I expect you to disagree with some of this list, maybe even a lot of it.

No chapter on Jesse Owens, a guy whose prowess in track and field carried international import? Well, Jesse went to high school here, but he was born in Alabama and his biggest accomplishments took place far from Cleveland in an age when there was no radio or TV coverage. His greatest day didn't even come in the United States. Jesse's triumphant moment in Hitler's Germany was not unique to Cleveland, nor even shared by Clevelanders at the time it happened. Jesse is simply not provincial enough. He's not a *Cleveland* sports legend, but an *American* sports legend.

Why not Max Schmeling's big heavyweight title fight at the Cleveland Stadium in 1931? Why not the end of Joe DiMaggio's incredible 56-game hitting streak at the hands of the Indians in 1941? Or Jack Nicklaus winning the PGA Championship at Canterbury in 1973 to break Bobby Jones's record for wins in majors? How about Tiger Woods sticking a 168-yard eight-iron next to the 18th pin in near-darkness to win $1 million at Firestone Country Club in the summer of 2000?

Well, those noteworthy feats were done right here, but they weren't done by our guys. Woods is from California, lives in Florida, and plays 95 percent of his tournaments somewhere other than here. DiMaggio was a Yankee, for heaven's sake. Anyone who grew up in Cleveland in the 1950s and '60s would sooner chew pine tar than write extensively about a New York Yankee. This book is provincialism at its finest. And *prooouuud* of it.

Okay, I hear you. Bob Feller lived in Cleveland for more than half of the 20th century and you don't have a chapter about his no-hitters, not even the one he fired on Opening Day of 1940? No-hitters are great. But they're not perfect. In the modern era, no-hitters outnumber perfect games 20 to 1. So Len Barker edges Rapid Robert.

No 1950 Browns? Yes, winning the NFL title the first year out of the All-America Football Conference was highly impressive. But don't forget that professional football didn't really come of age until the Colts–Giants championship game of 1958. The attendance at the 1950 title game, held at Cleveland Stadium, was a mere 29,751.

At first glance, the firing of Paul Brown seems to be a glaring omission. But that 1963 trauma has been folded into the chapter about an even more shocking move by Art Modell, the move to Baltimore.

The big charity high school football games at the stadium? The big Soap Box Derby series in Akron? Close. No cigar.

No LeBron? Maybe some day. Not yet.

My final list of local legends is from the gut, the same gut that tells me with certainty that there was no better football player—ever—than Jim Brown. In fact, Brown would serve quite nicely as the embodiment of Cleveland sports.

At the time of the 2003 banquet, he had aged remarkably well. When JB took the stage to collect a Lifetime Achievement Award only three weeks shy of his 67th birthday, he looked 37. The shoulders were still broad, and they still tapered quickly to a narrow waist. The neck was still as thick as any oak at Lake View Cemetery. The gaze was still steely. The man still had a presence. You looked at him and figured he could still take anyone in the room. And people were still fascinated. Even fellow sports stars turned and stared when the old fullback walked in.

Big Jim has his faults, and they've been well documented. But, like Cleveland's well-documented athletic woes, the bad stuff is far overshadowed by the pleasant memories stashed in the special files of our minds where we keep material that is not central to our existence but helps make us who we are. It is my hope that this book will enhance those memories and perhaps even draw the generations a bit closer together.

JOHNNY MARCHES HOME

THURSDAY, FEBRUARY 22, 1912

In an era when boxing was king, a little guy from the West Side, the son of a blind man, stunned the boxing world by winning the World Featherweight Title from a fighter who had held it for more than a decade. The welcome-home parade for Johnny Kilbane brought out a wild crowd of 200,000 ecstatic Clevelanders.

AS THE 19TH CENTURY turned into the 20th and European immigrants continued to flood into Cleveland, every neighborhood had at least one little guy you didn't want to mess with. The Irish enclave had two. Both of them were named Kilbane. But they weren't related, and they didn't much care for each other.

Johnny Kilbane and Tommy Kilbane grew up one street apart in a tough West Side neighborhood known as "the Angle." Residents of the Angle worked mostly on Whiskey Island, where iron ore and other cargo was unloaded from ships and transferred to land transportation—mules in the early years, then later trains and trucks.

The island had been artificially created in 1825 by civil engineers who straightened the mouth of the Cuyahoga River to smooth the way for commerce. The old riverbed, which curved to the west, suddenly was dry, and that angled piece of new land was quickly gobbled up by Whiskey Islanders, mostly hard-drinking dockworkers who slapped together crude, tiny houses.

It was a good time and place to be handy with your fists. The city was growing rapidly as the age of industrialization came into full swing. Nearly a third of the population was made up of people who were born in another country, and friction was the norm. Nationalism among the Irish was particularly strong, fired by the continued refusal of England to let Ireland manage its own affairs.

Finding a job in Cleveland wasn't terribly difficult, but the work was tough and the pay and conditions were usually lousy. Labor unions were beginning to thrive.

A decade into the new century, strikes and riots seemed to be breaking out all over the Western world—textile workers in Massachusetts, gold miners in Russia, cab drivers in Paris, coal miners in Germany and London and Cleveland.

The people who owned Cleveland's factories were already beginning to move their homes farther from the central city. Eleven years into the new century, a couple of brothers incorporated a place called Shaker Village, about six miles east of downtown, and were planning a big, upper-class housing development on land once populated by a sect of Christian communists.

The growing inequities between owners and workers bred growing resentment. Struggling immigrants needed to look no farther than Forest Hill, the summer retreat of John D. Rockefeller, on 700 acres of what is now East Cleveland and Cleveland Heights.

Rockefeller was the wealthiest man in the world. At the turn of the century, he constructed a nine-hole golf course at Forest Hill. That was the height of sporting decadence, because, in those days, golf was perceived as some kind of weird British affair that hardly anyone played.

Cleveland's upper crust also was indulging in another odd British pursuit, chasing foxes around on horseback. The Chagrin Valley Hunt Club was founded for that purpose in 1908.

Back in the working-class neighborhoods, people began to view the sport of boxing as a way out, a ticket to riches and fame, in much the same way that many African-American kids viewed basketball a century later.

Basketball was a nonentity in those days, and football was so new that organizers were still tweaking its fundamental rules. Not until 1912 was the length of the field changed from 110 yards to 100, the number of downs changed from three to four, and the number of points awarded for a touchdown changed from five to six.

The Irish quest was complicated by the fact that boxing was technically illegal in Ohio from 1830 to 1923. The enthusiasm with which that ban was enforced in Cleveland depended greatly upon the philosophy of the person who occupied the mayor's office at any particular time.

When do-gooders held sway, much of the boxing action was relegated to Whiskey Island, where "normal" folks didn't go. Many of those bouts consisted of liquored-up dockworkers trying to settle scores.

Johnny Kilbane started that way, and no wonder. When he was six years old, his father lost his eyesight, and the boy had to drop out of school after the sixth grade to get a job and help support his family. By age 17, he was working as a switchtender on the NY, P&O Railroad. He was in charge of a big switch at the center of the yard where more than half a dozen tracks came together. But he spent much of his time walking around shadowboxing. On summer evenings, he would throw jabs at the moths that were drawn to the light of his lantern.

Although Kilbane was not exactly an intimidating presence, weighing all of 90 pounds, people who crossed him found out the hard way that he was incredibly quick and not the least bit reluctant to mix it up.

That same year, a well-known boxer named Jimmy Dunn began training nearby. Johnny watched Jimmy spar and caught the boxing bug. He became friends with Dunn, a lightweight who had moved to Cleveland from Newcastle, Pennsylvania. Johnny badgered the fighter to show him the ropes. Dunn gave him lessons at his gym, at West 25th and Franklin, and eventually became his manager.

Neither one of them had any idea at the time that within just a few years they would be the recipients of an unprecedented display of public affection that would bring 200,000 people out onto the streets of Cleveland for a wild victory celebration.

Kilbane's first pro fight took place on December 2, 1907. By then he had grown to 5-foot-5, 120 pounds—a perfect featherweight. Kilbane won his debut, a three-round affair, and happily pocketed his $1.50 purse. He won again two weeks later, then captured his third straight fight on Christmas Day with a sixth-round knockout.

On New Year's Day, Johnny squared off in Lorain against his old neighborhood nemesis, Tommy Kilbane. Tommy, about the same size as Johnny, had resented the attention Johnny was drawing in the 'hood for his boxing prowess. Having held his own in street fights, he was eager to climb inside the ropes and see what he could do.

Johnny won that first fight, a three-rounder. On February 10, they went at it again, this time in Cleveland. The four-round bout was ruled a draw. By staying even with his more famous namesake, Tommy had proven something to himself and to the neighborhood.

During the next eight months, Johnny met six other opponents without losing, setting the stage for a rematch. That took place November 25 in Cleveland. It was a war, a 25-round bout that drew a big crowd. And Johnny reasserted himself, knocking Tommy to the canvas in the 23rd round before winning by decision.

The Kilbanes didn't meet again for more than a year. Johnny started having trouble landing fights, and began working as a tree-trimmer for the city, making $1.65 per day. He told Dunn he was going to quit boxing because he just couldn't make enough money.

But Dunn talked him out of it, and Johnny managed to land 10 more fights in 1909. He disposed of most of those opponents, and developed quite a local following. Northeast Ohio boxing fans were getting hyped for his big rematch with Tommy on New Year's Eve, 1909, in Canton.

Johnny won again, again by decision, in 15 rounds. That bout launched him into regional prominence. He was invited to fight in places like Boston and Pittsburgh, and never lost. Finally, in Kansas City, he met his match: the Featherweight Champion of the World.

Abe Attell, five-foot-four, 122 pounds, had been the world champ since 1901. Although Attell grew up 2,200 miles from Kilbane's childhood home, he experienced a hauntingly similar childhood. As a Jew living in a predominantly Irish neighborhood in the South of Market district of San Francisco, Attell got into scrapes every day. And, like Kilbane, he was pressed into the workforce at an early age.

Attell's father left home when Abe was 13, and the boy took a job selling newspapers. One of the intersections where he hawked his papers was near the site of a professional boxing match. Attell watched the fight and vowed that someday he would make his living that way.

His first pro bout came only three years later, in 1900. He quickly drew the attention of boxing aficionados, knocking out 24 of his first 28 opponents. By 1901 he had a share of the featherweight title. He became the undisputed champ in 1908, and defended his belt 22 times. Attell destroyed so many featherweights that he often ventured out of his weight class, all the way up to middleweight.

He took care of Kilbane that first night, winning a 10-round decision. But Kilbane quickly got back on track, climbing into the ring 12 more times without losing—including a "no contest" decision in a non-title bout with Attell.

Kilbane wasn't knocking many people out, though. His forte was speed and skill, rather than a thundering fist. In fact, he was growing a reputation as someone lacking a knockout punch, someone who could never be a great champion.

That view changed a bit on September 15, 1911, when Johnny took out "Indian" Joe Rivers in the 16th round in California. The impressive performance led to a championship rematch with Attell, referred to in the papers as "the little Hebrew."

On February 22, 1912—four months after William Durant and Louis Chevrolet got together to form the Chevrolet Motor Company, two months after the first explorer reached the South Pole, and eight days after Arizona became the nation's 48th state—Johnny Kilbane got his second shot at the champ, at the Vernon Pavilion near Los Angeles.

A year had passed since they last met. During that time, two significant events had taken place. Attell had fought against the other Kilbane, an up-and-comer himself, and sustained a broken shoulder. That put his training on hold for several months, and may have taken away a bit of his edge.

Something even more remarkable had happened as well: at the urging of a *Plain Dealer* boxing reporter named J. P. Garvey, the Kilbane boys, who had gone to great lengths to avoid each other outside of the ring, got together and talked. They found they had plenty in common, and began to get along. In time, they clicked so well that, when Johnny began to train for his second fight with Attell, Tommy served as a sparring partner and training mate.

The sessions helped them both. Tommy had grown into a lightweight with a powerful punch, and Johnny learned from Tommy how to improve his power. Meanwhile, Johnny's speed and techniques were rubbing off on Tommy.

When Johnny headed to California for a month to train for his championship bout with Attell, Tommy went along.

The afternoon of February 22, a Thursday, is hot and steamy. A crowd of nearly 9,000 is filing into the pavilion, the biggest group ever to watch a fight in Southern California. Another 3,000 to 5,000 are turned away.

Fight fans are eager to see whether Attell still packs his usual punch. Although he's relatively young, at 28, he has fought so many times that he looks like the boxing equivalent of a demolition derby car.

This fight is scheduled for a grueling 20 rounds.

Kilbane is dressed in skintight dark trunks and black socks. Attell's trunks are so small they look like briefs. He is wearing dark, calf-length socks.

Back home in Cleveland, the whole city is holding its breath. Johnny Kilbane is no longer just a guy from the Angle. Now he is a guy from Cleveland, the nation's sixth-largest city, and the populace is pulling nearly as hard for him as it would ever pull for the Browns, Indians, or Cavaliers.

Johnny's father, having moved to Hermann Avenue near West 70th Street, is joined by a horde of relatives and friends who are awaiting bulletins from the West Coast. As each one arrives, it is read aloud to the blind man, who sits in a big chair, listening with rapt attention.

At 2 p.m. Pacific time, the bell rings and the fight is on.

Attell and Kilbane approach each other cautiously, dancing and feinting. Finally, Attell leads with a left, but misses. He comes back with another left and scores, nailing Kilbane on the mouth. They tie each other up, and the referee pulls them apart.

As they break, Kilbane drills Attell in the chin with a right hook, spinning him halfway around. Attell smiles, as if to say it didn't really hurt. After some dancing, Kilbane gets in a couple more shots, but no significant damage is done, and they're both feinting as the round ends.

In his corner, Kilbane goes into a ritual he will continue after every round. He sits on his stool, eyes closed, slumped backward, unmoving, as if he's asleep. His trainer, Dunn, is peppering him with advice and encouragement while others are dousing him with water and toweling him off.

Attell is the aggressor at the start of Round Two, but Kilbane holds him back with a left and a right uppercut. As the fighters grab each other, Kilbane slips his left hand free and smacks Attell in the mouth, drawing the first blood of the fight. Kilbane continues to score regularly until the close of the round, when Attell suddenly begins raining down rights and lefts, a flurry that is stopped only by the bell. But as the fighters return to their corners, Attell is the only one bleeding.

In Round Three, the crowd begins to turn on Attell. Early in the round, he heels Kilbane. Later he throws a head-butt. By the time he tries to elbow Kilbane in a clinch, the crowd is hissing. The round clearly belongs to Kilbane.

So does Round Four, which ends with Attell backing away from a big exchange, drawing jeers from the fans.

As the champ stands up for Round Five, his left eye is swollen nearly shut. Kilbane unleashes a bunch of jabs that land on Attell's jaw and mouth. Attell fights back with a flurry that is capped with a solid left-right combination. Standing toe to toe in the middle of the ring, they swing wildly, only grazing each other, until just before the bell, when they each connect to the chest and face.

The sixth round is nearly even. Plenty of dancing, not much connecting.

The seventh round features lots of left jabs to Attell's face, and a fair number of rights and lefts to Kilbane's stomach. By the bell, blood is running down Attell's face from a cut over his swollen eye.

Attell spends much of the eighth round trying to escape. Kilbane jabs repeatedly and scores every time—more than a dozen consecutive punches without an effective counterpunch. When Attell ducks too close, Kilbane pounds him with a left to the face that leaves the champ wobbly.

Kilbane is clearly in control as Round Nine begins. Not much damage occurs early on. Then, suddenly, after Attell lands a right hook to the jaw, the challenger unleashes a right-left combination that staggers the champ again.

In the 10th, Attell repeatedly complains to the referee that Kilbane is holding, but Attell is holding at least as much as Kilbane. He also begins to butt the challenger, and the crowd hisses.

Round Eleven is saddled with frequent clinches. On the breaks, though, Kilbane manages to score often.

Midway through Round Twelve, Kilbane is warned for holding. He nods his head to acknowledge his error, and bores in on the champion, scoring often but not strongly. The crowd is now squarely in Kilbane's corner. Many are shouting for him to knock out the champ.

The 13th round becomes notable when Attell dodges a big right by ducking through the ropes. Kilbane helps him back in, and promptly socks him in the face. Kilbane easily wins the round.

Attell is tiring noticeably as the 14th progresses. After landing one early blow, he is completely out-pointed.

Other than a left and right to Kilbane's stomach, the Cleveland man dominates the 15th. At the bell he unleashes a left that rocks the champ.

Round Sixteen is a circus. Soon after the action begins, the ref stops the fight, calls for a towel, and rubs a foreign substance from Attell's back. After the fight, Kilbane will accuse Attell of coating his back with chloroform to try to daze the challenger. Attell will claim the substance was cocoa butter, which he used to try to cool himself off. In any event, after the time-out, they go at each other with renewed enthusiasm.

Each man lands some decent shots, then Attell blatantly head-butts Kilbane, opening a big gash above his right eye. Kilbane wipes at the blood and complains to the ref, but no action is taken. So Kilbane begins to head-butt Attell all over the ring, much to the disgust of the crowd. The round ends with a flurry of shots by Kilbane to Attell's face. But now the crowd is hissing both fighters.

A reserve of adrenaline kicks in during the 17th round. The men bash each other back and forth until, during a clinch, Attell complains to the ref that Kilbane is holding. The ref's response is not a warning to Kilbane, but a warning to Attell to quit butting.

Attell is growing increasingly desperate, and tries to bear in on Kilbane, but he is rejected each time with straight lefts. As the round winds down, Kilbane throws a thundering right hand into Attell's gut, lifting him onto his toes.

Both fighters are scoring to the mouth at the start of Round Eighteen. But Kilbane soon takes control, connecting frequently with lefts. He clearly is in command—so much so, in fact, that during the 19th round, when Attell tries repeatedly to deliver a blow to his stomach, the challenger laughs.

The final round begins with the boxers shaking hands. Immediately after that token nod to good sportsmanship, Kilbane corks Attell in the mouth with a flat-footed left. Kilbane repeatedly catches Attell's punches with his left glove, and reaches the champ's face with lefts and rights. Attell, in his last-ditch effort, briefly comes to life, connecting with a left and right to the challenger's mouth. The action intensifies, but Kilbane is responsible for most of the scoring. By the end, Kilbane, still relatively fresh, is making Attell miss routinely. The decision isn't even close. The judges declare that John Patrick Kilbane is the featherweight champion of the world.

The referee raises Johnny Kilbane's hand above his head, and his fans stream into the ring to congratulate him. The entire canvas is jammed with people, some of whom put the little Clevelander on their shoulders and carry him to his locker room and on into boxing history.

Kilbane pocketed $3,500 for his efforts (about 40 grand in today's money) and wasted little time in further capitalizing on his newfound glory. He told reporters he wouldn't be back to Cleveland for about a month because he was going to explore his options in the entertainment industry.

Modern sports heroes get TV gigs; in 1912, they got vaudeville shows. The week after the fight, Kilbane opened a seven-day engagement at a Los Angeles playhouse. He was looking at an offer to do the same in Chicago. But he wasn't leaving L.A. until after he served as a cornerman for Tommy Kilbane.

Johnny also agreed to a photo shoot by a Los Angeles company that paid him $2,000 for one session. He was quite photogenic for a boxer. His blue eyes sparkled, and his smile was infectious and also, somehow, still intact. From the front, his battered nose looked reasonably healthy. And, as the *Plain Dealer* put it, his "every action [was] peppery, effervescent, indicative of a lightning brain and panther body."

In early March, Kilbane began a one-week engagement at a San Francisco playhouse. The money was flowing. He was in no hurry to defend his title and take the risk of cutting off his financial geyser.

The new champ wasn't above a bit of gloating. The day after the fight, he said he didn't work as hard against Attell as he worked every day in training camp. He said he didn't think Attell deserved a rematch because of his dirty tricks. Besides, he scoffed, "the public knows Attell would stand no chance with me, and that would hurt the gate."

Those comments triggered a doubled-barreled blast by a writer for the *New York American*: "Not unlike a few titleholders, Kilbane is becoming offensive to the public. The latter supports fighting, and always loves to string with a winner. When a one-day champion, made such by a twist of fate, belittles one who was a marvel for 11 years, it is rather disgusting. Kilbane will receive proper appreciation only after he does more than beat a boy who stood them all, small and large, on their heads for many years."

In boxing circles, Kilbane was drawing raves for his speed and technique. The referee, Eyton, said the new champ was the fastest man he had ever seen. But Eyton also said he had noticed a significant drop-off in Attell's game. "He seemed at times to be nailed to the floor," Eyton said.

The ref didn't expect Attell to be as fast on his feet as Kilbane, but he was shocked that the defending champ wasn't better with his hands. "I had given him credit for being the more clever of the two in this respect. He failed utterly, however, to live up to his reputation. There was not a round except two in which Kilbane was not far in the lead. In fact, out of the entire 20, Abe was entitled to but two."

For Attell, the fight was a disaster. Not only had he lost the crown, he had severely damaged his image with his desperate dirty tricks, the butting, grabbing, and heeling. Nor did Attell win any new admirers with a sour-grapes post-fight interview in which he ridiculed Kilbane's evasive style and claimed the ref had "robbed" him.

According to Henry P. Edwards, writing in the *Plain Dealer*, Attell's outburst was "the cheap excuse of a beaten man, a man beaten from every angle, a man who was outboxed, outpunched, outgamed and outgeneraled, a man who never had a real chance to win from the time he crawled through the ropes until Referee Charles Eyton raised Kilbane's hand aloft, indicative of victory. The detailed description of the contest shows that Johnny landed 105 blows on Attell's head, face, and jaw, and escaped with but 23 in return, and light taps at that.

"From the third or fourth round on, the ex-champion was bleeding from the mouth and eye, while Johnny went through the entire bout without a mark—with the exception of the gash inflicted when Attell deliberately butted him with his head. The chances are that Attell, seeing he was doomed to defeat, sought to lose the decision on a foul. Johnny's margin, however, was so great that Referee Eyton allowed the bout to continue to the finish."

The city's newspapers were choked with fight-related stories and illustrations for weeks. One edition carried a drawing of two torsos with numbers that corresponded to how many blows had landed in various locations. Numerous stories retraced Kilbane's life and the lives of his associates. Editorials praised him. Cartoonists joined in the fun too.

The owner of the Cleveland Naps, the professional baseball team that played in League Park, half-jokingly said he was disappointed in Kilbane's victory because he wanted to be the man to bring the first championship to Cleveland. He said he was consoling himself with the notion that "such things go in threes."

Right. In Cleveland's case, maybe three centuries.

Professional wrestling—legitimate wrestling—was big during the era, too. Alongside all the boxing news were breathless reports about the "clever grapplers" who were going to meet at Gray's Armory. But Kilbane's victory was unprecedented. On February 25, the *Plain Dealer* declared:

> Clevelanders are provincial in sporting affairs and they are glad of it, for such a fault, if it is a fault, gives them a chance to enthuse and demonstrate that red blood flows in their veins. That Clevelanders are provincial was shown most clearly by the great interest manifested in the victory of Johnny Kilbane over Abe Attell, the triumph carrying with it the featherweight championship of the ring.
>
> The two leading titles in fistiana are the heavy and lightweight honors. Kilbane is neither, yet. [But] Cleveland made just as much of a fuss and will continue to do so as if he had whipped Jack Johnson. . . .
>
> [Clevelanders] will enthuse to an even greater degree when Kilbane returns to the tune *When Johnny Comes Marching Home*. Have the band out? You know it. We will have several bands out, and Johnny's admirers, from Patsy Lavelle, the legless newsboy, to Mayor Baker, will be there to congratulate the boy who brought home Cleveland's first boxing championship. . . .
>
> The time may come when Cleveland may become ennuied with championships as have Chicago, Detroit, New York and Philadelphia; but until that time, the residents of the Forest City are going to make the most of the one championship they do possess.

Sound familiar?

The former champion had been a heavy favorite among both serious and casual bettors. Among the more casual wagers was one placed by two residents of the Lincoln Hotel in downtown Cleveland.

Neither had much money, but both were boxing fanatics and wanted to put a significant wager on their favorite. So they agreed that the loser would roll a peanut from their hotel to Public Square using a 15-pound crowbar.

The *Plain Dealer* turned out to document the payoff. A fellow named Clarence Webb placed his peanut in the middle of Ontario Street and carefully pushed it along, sometimes through ice, slush, and mud. He made it to St. Clair before the peanut got stuck in the trolley tracks. He pried it out and continued on, but the peanut didn't last as long as he did. It was accidentally crushed, as was the next one and the next one. Webb was working on his sixth peanut when he finally arrived at the square, one hour after the journey began.

Soon, Johnny Kilbane would appear in that same square in front of so many people that they would all look like peanuts.

The welcome-home bash was held, appropriately enough, on St. Paddy's Day, a Sunday. Although the *Titanic* had sunk two days earlier in the North Atlantic, the mood in Cleveland was absolutely joyous. Women along the parade route were so happy they cried at the sight of Johnny Kilbane holding his baby in one hand and a flag in the other.

Reports called it the largest gathering in Cleveland's history, in the neighborhood of 200,000, bigger than the turnout for any president—bigger, even, than the throng that had lined the streets to witness the funeral procession the year before of legendary five-term mayor Tom Johnson.

The fun began at Union Station, an aging train depot on the lakeshore between West Sixth and West Ninth streets. Police had cleared the area where Kilbane's train was to arrive, but people were so excited when they saw him that they rushed forward and crushed a wooden partition.

As Kilbane slowly worked his way outside to an automobile, in which he would ride with his wife, his two-year-old daughter, and his manager, Dunn, he saw thousands of people on the streets and hillsides.

Police on horseback cleared the path to Public Square, where the parade was to begin. A number of other cars lined up behind Kilbane's. They carried his father, other relatives, close friends, and in-laws.

The crush of humanity brought streetcars to a halt, and men climbed on top of them for a better view. Vendors did a brisk business in green flags and green carnations.

At the square, an excited eight-year-old boy ran across Superior Avenue to get a closer look at the fighter and was hit by a car, which ran over him and left him badly injured. As police began to rush him to Lakeside Hospital, he pleaded with them to stay: "Don't take me away! I want to see Johnny! He will go by and I won't see him!"

The boy was unconscious by the time he reached the hospital, and later died.

At a bowling alley in the Angle, mishandled fireworks were blamed for an explosion and fire that resulted in half a dozen injuries.

With those notable exceptions, the parade along Detroit Avenue was a love-fest that extended all the way to West 75th Street, near Kilbane's father's house. People sat on their roofs. People cheered and applauded. Men threw their hats in the air. Kilbane's eyes watered at the realization of how popular he had become.

Even the mayor, Newton D. Baker, dispensed with his rule against making public appearances on Sundays and reviewed the parade from a stand in front of city hall. His wife and young children were there, too, and his kids exchanged waves with Kilbane's little girl as the procession passed.

When the parade neared its end, so many people were jammed into the neighborhood that Johnny was shepherded out of town for an hour so police could disperse the crowd. A throng standing right outside his father's house turned the lawn to mud. After nightfall, the boxer sneaked back to a quiet family gathering. Among family, the excitement over his presence was rivaled by that over his daughter, Mary Coletta, who was just beginning to stand up on her own.

Johnny Kilbane was stunned by the enthusiasm of his reception, far more stunned than he had been by any punch thrown by Abe Attell. Perhaps he should have gotten a hint of the fervor as his train passed though western Ohio. He had been cheered through the train windows by hundreds of gawkers at depots in Toledo, Sandusky, and Elyria.

Part of the young man's appeal was the fact that he appeared to be a good husband and father and didn't hang out, like many boxers did, in pool halls and bars.

Kilbane's popularity had legs. Long after he quit boxing, well after he bought a gym and worked as a boxing referee, he went into politics and was elected clerk of courts for Cleveland.

The boy from the Angle held on to his title for 12 years, longer than any featherweight in history. Although he fought regularly—averaging a dozen bouts per year for the next six years—he was reluctant to put his title on the line. Only seven times in those 12 years was a fight designated as a title bout.

In 1918, at the climax of the World War (as they naively referred to it in those days), Kilbane spent a year as a boxing instructor for the Army. He returned to the ring the following year, but gradually slowed his pace. After he didn't fight at all in 1922, the boxing authorities threatened to strip him of his title if he didn't get back into action. So finally, on June 2, 1923, for $75,000 (about $825,000 in modern dollars), he put his crown on the line at the Polo Grounds in New York.

His opponent was Eugene Criqui, a French hero who had been severely injured during the war. Criqui had healed sufficiently to knock Kilbane out in the sixth round. Kilbane was now 34, and out of gas.

Cleveland's greatest boxer didn't fight again until a three-round exhibition in 1943—refereed by Abe Attell.

WASHING THE BLACK SOX

TUESDAY, OCTOBER 12, 1920

One season after the Black Sox tanked the World Series, a Cleveland Indians' roster full of good guys helped repair the game's image. The Tribe not only won the first World Series in Cleveland history, but did it just a couple of months after losing their star shortstop, Ray Chapman, who was killed by a fastball to the skull.

AT THE START OF A DECADE that would come to be known as the Roaring Twenties, the city of Cleveland was firing on all cylinders. It was the fifth-largest city in the United States, and jobs were growing on trees. Changes—big changes—seemed to be arriving as often as the streetcars that plied the city's many rails.

The powerful Van Sweringen brothers were in full swing. Their upscale housing development, Shaker Heights, was a smash hit. So was their rapid-transit line, which carried well-to-do professionals from the East Side to their work downtown. Now, with overflowing wallets, "the Vans," as they were called, were ready to make their biggest mark of all.

For some time, the city had been trying to replace the dilapidated Union Terminal on the lakefront. City leaders also were trying to figure out a way to draw all of the competing train companies together under one roof. World War I had put the debate on hold. But soon after the war ended, the Vans managed to push through a radical new plan.

On 35 rundown, crime-infested acres at the southwest corner of
Public Square, they were going to build not only a new train terminal but a huge office tower.

The square had been in steady decline as businesses moved east-
ward along glamorous Euclid Avenue. But the Vans' rapid-transit
line ended at Public Square, and they were eager to rejuvenate the
area.

Complicating their effort was the fact that the 35-acre tract was
anything but abandoned. More than 2,000 separate buildings stood
on the land between the square and the Cuyahoga River, housing as
many as 15,000 people, and all of the structures would have to be
demolished.

Throughout 1920, the downtown was filled with the dust and
noise of falling walls—some of them belonging to historic buildings.
Among the ramshackle houses and stores were a number of gems:
three old hotels, two breweries, the headquarters of Ohio Bell Telephone, and the old Central Police Station. Entire streets disappeared, including one called Diebolt's Alley that was famous for its
restaurants. Three aging cemeteries were in the way as well. The
bodies were dug up and transferred elsewhere.

Cleveland's baseball company was in flux too. Only five years earlier, the team had changed its name. The former name, the Cleveland Naps, no longer worked because it was drawn from the first
name of longtime manager and star Napoleon Lajoie. As Lajoie's
Hall of Fame career wound down and the 1914 Naps imploded, losing 102 games, he was unceremoniously dumped by an owner who
was struggling financially. Another victim of cost-cutting was a hard-
hitting outfielder named "Shoeless Joe" Jackson. Jackson was sent to
Chicago for three players and a pile of cash.

That winter, a new owner, "Sunny Jim" Dunn, took over. The
new guy had money. And he spent enough of it to start turning things
around. For the 1916 season, Dunn picked up superstar Tris Speaker,
who had been in a contract dispute with Boston. The Tribe sent the
Red Sox two players and $55,000. The acquisition of Speaker was a
thrill for the fans, who had suffered through 14 consecutive years of
lousy American League baseball.

Clearly, the team needed a new name to go with its new direction.
Dunn turned the task over to the city's top sportswriters. They settled on "Indians," a name used 20 years earlier when Cleveland was
a member of the National League. The writers not only liked the his-

torical tie-in, but also figured the name would celebrate the career of
Louis Sockalexis, who starred briefly for the team in the late 1890s.
The *Plain Dealer* reported on January 18, 1915:

> Many years ago, there was an Indian named Sockalexis
> who was the star of the Cleveland baseball club. As bat-
> ter, fielder, and baserunner, he was a marvel. Sockalexis
> so far outshone his teammates that he naturally came to
> be regarded as the whole team. The fans through the
> country began to call the Clevelands the "Indians." It was
> an honorable name, and while it stuck the team made an
> excellent record.
>
> It has now been decided to revive this name. . . . There
> will be no real Indians on the roster, but the name will re-
> call fine traditions. It is looking backward to a time when
> Cleveland had one of the most popular teams of the
> United States. It also serves to revive the memory of a
> single great player who has been gathered to his fathers
> in the happy hunting ground. . . .

One year after the name of the team was changed, the name of the
ballpark was, too. Originally it was dubbed National League Park.
When the team joined the AL in 1901, the "National" was dropped.
And in 1916, with Dunn as the owner, it was changed to Dunn Field,
as it would be called through 1927.

Believe it or not, those name changes were the *least* of it. Few
other baseball teams in history witnessed as much change—both in
the game and in society at large—as the 1920 Cleveland Indians.

Before the 1920 season started, American women were not allowed to vote. By the end of the season, they were.

Before the 1920 season, Americans were legally permitted to
drink alcohol. Now, they weren't, as Prohibition kicked in on January 16.

Before the 1920 season, Babe Ruth was pitching for the Boston
Red Sox. This year, he was playing for the Yankees.

At the start of the 1920 season, Cleveland had a wonderful shortstop named Ray Chapman. By the end of the 1920 season, he would
be dead.

Another casualty of the time: the good name of baseball.

During the 1920 season, a grand jury in Chicago indicted eight players, including Shoeless Joe, on charges they had purposely lost the 1919 World Series to win bets for gamblers in exchange for cash.

Although the indictments didn't come until near the end of the 1920 regular season, rumors had been swirling ever since the Sox lost the series, five games to three, to the Cincinnati Reds. It became the darkest hour in baseball history, forever earning the White Sox the derisive nickname "the Black Sox."

Still, in Cleveland, baseball was looking up. Since the disastrous season of 1914, the Cleveland club had been on a steady climb, finishing eighth, seventh, sixth, third, second, and second. Its winning percentage had risen every year, moving from .333 to .604.

The ascent began with the arrival of Speaker. The future Hall of Famer was a hitting machine and the best defensive outfielder in the game. Since his first full year in the bigs, 1908, he had batted better than .300 every season—including an astonishing .386 during his last year in Boston. Speaker also was an excellent base stealer, averaging 37 swipes during his first seven full seasons. His combination of hitting and speed also enabled him to pile up a record number of doubles.

Defensively, his approach was downright revolutionary. He was so good at going back on balls hit over his head that he was able to play extremely shallow and take away balls that would normally drop as singles. With his shallow positioning and rocket arm, he routinely led the league in double plays by outfielders.

After arriving in Cleveland, Speaker continued to pound the ball, blaze around the basepaths, and serve as the prototype for fielding excellence. Partway through the 1919 season, owner Dunn thought so highly of him that he gave him a second job: manager.

Speaker, from the plains of Texas, was a six-foot lefty weighing 195 pounds, with a wide batting stance and a huge stride into the ball, A teammate gave him his widely used nickname, the Grey Eagle. Others called him "Spoke." Anything but his real name, Tristiam E. Speaker.

The only man faster than Speaker was the team's veteran shortstop, Ray Chapman. Chapman was smaller than Speaker, at five-ten, 170 pounds, but he may well have been the fastest man in the American League.

Chapman's speed helped him become a good, but not great, base stealer. His wheels were more noticeable in the field and at the plate. He had great acceleration out of the batter's box, which helped him add plenty of points to his batting average and slugging percentage.

Routine infield rollers could turn into singles, and routine singles could turn into doubles.

"Chappie," as he was universally called, hit near .300 every year and was known as a clutch hitter. He also was a fan favorite, a pleasant, engaging, team-oriented player who had been around for eight full seasons. He had a nice tenor voice and often gathered teammates together in song.

The shortstop was no dummy. His off-season job was secretary-treasurer of the Pioneer Alloys Company.

In the fall of 1919, Chapman married Kathleen Daly, daughter of the president of East Ohio Gas. She didn't seem to mind that his ears stuck out wide. The couple began to build a house on Alvason Road in East Cleveland.

Chapman and Speaker were close friends. The player-manager traveled from his home in Texas to serve as best man at the wedding. During the season, the two players were inseparable. Speaker enjoyed Chapman's humor and storytelling ability.

Chappie was a bit of a practical joker, sometime staging elaborate—and usually harmless—pranks. One of them took place during spring training, when he organized a long-drive contest among the players. As the talk built and the braggadocio kicked into high gear, the players began to bet on who could hit the golf ball the farthest. Catcher Steve O'Neill was pumped up; he was convinced he could rip one over a distant fence in three tries. Chapman pretended to have money on O'Neill. When the moment arrived, the shortstop brought out a shiny new ball and placed it carefully on a mound of grass, telling O'Neill, "Now Steve, boy, I'm betting all I got on you. Take a healthy swing on it."

It was, of course, an exploding golf ball. O'Neill ripped into it, white powder flew everywhere, and the players erupted in laughter at the stunned look on O'Neill's face.

With the Eagle soaring in centerfield and Chappie presiding over the infield, hopes were high at the corner of East 66th and Lexington.

The site was originally chosen because the fellow who owned the team also owned two major streetcar lines that intersected there. In 1920, streetcars were still the primary mode of transportation. From as far south as Akron, fans could hop on the interurban line and arrive within 90 minutes.

Dunn Field was a fun place to watch a game. It had been expanded from 9,000 to 21,000 seats a decade earlier, when wooden stands were replaced with concrete and steel. The place was surrounded by an upper-middle-class neighborhood with big houses and inviting front porches.

The sightlines were great. And some of the sights were improving. As the *New York Times* reported April 11, "Women's hemlines are escalating so much lately that they are astonishingly closer to the knee than the ankle."

Still, you didn't find any kissing bandits in this crowd. A day at the ballpark was a semiformal affair. The uniform for men was dress shirts (selling for $1.45 at Higbee's), ties, and hats. Hemlines may have been rising, but women still wore dresses.

The most intriguing aspect of the ballpark itself, at least for fans, was the right-field fence. It was absurdly short, 290 feet, a full 20 feet shorter than the notoriously short left-field fence at Fenway Park. Pitchers hated it because routine fly balls turned into homers. Outfielders weren't exactly enthralled, either. The wall was 40 feet high, with three types of surfaces: concrete at the base, chicken wire at the top, and steel support posts. The ball might ricochet off the concrete or drop straight down from the chicken wire or career away at a crazy angle after hitting one of the posts.

By contrast, left field was a whopping 378 feet from home plate and center was an ungodly 460. For big games, ropes were strung inside the center- and left-field fences so fans could stand on the field. And when a game ended, youngsters were allowed to run around the bases.

Kids who didn't have a ticket could lie on their stomachs and watch through a gap between the ground and the bottom of the right-field fence. If a kid was really lucky, he could scoop up a batting-practice homer and return the ball to management in exchange for a free ticket.

Dunn Field was full of smiles in early 1920 as the Cleveland Indians shot out of the gate with a 6–1 record. They bumped it out to 21–8 by late May. At the start of June, though, the wheels began to wobble. The team lost five of six to start the month. But then, just as suddenly, the boys won six straight.

Through the middle of the summer, the team hung around first place, only percentage points ahead of the Yankees and White Sox.

On August 16, the Tribe arrived at the Polo Grounds for a crucial series against the Yanks. Ace spitballer Stan Coveleski was on the mound for Cleveland, facing New York's top pitcher, Carl Mays.

A crowd of 20,000 filed in for the opener on a Monday afternoon. They were quiet in the early going as Cleveland jumped out to a lead. But they were stunned by what they saw in the top of the fifth.

The leadoff batter for Cleveland that inning was Ray Chapman. Wearing the road gray with thin pinstripes and a block "C" on his left chest, the Cleveland shortstop finished swinging two bats in the on-deck circle, tossed one aside, and dug into the righthand batter's box.

Like Chapman, Mays was born in Kentucky. Unlike Chapman, Mays was universally regarded as a pain in the ass. He had an un-orthodox "submarine" delivery, in which he slung the ball with his arm hanging almost straight down. In those days, it was called a "shoot." He released the ball somewhere near his knees.

Mays also was a surly guy, widely disliked, and known as a head-hunter. A few years earlier, he had led the league in hit batsmen, with 14. During the previous three seasons, he drilled an average of 12 batters each year.

One of those had been Speaker. In 1918, Mays hit Speaker right in the head. Even though batting helmets were still far off in the fu-ture, Speaker wasn't hurt. He was, however, livid. He was convinced Mays hit him on purpose.

As Chapman looked out at Mays on the afternoon of August 16, 1920, he tugged on his cloth cap and pawed the ground with his metal spikes, getting comfortable. Then, as was his custom, he crowded the plate.

Mays stood on the mound with his hands together, chest high. He swung them over his head, dropped them down, pulled his right hand out of his glove, then let loose with his blazing "shoot." It was an inside pitch, and at the last instant it began to tail in. Chapman tried to get out of the way but couldn't. The ball hit him directly in the left temple.

He immediately collapsed. Speaker sprinted from the dugout, and Mays ran in from the mound. The umpire quickly summoned a doc-tor. As players from both teams gathered around, Chapman regained consciousness and was helped to his feet. But when he tried to stand by himself, he couldn't. With a teammate on either side, he tried to walk off the field, but his knees buckled and he had to be carried the rest of the way. He was unable to speak.

The game continued. Cleveland was cruising along with a 4–0 lead, but New York rallied for three runs in the ninth before falling short. Coveleski got the win and Mays took the loss.

When night fell, the Indians held a 1½-game lead over the Yankees and a half-game lead over the White Sox. And when the sun rose the next morning, Ray Chapman, 29, was dead.

New York's finest surgeons worked through the night to try to save him, but his skull was fractured, his lateral sinus was ruptured, and a massive quantity of blood had built up in his brain. Doctors removed a small part of his skull, but he passed shortly before 5 a.m.

The incident shocked the city and rocked the Indians' clubhouse. "He was the best friend I ever had," said Speaker. Back in Cleveland, amateur sports events were canceled. At the field where a sandlot game had been scheduled, someone laid a funeral wreath at the shortstop's position.

Many fans and players believed Mays had been aiming in the general vicinity of Chapman's head. Some Indians pressed the league office to ban Mays from baseball. But the American League president said he didn't believe the pitch was intentional.

While the *Cleveland Press* stopped short of accusing Mays of intentionally hitting Chapman, the newspaper did call for his ouster on the grounds that he was too wild: "Carl Mays has demonstrated that he does not possess the proper control to continue as a pitcher in the American League. So far this year, Mays has hit six batsmen. Since Mays entered the league in 1915, he has hit 55 batsmen. . . . His control is so poor that it is a menace to the welfare of baseball."

Most pitchers would have become psychologically scarred after killing a batter. Mays didn't seem the least bit fazed. In his next start, he shut out the Tigers, 10–0, and went on to finish the season with 26 victories.

The day after the beaning, the Indians–Yankees game was canceled. But the show must go on, and the following day, a Wednesday, the second game of the series got under way. Chapman's backup, a third-year player and former pal named Harry Lunte, was inserted into the lineup. In his debut, he fielded two easy chances without problems but went hitless in four at-bats.

Lunte was only a temporary solution. In early September, the call went to the team's minor league affiliate in New Orleans, where a hot prospect named Joe Sewell was burning up the Southern League. Sewell, whom the Tribe had discovered at the University of Alabama, joined the Indians September 10 and went on to hit .329 in 70 at-bats. He was shaky in the field, though, committing 15 errors in only 22 games.

Cleveland newspapers were full of speculation about whether the team would fold after the tragedy or gain renewed strength from it. The latter happened. But it took a while. Chapman's teammates were devastated. Speaker was so distraught he was unable to attend the funeral, held at St. John's Cathedral at East Ninth and Superior.

The ceremony was originally planned for St. Philomene's in East Cleveland, where Chapman had wed just 10 months earlier. But too many people wanted to attend.

Even at the much-larger St. John's, 3,000 folks had to be turned away. Some of them climbed on top of cars or set up ladders to try to see through the church windows. Another 2,000 people were packed inside for the 40-minute mass.

Burial took place in Section 42 of Lake View Cemetery, the lush final resting place of internationally known statesmen, inventors, industrialists, authors, and even a U.S. president, James A. Garfield.

Ironically, Chapman had promised his wife that 1920 would be his final season. They were comfortable financially, and, although she was a baseball fan, she constantly worried about him getting seriously injured.

The Indians lost seven of their next nine games. But at the end of August, they began a hot streak, capturing eight of nine. They won seven straight in mid-September, and took the American League pennant by two games over the White Sox and three over the Yankees. But after the beaning, a team that had been playing .639 baseball played its remaining games at exactly .500.

In baseball's earliest days, a team had to win five games to become the World Series champion. The format was changed to a best-of-seven in 1905, but changed back to a best-of-nine in 1919, where it would stay before switching back for good in 1922.

The Indians' opponents in their first World Series were the Brooklyn Robins. Seriously. The *Robins*. The name "Dodgers" was a secondary nickname that was not yet official.

The Robins had chirped their way to the National League pennant by seven games. The team was known for its deep and talented pitching staff—the "Big Seven," they were called.

The first three games were held in Brooklyn. For Game One, on a Tuesday afternoon, 23,573 people filed into seven-year-old Ebbets Field. Manager Speaker sent out the following lineup:

1. Joe Evans, LF
2. Bill Wambsganss, 2B
3. Tris Speaker, CF
4. George Burns, 1B
5. Larry Gardner, 3B
6. Joe Wood, RF
7. Joe Sewell, SS
8. Steve O'Neil, C
9. Stan Coveleski, P

The Robins took the field like this:

1. Ivy Olson, SS
2. Jimmy Johnston, 3B
3. Tommy Griffith, RF
4. Zack Wheat, LF
5. Hi Myers, CF
6. Ed Konetchy, 1B
7. Pete Kilduff, 2B
8. Ernie Krueger, C
9. Rube Marquard, P

Coveleski was one of his team's top aces. Marquard was not. The Brooklyn starter was in his 15th season, and his best years were well behind him. His 10 wins were only sixth best on the Brooklyn staff. But Marquard, tall and thin at six-three, 180, did have plenty of experience.

That didn't help him in Game One. The Tribe scored two runs in the second inning on two singles, an error, a walk, and a double by O'Neill. That would be plenty, because Coveleski was virtually unhittable.

The Tribe added an insurance run in the fourth on another O'Neill double. Coveleski, who scattered five hits, gave up one meaningless run in the seventh, and the Tribe cruised home with its first World Series win ever. The game took a mere one hour, 41 minutes.

Easy Street got considerably tougher the following day. The Tribe's superstar pitcher, Jim Bagby, winner of an incredible 31 regular-season games, coughed up more runs in the first three innings—two—than Coveleski gave up all the previous day. Brooklyn knicked him for another in the seventh.

Not that it mattered. You can't win without any runs, and Brooklyn's 23-game winner, Burleigh Grimes, kept Cleveland's feet away from the plate all day despite allowing seven hits. A Brooklyn crowd of 22,559 saw another sub-two-hour contest, but enjoyed this one much more.

Game Three brought the biggest crowd yet—25,088—and another swift pitchers' duel. The Robins got all the runs they needed in the first on a walk, a boot by Sewell (what else was new?), and two singles. Only five batters into the game, Speaker had seen enough. He jerked out 20-game winner Ray Caldwell and brought in Duster Mails, who worked six solid innings.

Cleveland's only run off Sherry Smith came late in the game when Speaker ripped a double to left field, to which Wheat added a two-base error. Smith made Brooklyn's manager look like a genius. The southpaw had been a relief pitcher most of the year and had only worked 136 innings.

Although the Tribe returned home trailing two games to one, 25,734 fans piled into Dunn Field on Saturday, October 9, for Cleveland's first World Series game. Coveleski was back on the hill, facing Leon Cadore, Brooklyn's third-best arm. It's a wonder Cadore still had an arm; earlier in the season, he had worked all 26 innings—yes, 26 innings—in a game against Boston that was finally declared a tie.

Tickets were so hard to come by that some people resorted to extreme measures. An 11-year-old kid, dubbed "Tree Boy" by the *Cleveland Press*, climbed high into a tree that overlooked the field. And, just to make sure nobody took his seat, he climbed the tree the night before. Tree Boy watched the second game from the same location before the *Press* pulled some strings and got him a ticket.

Those who weren't as adventurous could listen in on the "wireless." The U.S. Naval Station in Cleveland was pumping out a play-by-play account of the games, reachable as far away as 750 miles. On the fringe of the reception area, hundreds of ham radio operators picked up the signal and pumped it out farther. One report cited listeners from New York to San Francisco and from the Gulf of Mexico to Canada. (The first broadcast over commercial radio would not take place until 1928.)

In Game Four, Coveleski continued his Game One magic, retiring the side in order. Then Cleveland went to work. After Charlie Jamieson lined back to the mound, Wambsganss walked, Speaker singled, and Smith singled, scoring Wamby (as the media thankfully called him). Speaker moved to third and scored on a sacrifice fly.

When Cleveland started the second inning with two singles, Iron Man Cadore was sent to the showers, having retired a grand total of three Indians.

The Tribe added to its lead in the third. Wamby led off with a single and Speaker ripped his second straight hit. Brooklyn went to the bullpen and called in Marquard, who promptly surrendered a two-run single to Burns to give Cleveland a 4–0 cushion.

Brooklyn managed a run in the fourth on a single and a double, but Coveleski continued to throw darts. He not only shut the Robins down the rest of the way, but delivered a hit in the sixth and scored Cleveland's last run in a 5–1 beauty.

The Series was tied, with the next three games to be played at East 55th and Lex. For Tribe fans, all was right with the world.

By contrast, Brooklyn's Marquard was not having fun. He was arrested Saturday at the Hotel Winton and charged with ticket-scalping. He had tried to peddle six tickets for $300. A few days later, he was fined $1 and costs by a judge who noted that Marquard had already paid a hefty price in bad publicity.

The visitors weren't faring much better on the ballfield.

Game Five was essentially over after one inning. On a glorious Sunday afternoon, the home team unleashed a four-run opening frame. Jamieson singled. Wamby singled. Speaker singled. Bases loaded. Elmer Smith stepped up and crashed the first grand slam in the history of the World Series. When the ball cleared the right-field wall, the grandstands shook with noise.

Meanwhile, Cleveland's starter, Bagby, had reverted to his All-World form. In addition to shutting down the Robins, he jacked a fourth-inning homer that gave him a seven–zip lead. His blast not only put three more runs in Cleveland's column but marked the first homer by a pitcher in World Series history.

The very next inning, the Indians wrote yet another new entry in the World Series record book. This one would stand up for a long,

long time. In fact, Bill Wambsganss accomplished something that hasn't been duplicated to this day.

With Brooklyn runners on first and second and moving with the pitch, the little second baseman caught a line drive off the bat of Clarence Mitchell, tagged the runner coming from first and stepped on second to catch the runner who had left early. An unassisted triple play. The fans went wild, and Brooklyn was toast.

Mitchell, the batter on the triple play, hit into a double play in his next at-bat, giving him the dubious honor of making five outs with two swings.

The Indians won 8–1, taking a 3–2 lead in the series, and had more momentum than an avalanche.

Unfortunately, Monday afternoon looked nothing at all like Sunday. For a while, it seemed as if the two teams were going to play until Thanksgiving without scoring. Cleveland starter Duster Mails gave up only two hits in the first seven innings. The only time Brooklyn mounted even a minor threat was in the second, when a single and an error by—you guessed it—Sewell put runners on first and second. Sewell's antics then rubbed off on third baseman Gardner, who booted a grounder to load the bases. But Mails snuffed the threat by getting the opposing pitcher to fly out.

Cleveland wasn't faring much better against Sherry Smith. After a close call in the second, when a Tribe runner was thrown out at home on an infield grounder, Brooklyn's pitcher settled down. His only real problem came in the sixth. With two outs, Speaker singled. Then Burns ripped a double to left, scoring Speaker.

Cleveland took that 1–0 lead into the bottom of the ninth. The starter, Mails, was still going strong. He got the first batter to ground out to second. The next batter hit another routine grounder to short. But Sewell—yep, afraid so—kicked another one, and Brooklyn had the tying runner on first. He was forced on a grounder to third, though, and Mails nailed down the win when the last hitter flied to left.

The Indians were in command. They needed only one win in three chances, with yet another home game on Tuesday.

Why mess around? Coveleski lubed up his spitter yet again, and the Robins still couldn't hit it.

The visiting batters did absolutely nothing of consequence until the seventh. And even then they didn't do much. With two outs, Konetchy beat out a grounder to Sewell at short. No big deal, except the next guy hit a grounder to Sewell, and the rookie shortstop rang up yet *another* E-6. Fortunately, the next batter hit one to Wamby at second, and Coveleski was out of the inning.

The Indians' offense was struggling too. The home team scratched out a run in the fourth on two singles and a sacrifice fly. An inning later, a single, a stolen base, and Tris Speaker's triple nudged the lead to 2–0.

After the seventh-inning stretch, a double by O'Neill and another by Jamieson put another run on the scoreboard, easing the tension in the Tribe dugout and ratcheting it up a notch on Brooklyn's bench.

The home crowd of 27,525 is roaring as Coveleski returns to the mound for the bottom of the ninth. The thin right-hander from Shamokin, Pennsylvania, has turned into Brooklyn's worst nightmare. In two full games and eight-ninths of another, he has yielded a grand total of two runs. He already owns two complete-game victories and is on the brink of a record-tying third.

The first batter is the cleanup hitter, Tommy Griffith. He has had a miserable series, and he promptly flies out to left.

Next up is the left-fielder, Wheat, one of Brooklyn's bright spots. He has eight hits in 26 at-bats. He continues the trend with a single to center.

The next hitter smacks a roller to Sewell. The fans hold their breath. But the shaky rookie picks it up and flips to Wamby for the force at second.

One more out to go.

The batter is the first baseman, Konetchy, who is only 4-for-22 in the series but hit .308 during the regular season. He swings and hits a bouncer to—egads!—shortstop. But Sewell snags this one, too, and flips to Wamby for the force.

The crowd erupts. The Indians are the champions of baseball.

Speaker dashes from centerfield to the front of the grandstand, jumps the railing, and hugs his mother. At first, fans can't figure out what he is doing, and a weird silence hangs over the park. But after he accomplishes his mission and everyone realizes his motives, a huge cheer erupts again.

Coveleski has recorded his third consecutive five-hitter. His ERA in the Series: .067. In 27 innings of work, he has walked exactly two batters.

In winning the series five games to two, Cleveland has beaten Brooklyn at its own game—pitching. The Robins scored a mere eight runs in seven games.

Northeast Ohio was excited, but hardly delirious. The day after Cleveland's first World Series championship, the *Akron Beacon Journal* carried the news on page 17. The *Cleveland Press* ran its story on page 22. The *Press*'s sports pages also ran this headline: "With the World Series out of the way, we are beginning to wise up to the fact that football is kicking in."

So much for delirium.

To be fair, part of the reason for downplaying the story was timing. In those days, both newspapers came out in the afternoon, and the deciding game ended shortly after that day's editions hit the street; by the following day, the news was nearly 24 hours old. The morning *Plain Dealer*, by contrast, ran a two-deck, front-page headline trumpeting the victory.

Still, something short of wild celebration followed the win. Part of the thrill may have been dulled by the Black Sox scandal.

Cleveland had certainly done its part to put the game back on solid ground. Its players were widely viewed as good guys, and they were sentimental favorites in the aftermath of Ray Chapman's death. Even Babe Ruth thought the Indians were a good antidote for baseball's troubles.

"It is gratifying that a hard-fighting, clean-playing club such as Cleveland should bring the highest baseball honors back to the American League," Babe was quoted as saying. "There can be no doubt that the best team won."

Many a glass was raised to Chappie, whose invisible presence seemed to hover over the Cleveland bench. The players showed their class by voting a full World Series share, $3,986.34, to his wife.

For the next five years, baseball fans flocked to Ray Chapman's gravesite to stare at his big headstone. Then the visitors began to dwindle. Today, hardly anyone comes around.

The saga of Chapman's replacement, Joe Sewell, is considerably happier. Not that his glove got any better. During the next eight years, Sewell would average 42 boots a year. In 1923, he butchered an astounding 59 chances. Finally, in 1929 he was shifted to third base, where he couldn't do as much damage.

But Sewell was a born hitter, and, starting with his September 16 debut, he would play in every Indians game until April 30, 1930. That's 1,103 consecutive games, a team record that still stands.

Seventy-one years later, he would be voted one of the greatest 100 Indians of all time—right alongside his fellow 1920 shortstop, Ray Chapman.

MASTERING HOGAN

SUNDAY, APRIL 7, 1946

It was the first Masters held after World War II, and the leadership at Augusta National was eager to reestablish the tournament as one of the elite events in the world of sports. What better way to do that than by handing over the green winner's jacket to a superstar? Ben Hogan was doing his part, flirting with the lead. But a little-known golfer from Akron, Herman Keiser, kept messing up the script—and the folks at Augusta National didn't like it one bit.

COPLEY TOWNSHIP, a mere 30 miles from downtown Cleveland as the Titleist flies, a straight shot down Interstate 77, was one of dozens of Northeast Ohio communities to be completely transformed in the final decade of the 20th century.

Farm fields that for centuries had produced wheat, oats, corn, and hay were suddenly sprouting four-bedroom houses with three-car garages.

As late as 1986, the Akron suburb had featured a 50-acre drive-in movie theater. That turned into a Super Kmart. A horse farm on a pastoral hill overlooking Crystal Lake morphed into "Restaurant Hill," where every mid-priced national chain set up shop. Just down the road, a glorious row of majestic oak trees was decimated to make way for a Wal-Mart.

One of the precious few things that didn't change during this rapid makeover was Herman Keiser's driving range. Herm's place, down on Cleveland-Massillon Road south of Copley Circle, wasn't quite as tired as the driving range Kevin Costner ran in the movie *Tin Cup*. But it wasn't exactly state-of-the-art, either. It faced the wrong way, into the afternoon sun, so you couldn't follow the flight of your shots. The golf balls were a motley crew, scuffed and cut and sometimes even misshapen. A few poles were stuck out back in the uneven turf, doing a marginal impersonation of flagsticks. And out front, the gravel parking lot guaranteed that your car would be dust-covered by the time your bucket was empty.

As the 20th century wound down, visitors to the exceedingly modest clubhouse would find a salty old guy inside, running his range and happily running his mouth for anyone who inquired about events nearer to the middle of the century.

The proprietor would talk more about his years in the Navy than his years on the golf links. He would talk about the fear that enveloped the men, about the ongoing seasickness, about how they felt so horrible for so long, back there during World War II, on those dangerous Atlantic crossings, that sometimes the guys considered jumping overboard and being done with it.

Most of Keiser's new patrons, the folks who filled the bedrooms in this new bedroom community, didn't know anything about him. He was just an old geezer sitting in the clubhouse, fingering a putter, occasionally dipping a battered metal bucket into his battered collection of golf balls, at night sleeping in the dormer apartment upstairs.

But the old-timers knew. They knew all about Herman Keiser and his amazing feat. They would happily recount the saga of the dirt-poor loner who, on a magical spring weekend in 1946, defeated one of golf's greatest legends in golf's single greatest tournament.

You mean that crumpled old guy once beat Ben Hogan at the Masters? That would be him. The guy in the corner. Herman Keiser— born October 7, 1914, peaked April 7, 1946.

Even in his golfing prime, Keiser wasn't much of a national name—which may have been the precise reason why the people running Augusta National Country Club in 1946 were doing everything in their considerable power to unnerve him and wrap the green winner's jacket around Hogan.

Call it the Tiger Woods Syndrome. The folks who stage golf tournaments want their tournaments to be won by superstars, not unknowns, because superstars give an event more prestige and draw more attention, in turn bringing more fans and more money.

The 1946 Masters was the first after a war-era gap of three years, and the Augusta National honchos were determined to return the event to its former level of glory. One way to ensure that was a win by one of the golden boys.

Keiser always had a suspicion there was more to his mistreatment than that. Augusta, despite its polite galleries filled with men in ties and hats and women in dresses, had rougher edges in those days. High-stakes wagering by the membership was a poorly guarded secret. Some members reportedly had as much as $50,000 on Hogan, whom the bookies listed as a 4-to-1 favorite. After all, Hogan already had won 100 professional golf tournaments and was the tour's leading money-winner.

Keiser, by contrast, was 20-to-1 against, with little betting money behind him. And some of that money was Keiser's. He borrowed $50 from two bookies and put a wager on his own skill and determination.

It turned out to be a solid bet. Keiser led from the third hole of the opening round, played in brisk winds, through the final day. That's 69 consecutive holes. Given the strength of the field, which included not only Hogan but Bobby Jones, Sam Snead, Byron Nelson, and Jimmy Demaret, it was a remarkable athletic feat. Given the extra obstacles thrown in Keiser's path, the win was nothing short of miraculous.

The most blatant insult by Augusta's royalty was a stunt that had never been pulled before and has never been pulled since. On the climactic day of the four-day competition—the nerve-wracking Sunday afternoon when a golfer's throat goes dry, his hands get jittery, and every shot seems harder than calculus—tradition dictates that the leaders go off in the final group. It's done for the sake of drama. But it's also a significant competitive advantage. As the last two players come down the home stretch, they know what all the other golfers have done and exactly what score is required to win.

Keiser, who was leading by five shots on Sunday morning, was not sent out in the last group. He was not sent out in the second-to-last group. Nor was he in the third-to-last group, or the fourth-to-last group. The pro from Northeast Ohio was placed in the group that teed off fifth-to-last.

His unpopular surge had begun in earnest during the second round, played in ideal weather, when he carded a sparkling 68, four under par. That gave him a four-stroke lead over Jimmy Thomson of Los Angeles. Tied for fourth after two rounds was the hotshot from

Hershey, Pennsylvania—Hogan, a Texas native known for his surliness and obsessive practice habits. Fellow superstar Bobby Jones, nearing the end of his glorious career, was 10 strokes back.

Keiser got a foreshadowing of the last round's dirty tricks on Saturday, when his starting time was switched without anyone bothering to notify him. He nearly missed his tee time, which would have disqualified him, and was forced to hustle to the first tee without even warming up. Somehow, deep behind the scenes, Keiser had been switched to a pairing with the popular "Slammin' Sammy" Snead, who typically hit the ball half a football field farther than Keiser. Never mind that Snead trailed Keiser by an astronomical 12 shots and should never have been playing with him.

Keiser got another hint that something was amiss when his previous caddy was suddenly unavailable that day, replaced by a 13-year-old kid. By the second hole, the kid was gassed. He was dragging Keiser's clubs along the ground, barely able to keep up. Keiser demanded that officials provide him with a real caddy, but was told nobody else was available.

Although Sneed's booming drives consistently outdistanced Keiser's, and the mismatch could have been demoralizing, Keiser stuck to his knitting and finished the third round with a solid 71, stretching his lead from four to five.

As always, putting was his forte. He would stand nearly straight-legged, bent over at the waist, eyes directly over the top of the ball, hands close to his body, and, gripping a simple blade putter, use a smooth, consistent stroke. Through the first three rounds, Keiser three-putted only once. His drives were relatively short, about 230 yards on average, but he could get up and down, as they say.

In the final round, Keiser was not his usual consistent self. On the front nine, he birdied the second, sixth, and eighth holes—nailing a 30-foot putt on the par-three sixth—but bogeyed one, five, seven, and nine.

On the 10th, he took a major gamble. Sitting behind a pine tree, he whacked an approach shot that missed the trunk of the tree by the length of a dimple and came to rest six inches from the cup.

The final affront by the Augusta National membership was lurking on that back nine. With his lead down to two strokes, Keiser was playing the 14th hole when legendary sportswriter Grantland Rice— a charter member of Augusta—sidled up and, without introduction, told Keiser to speed up his pace or he'd be penalized two shots.

Keiser promptly threatened to wrap his putter around Rice's neck if he came anywhere near him again. Keiser was a big man, six-foot-two and 190 pounds, and Rice didn't press the matter.

After 37 months at sea, battling both the Atlantic Ocean and the Nazis, Keiser was not about to be intimidated. The game of golf no longer seemed like life or death, and nobody was going to tell him how to play it.

The only person who didn't seem to be sneering at Keiser was his final-round playing partner, the gentlemanly Byron Nelson. On the final hole, when Keiser pulled his tee shot into the left rough, then drilled a marvelous seven-iron that hit the flagstick and stopped within 25 feet of the cup, Nelson said, "Herman, that's the one I wanted to see you hit."

As they approached the final green, Nelson tried to calm Keiser's nerves by saying, "You haven't three-putted all day." The comment may have had the opposite effect, planting a seed of doubt, because that's exactly what Keiser did.

He got reasonably close on his first putt. Then, his blue eyes peering out beneath his white visor, he studied the slick green carefully, and set up in his customary stance for the biggest putt of his life. He stroked the par putt smoothly . . . but it rimmed out.

Keiser tapped in the bogey to finish the day with a 74, for a tournament total of 282. Now he had to wait around and see what Hogan would do.

And now, of course, Hogan knew exactly what he had to do.

The fiery competitor with the piercing eyes had been making a charge. As Keiser moved along the back nine, he repeatedly heard cheers erupting behind him.

Hogan birdied the par-three 12th.

He birdied the par-five 13th.

He barely missed an eagle on the par-five 15th.

Now, after pars on both 16 and 17, Hogan needs a birdie to win the Masters and a par to tie with Keiser.

His tee shot is fine, as is his approach. He has reached the 18th green in regulation, seemingly in perfect shape to at least tie.

With film cameras grinding away, documenting the action for the newsreels, Hogan studies his first putt for an eternity, seemingly trying to memorize the position of every blade of grass on the entire green. Finally, after lining up the birdie putt for nearly two minutes, he stands over his ball and strokes it gently. The ball rolls two feet past the hole as the crowd lets out an "oooh."

Now Hogan has an easy comebacker to tie the match and force a playoff. He studies the return putt . . . strokes it . . . and leaves it one inch short.

Herman Keiser, 31, is champion of the Masters.

Nelson, the winner of the previous Masters, continued the tradition by helping the new champion don the most famous green jacket in the world—in Keiser's case, a 42-long. The club members, already grinding their teeth about the upset victory, were even more displeased that Keiser was wearing the same white shirt he had worn the previous three days. If something is working, thought Keiser, why change?

Into the pocket of the green blazer he stuffed his winner's check, a hefty $2,500. That pushed his season total to $6,076.24, fifth best on the tour behind Hogan, Nelson, Snead, and Demaret. And before he left town, Keiser put $1,000 in cash in his pocket, compliments of the bookies.

Not bad for a guy who not only didn't have an equipment sponsor but won the tournament with a mismatched set of clubs. Not bad for a guy who played the first round watched only by his caddy. Not bad for a guy who had $10 in his pocket on the final day, and would have had trouble paying his caddy had he not won.

Even in those days, major golf tournaments were big business. More than 10,000 people paid to see the final round. And every last one of them seemed bitter about Keiser's win.

The story in the next day's *Augusta Chronicle* began, "Plodding Herman Keiser won the 10th Masters tournament here yesterday afternoon with a 72-hole total of 282 when little Ben Hogan used up three putts to hole out on the 18th."

In the story's second reference to Keiser, the writer called him "the methodical Akron professional." Well, Hogan was not exactly a speed demon himself.

A reporter from the United Press wire service was even less of a Keiser fan: "As long as there is a Masters tournament at the Augusta National Golf Course, the 18th hole will be remembered as the one where in 1946 Ben Hogan lost a Masters title and where Herman Keiser 'backed' into one."

He also wrote that Keiser "blew" his title chance with the three-putt. Never mind that Keiser's second putt barely rimmed out, and that Hogan's stopped short—a cardinal sin with a match on the line.

A writer for the International News Service called Keiser "a sort of latter-day intruder on the golfing big time."

Only the reporter for the *Plain Dealer* pointed out that Keiser "gave one of the most spectacular exhibitions of putting ever seen anywhere."

In most stories, Hogan got far more ink, even with a second-place finish. The guy was so famous that, the week following his loss to Keiser, he stayed in Augusta to star in a movie called *The Mighty Atom of Golf.*

Hogan had plenty of nicknames, and none of them was particularly warm and fuzzy. He was "The Hawk" and, most commonly, "the Wee Ice Mon."

Oddly enough—or perhaps not, given the feistiness of both men—Keiser soon befriended Hogan.

The relationship began on a sour note, as was so often the case with Hogan. The two were paired at the Phoenix Open. On the front nine, Hogan was hitting one great shot after another, and Keiser kept complimenting him. At the turn, Hogan said he didn't want to hear any more compliments.

Keiser obliged.

Later that year, at the Jacksonville Open, they were paired again. Keiser stayed largely mute until the 11th hole, when Hogan's wheels fell off. The golf icon butchered the hole, plunking a ball into a water hazard en route to an unbelievable 11.

As the men walked toward the 12th tee, Keiser said to Hogan: "Now I'm gonna tell you those were the worst [bleeping] shots I've ever seen a golfer of your caliber hit."

Hogan smiled. It was a thin smile, but that's about the best you'd get from the man.

Keiser was something of a loner himself. Although he was repeatedly described as "handsome" and "tall" in newspaper articles, in those days, he was a man of few words. One of the reasons he got lousy publicity was that he was a lousy interview. When he made his big competitive breakthrough in 1942 at the then-prestigious Miami Four Ball tournament, teaming with Chandler Harper to knock off Hogan and Gene Sarazen, he was asked how it felt to make his mark. He responded, "Great," with no further elaboration.

Another thing Keiser and Hogan had in common was a rough

childhood. Since his earliest days in Springfield, Missouri, Keiser felt as if it was him against the world. He never knew his father. He took a job at age 12, dealing with the no-nonsense types who worked on the railroad. He would deliver papers to them every day and carry home a grand total of 25 cents. The money helped support his mother and grandmother.

Later, Keiser got a job as a caddy at a club where renowned putter Horton Smith played. Keiser was a good caddy, and worked his way up to caddie master. He began to assemble a collection of non-matching golf clubs. He hit them well, and caught the attention of Smith, who won the first Masters in 1934. In 1939, Smith got Keiser a job as assistant pro at Portage Country Club, the ultra-exclusive preserve of Akron's rubber barons.

Within a year, Keiser tamed the tricky Portage layout with an unheard-of round of 60, a matching 30 out, 30 back, good for 11 under par. In 1941, he reached the pro tour, and soon was hired away by Firestone Country Club across town. He was the head pro at Firestone until he joined the Navy in 1943.

When Hogan was involved in his near-fatal traffic accident in 1949, Keiser was riding a couple of cars behind him. Keiser went to see him in the hospital. Hogan asked for his clubs. Keiser brought them in and set them next to the bed.

Again, Keiser could relate. During his three years in the Navy, he had stowed his own clubs under a bunk on the USS *Cincinnati*, much to the amusement and occasional derision of his shipmates.

Years later, Hogan knocked on the front door of Keiser's mother's home in Akron, saying he needed a putting lesson. Later he would show up at Keiser's driving range unannounced and hit balls until his hands bled.

When Keiser talked about putting, people listened. That's why the three-putt on the final hole of the '46 Masters was ironic and disappointing.

The putter was the weapon that got him there. Over the first three rounds he averaged only 26 putts, or 1.4 per hole. On the last day, on the 14th hole, he faced a brutal putt over two big mounds in the middle of the green. He sent the ball on a gentle roller-coaster ride that stopped only two feet away, and easily made two.

Until the final hole, Keiser's only three-putt had come from 90 feet out. So it annoyed him that he didn't finish in typical style.

He was even more annoyed by the widespread perception that he was a second-rate player who wasn't fit to pick the lint off a green jacket.

Keiser was not totally unknown—or, at least, he shouldn't have been. Earlier the same season, he had tied Hogan after 72 holes in Phoenix, firing a 66-68-69-69. In the 18-hole playoff that followed, Keiser shot yet another sub-70 round, but Hogan pulled away on the final half-dozen holes, sinking putts of 40 and 35 feet.

Golf aficionados should also have remembered that, in 1942, before he sailed off to World War II, Keiser finished 10th among all the pros in prize money. That was the year he and Chandler won the Miami Four Ball.

Nor was the 1946 Master's win a flash in the pan: Keiser stayed hot the rest of the year, finishing second in two tournaments and averaging a stellar 70.25 strokes per round. He would up the season with $18,934 in winnings, fifth on the tour. The next year he was 10th, with $12,703.

So it galled him no end that, well into the 1960s, the nation's golf writers continued to refer to him as "the only surprise winner" in Masters history.

He was galled about a lot of things after his Masters win. He was mad at himself for failing to two-putt the final green, which would have added more legitimacy. But mostly he was riled at Augusta National. In fact, every year for the next half-century, he took more shots at the people who ran the Masters than Martha Burk.

Keiser would return annually for the winners' reunion dinner in the middle of Masters week, where he would pick up a $1,500 check, given each year to all previous winners. But many of those years he'd just grab his check and head back to Ohio before the tournament even started. Some years he wouldn't even stay for the dinner.

Keiser's bitterness toward the Masters power structure—people like Augusta National chairman Clifford Roberts—was not difficult to understand, given the way he was treated in 1946.

Any time he came within half a mile of a reporter, he would say the same thing: "If I hadn't won, I would have sued the shit out of them." He'd relish the annual payback, those $1,500 checks. "I want to cost them as much as I can," he would say.

Money was usually tight for Keiser, and he never forgot the financial misery of the Great Depression. But the people who knew him best knew that his return visits to Georgia were not just about the money.

For more than half a century, Keiser would carefully pack the green blazer in the trunk of his car and head back to the land of blooming azaleas. The winners were supposed to store their blazers at Augusta National, but Keiser figured those people tried so hard to take it away from him that he'd just hang on to it himself.

More than 20 times, when he was still healthy, Keiser took advantage of his lifetime exemption and actually played in the tournament. Once he even played when he wasn't healthy.

In 1982, at the age of 67, he ventured out with aching hands into a cold rain for Thursday's opening round and slogged off the 18th green with a hideous 93. It was an all-time high for the tournament. Again, he was the outcast. He refused to sign his scorecard, climbed into his car, and drove home.

After winning the Masters, Keiser spent most of the rest of his life in Northeast Ohio. The exception came when the 1940s gave way to the 1950s and he left to become the head pro at Lost Creek Country Club in Lima. Just a few years later he was back, buying Loyal Oak Golf Club just south of Copley. He sold the golf course and created Keiser's Golf Range.

Keiser kept threatening to move to the warm weather of Florida, especially after his wife died in 1972, but he never did.

At the turn of the century, after Herm had retired, a fancy new driving range was built about five miles away from his, closer to the Wal-Mart and the Super K and Restaurant Hill. The new range had heated tees and a putting green and sand traps and video lessons and automatic ball dispensers. It made Herm's old range look even shabbier.

Many of the existing customers defected. But some stayed. After all, if Herm's little patch of fescue was good enough for Ben Hogan, it was good enough for them.

Rank: #2

ONE-GAME SEASON

MONDAY, OCTOBER 4, 1948

Cleveland's baseball franchise had been buffeted by change as the 1948 season opened. One of the few links to the past was player-manager Lou Boudreau, a longtime fan favorite. Boudreau guaranteed himself that status for life when he led the Tribe to victory in the first one-game playoff in American League history.

THE EYEWITNESSES ARE no longer around, so we can't be certain exactly when little Lou Boudreau of Harvey, Illinois, took his first baby step. But it was probably within five minutes of leaving the womb.

This guy did everything early. He was named captain of his high school basketball team as a sophomore and captain of his college team as a junior. He got married at the age of 21. He became a big-league baseball manager at 24. And he was nearly fired at the tender managerial age of 29.

But he wasn't. And sometimes it's the things that don't happen that make all the difference.

The non-trade of Boudreau in the winter of 1947–48 ensured that at least one thing associated with Cleveland Indians baseball remained unchanged during the years that followed World War II

Since buying out 19-year owner Alva Bradley in June of 1946, flamboyant Bill Veeck had picked up his new toy and shaken it like one of those holiday snow scenes, sending pieces flying everywhere.

At the end of 1946, he cut all ties to the Tribe's longtime home,

League Park. In 1947, he moved spring training from Florida to Tucson, Arizona, primarily because he owned a ranch there. That same year, he hired the first African-American player in American League history, Larry Doby. And in the winter of 1947–48, he nearly canned his most popular player, shortstop Boudreau, who doubled as his manager.

Veeck leaked the proposed trade and was immediately and roundly ridiculed by Tribe fans. The deal would have sent Boudreau, two Tribe pitchers, and cash to the St. Louis Browns for their shortstop, Vern Stephens, as well as pitcher Jack Kramer and outfielder Paul Lehner. Veeck was also lusting to have Al Lopez, who had just retired as a player, replace Boudreau as manager.

A two-month fan backlash ensued. It culminated in a one-sided reader poll in the daily *Cleveland News*, in which Boudreau received an approval rating of more than 90 percent. Veeck decided to back off. Either that or he never had any intention of trading Boudreau and just wanted to give his team two months of extra publicity.

Veeck was like that. He was the first person to introduce fireworks displays at ballgames. He brought in vaudeville acts. He hired baseball clowns such as Max Patkin, and even let one of them, Jackie Price, play in a few real games. Later, after selling the Indians and buying the St. Louis Browns, Veeck would pull the most famous PR stunt in baseball history, sending a three-foot, one-inch midget to the plate as a pinch hitter.

In any event, Boudreau was the core and the constant for an Indians team that was somewhere between "in flux" and "in chaos."

On top of a flurry of signings, trades, and cuts, Boudreau and Veeck were turning outfielders into pitchers, infielders into outfielders, relief pitchers into starters, and raw rookies into regulars. In the biggest game of the year—and quite likely the biggest single game in the history of the Cleveland Indians—Boudreau would take a lifelong outfielder and stick him at first base for the first time.

In other words, the 1948 Indians were not exactly the 1927 Yankees, a feared and fully formed powerhouse.

None of Cleveland's three daily newspapers picked the '48 Tribe to finish higher than second in the American League. And why would they? Since the start of World War II, Cleveland had finished fourth, third, fifth, fifth, sixth, and fourth. Any Tribe fan age 28 or younger hadn't even been alive the last time the Indians won a pennant.

The roster was jammed with question marks. Could Bob Lemon become a cornerstone of the starting rotation after making the bigs as a third baseman, moving to centerfield, and then finally converting to pitcher? Could second-year- man Doby, the second black player in all of baseball, make a meaningful contribution after moving from the infield to the outfield? Was there anything left in the right arm of Bob Feller, the veteran fireballer who had worked an incredible 670 innings the previous two seasons, including 56 complete games? Could rookie relief pitcher Gene Bearden get his pesky knuckleball over the plate?

Despite the fact that Boudreau was younger than many of his players and hadn't served in the war because of chronically bad ankles, he was the team's rock. He had been a star and leader everywhere he went. He won four letters in high school basketball in Illinois and, during his three years as captain, his team made the state finals every year. He went to the University of Illinois on a basketball scholarship. He was so good on the baseball field that he lost his college eligibility when the Indians gave money to his parents in hopes of influencing his postgraduate choice of professional teams.

In spite of that bad experience, Boudreau signed with the Tribe. He came aboard as a third baseman, but with superstar Ken Keltner entrenched at third, he was advised to switch to shortstop, and was a good enough athlete to do so smoothly.

That track record of success helped give Boudreau the audacity to campaign for a managerial job at the ridiculously young age of 24. Having been with the Indians only two full summers, he sat down after the 1941 season and wrote a letter to team owner Bradley, spelling out the reasons he should be put in charge.

Incredibly, Bradley did not dismiss the notion out of hand. Instead, he invited his precocious shortstop to meet with the team's board of trustees, a high-powered group that included people like the Van Sweringen brothers, founders of Shaker Heights and owners of the Terminal Tower. They grilled him for two hours and gave him the job.

Why not? He would be the fourth manager in six years. Might as well try a totally new approach.

Boudreau's own game didn't seem to suffer as the result of his extra duties, and, although not everyone was thrilled with his tendency to play hunches rather than follow the book, he was moving into his seventh year at the helm as the 1948 season dawned.

By then, Boudreau had developed an odd batting stance. He held the bat high, bent his knees, and bent over sharply at the waist. He developed that stance during his early years with the Tribe, when they played most of their games at League Park, which had an absurdly short right-field fence. He was a right-handed hitter, with a natural tendency to pull the ball to left. But when you see a home run porch only 290 feet from home plate—20 feet shorter than the Green Monster in Boston—you can't help but salivate, especially when your left-field fence is 378 feet and centerfield is 460.

Boudreau's stance served him well in any ballpark. He hit .258 in his debut season and .295 in his first full year as a starter. During the war, he established himself as a solid .300 hitter. And in 1948, he would unleash a monster season, one of the best in Cleveland history.

The home opener took place on a breezy, 73-degree day in front of the biggest opening-day crowd in major league history: 73,163. The Tribe ran onto the field in their white flannel uniforms with baggy pants and blue-over-white socks. The jerseys featured a script "Indians" across the chest, and Chief Wahoo on the left sleeve. This was the chief with the pointy nose, drawn in yellow instead of red.

The opening-day lineup looked like this:

1. Thurman Tucker, CF
2. Larry Doby, RF
3. Lou Boudreau, SS
4. Joe Gordon, 2B
5. Eddie Robinson, 1B
6. Allie Clark, LF
7. Kenny Keltner, 3B
8. Jim Hegan, C
9. Bob Feller, P

That group was good for 11 hits—three each by Hegan and Robinson—while Feller fired a two-hitter at the Boston Braves. The Indians sent the record crowd home happy with a 4–0 win in a snappy, two-hour game.

Cleveland won six straight games in April. But then it dropped the first four of May. Feller fell into a slump, and the whispers began. *Too many innings. Too much mileage on that right arm.*

Feller had been a local hero since strutting into town in 1936 as a 17-year-old phenom. He had a supersonic fastball and reasonably good control. Kids would mimic his acrobatic delivery, which involved taking his hands way back behind his head, lifting his front leg nearly straight in front of him, and bending backward so far you thought he was going to tip over.

Feller's first taste of professional baseball was not in the low minors, or even the high minors. He was thrown into action in an exhibition game against the mighty St. Louis Cardinals. This was the era of the Gas House Gang, the fearsome club that featured the Dean brothers, Joe Medwick, Pepper Martin, Leo Durocher, Frankie Frisch, and Rip Collins. He was summoned to the mound in the fourth inning for a three-inning stint. Catcher-manager Steve O'Neill told him to keep it simple: Nothing but fastballs.

Feller struck out eight batters in three innings.

A month later the Iowa native was given a start and responded by striking out 15 batters. Enough said. He would keep his starting job for 18 years.

Those years, unfortunately, were not consecutive. Right after Pearl Harbor, Feller enlisted in the Navy and lost more than three and a half seasons in the prime of his career.

In his first full season back, 1946, he won 26 games and led the league with 348 strikeouts. The next year he won 20 more games. So Boudreau had no reason to think Feller was finished, and the manager never even considered removing him from the rotation.

Along about that time, Boudreau did make an unorthodox pitching move, one that would transform the season.

Rookie Gene Bearden, a lefty who threw 80 percent knuckleballs, made the roster coming out of spring training as a relief pitcher. But Boudreau wanted a lefty to start the May 8 game against the lefty-dominated Washington Senators, and he wrote Bearden's name on the lineup card. The newcomer delivered a three-hit masterpiece. He was on his way—and so was the Tribe.

After moving in and out of the league lead throughout May, the Indians surged into first and stayed there for nearly two months.

Attendance was soaring, and only partly because of all the winning. Veeck was the most popular owner in team history. Although wealthy from buying and selling baseball teams, he acted more like a bleacher creature—and, in fact, spent plenty of time in the bleachers, talking to fans about what they liked and disliked about attending games. The Kenyon College dropout would talk to anyone, anywhere—in the bleachers, in bars, on the sidewalks of the city. "The Burrhead" refused to wear hats and ties at a time when they were the standard uniform. He just didn't give a damn.

Fans were given free stuff at the gate or in random drawings. Almost every game was designated as some kind of special "night," and many of the promotions were wacky. Veeck put midgets in miniature cars. He gave fans rabbits, guinea pigs, and live turkeys. He gave away stockings, orchids, and outhouses. He put full marching bands on the field before games. For one pregame exhibition, he set up black lights around the infield, turned off the main lights, and used specially coated phosphorescent bats and balls. He honored groups, players, former players, and even the team trainer. For the last game of his first season, he let everyone in for free.

Some of Veeck's best PR moves were far subtler. Before he took over, the fans had to return any foul ball hit into the seats. Veeck issued an order allowing the paying customers to keep their souvenirs. How could you not like this guy?

His predecessor had forbid radio broadcasts of the games, worried that free accounts of the action would dampen ticket sales. Veeck knew the opposite was true—people who were exposed to the team on a regular basis were actually *more* likely to shell out money to see the players in person. Immediately after taking over, he allowed all comers to air the games, free of charge. The next year, 1947, he drove a much harder bargain, selling the rights to WGAR for $1. Former player Jack Graney teamed with Van Patrick in the booth.

The 1948 season marked the first year for Indians TV broadcasts. Patrick moved out of the radio booth to call the occasional game for WEWS (Channel 5). He was replaced by Jimmy Dudley.

Local fans also appreciated the fact that, like many of them, Veeck was a war veteran. Anyone who laid eyes on him got a powerful reminder. His right leg was amputated just below the knee because of an infection that resulted from a wound he received while serving in the Pacific Theater with the Marines. He was fitted with a prosthesis after his 1946 surgery, but had a severe limp and usually used a cane. Not that it slowed him down any. Bill Veeck was in constant motion.

Boudreau was, too, despite ankles so bad that he had been classified as 4-F for the war, meaning he was physically disqualified. Both ankles were bad, dating back to his high school basketball days. Now they were weak and riddled with arthritis. And it didn't help that he broke an ankle during a game in 1945.

Perhaps feeling that his mates needed some outside help, Feller imported a bit of technology from his years in the Navy. He had returned home with a telescope used as a gun sight on his ship, and in 1948 loaned it to members of the stadium's grounds crew. They would sit inside the big scoreboard in centerfield, focus the telescope on the opposing catcher, and steal the signs. An Indian batsman could look for a signal on the scoreboard and see what type of pitch was coming.

Still, the 1948 season was hardly lopsided. For most of the year, four teams were slugging it out for first place—Cleveland, New York, Boston, and Philadelphia.

The mood on the lakefront was consistently electric. One of the best days in franchise history may have been June 20. On a nice Sunday afternoon, 82,781 fans made their way to 17-year-old Cleveland Municipal Stadium for a doubleheader against Philadelphia. It was the biggest crowd anywhere, at any time, in major league history.

Feller came out the first game and beat the A's, 4–3. Lemon followed that up with a 10–0 win. Most of those fans vowed to come back, and soon.

Three days after the Fourth of July, Bill Veeck gave local baseball fans yet another reason to come to the ballpark. He signed the legendary Negro League star Satchel Paige, who was 110 years old. Well, we actually don't know how old he was, because even he claimed not to know. But he was well past his prime. Most estimates had him somewhere between the ages of 48 and 50.

Boudreau wasn't thrilled with the idea. He thought it was another of Veeck's publicity stunts, and didn't want that kind of disruption during a hot pennant race. But he soon changed his tune.

Veeck asked Boudreau, who had occasionally played catcher in amateur ball, to catch Paige at a workout and judge whether he had any gas left. According to Boudreau's 1993 autobiography, Boudreau and Paige played pitch and catch for about 10 minutes. Then Paige walked in to Boudreau and handed him a folded-up handkerchief. The pitcher told him to put it somewhere—anywhere—on home plate, and vowed to throw the ball right over it.

Boudreau set it on the inside corner. Paige threw 10 hard pitches, mixing fastballs and sliders, and hit the hankie nine times. Then the catcher moved the hankie to the other side of the plate. Paige nailed the target seven more times, and barely missed on the others.

Finally, Boudreau went into the batting cage and took some cuts. After failing more often than succeeding, he told Veeck that Paige still had impressive stuff, and could help the team as a reliever and occasional starter. They all went into the clubhouse, where Paige signed a contract.

On July 9, the call went out to the bullpen. As the six-foot, five-inch Paige walked to the mound, a feeding frenzy erupted among photographers. In those days, newspaper photographers were allowed to stand right on the field during games, only a few feet from home plate or the bases. And when Paige came in to warm up, the shooters went right out on the mound next to him. It was a bizarre scene.

No wonder the first batter singled. But Paige, who sported a thin mustache and a hangdog look, got the next three outs, and the crowd gave him a standing ovation.

Three weeks later, the old man got his first big-league start. On a Tuesday night, an amazing 72,434 people turned out to watch. Satch had already become a fan favorite, not only because of his advanced age but also thanks to his colorful, homegrown philosophies. He was a low-rent, self-styled Confucius, trotting out such unique homilies as "Don't look back, somebody might be gaining on you." And, "Avoid fried meats, which angry up the blood." And, "Keep the juices flowing by jangling around gently as you move."

Paige pitched well that night, getting the win in a 5–3 decision over the Senators' Early Wynn, and he kept pitching well, ending the season with a 6–1 record and a 2.48 ERA.

What a summer. Three-quarters of the Indians' infield made the All-Star team: Keltner, Boudreau, and Gordon, along with two starting pitchers, Lemon and Feller, even though Feller was having a down year. Veeck decided to hold Feller out of the game, not giving the All-Star manager a chance to burn out two of his pitchers during a pennant race. In mid-July, at Sportsman's Park in St. Louis, Boudreau batted third, Gordon was the cleanup hitter, and Keltner hit sixth as the American League notched a 5–2 win.

By the second week in August, the standings showed a three-way tie among the Indians, Yankees, and A's. By Labor Day, Cleveland had slipped to third behind Boston and New York. Worse yet, they were four and a half games out with less than a month to go.

Then things got weird. Pitcher Don Black was batting during a September 13 home game when he collapsed at the plate with a brain hemorrhage. He survived, but just barely.

He was still in critical condition nine days later when Veeck held a "Don Black Night" that drew 76,772 and raised $40,000 for Black's medical bills. Getting that many people to the ballpark on a Wednesday night was nothing short of astonishing.

Attendance was fabulous throughout September. A key doubleheader against Philadelphia drew 75,382, and the Indians would wind up setting a new season record of 2.6 million people.

With seven games left, the Indians found themselves in another three-way tie for first. Four games later, they led by two games.

With only three games remaining and the so-so Detroit Tigers in town, the pennant looked like a lock. But sports are never a lock in Cleveland, even during the best of times. The Tribe tanked two of the three games.

Lemon lost the first outing, and Bearden got his 19th win in the second, leaving Feller in a position to wrap things up on the final day.

What a great script: the longtime local star, a war hero, uncharacteristically struggling on the mound for much of the season, but hanging tough and winning the pennant on the last day of the season in front of an enthusiastic throng in his home ballpark.

Feller got shelled.

He was knocked out in the third inning, and the game was never close. Tigers 7, Tribe 1. And when Boston beat the Yankees, Cleveland and Boston had completed all 154 of their games in precisely the same manner: with 96 wins, 58 losses.

For the first time in the history of the American League, a one-game playoff would be needed to determine which team would go to the World Series.

American League authorities knew the race could come down to this, so they had held a coin toss earlier to determine which team would have the home-field advantage. Naturally, luck turned its back on Cleveland. The game would be held at Fenway Park in front of Boston's roaring, cantankerous throngs. And it would be held the next afternoon. So the Indians boarded a train for a late-night journey to Beantown.

On Monday, Boudreau already knew which pitcher he was going to trot out for the biggest game of the season. But nobody else did, and he wanted to keep it that way. On a normal day, before the game, he would go into the locker room and stick a baseball under the cap of the pitcher who was starting. That habit was well known in baseball circles. So before the Boston game, instead of placing one baseball under one cap and giving the clubhouse attendant a chance to report back to the Red Sox manager, Boudreau put balls in the lockers of Lemon, Feller, and Bearden.

The real choice was Bearden.

It was a shock on the face of it. Feller was the best pitcher in club history, perhaps the best righty in *baseball* history, and had worked only three innings the day before. Lemon had gone 20–14. And Boudreau was going with a rookie?

Well, this "lowly" rookie had won 19 games himself, including his last start. Besides, he wasn't exactly a babe in the woods. He was 28 years old. His career had been delayed because he served overseas with the Navy in World War II, picking up a purple heart and metal pins in various body parts. Gene Bearden was well aware that baseball was not a matter of life and death.

But this was the biggest game of the year, and the eyes of the nation would be watching.

Back in Cleveland, life nearly ground to a halt. Even high school football teams delayed their practices until the game was over. Although the game was shown on television, hardly anybody owned one because they were too expensive. Most fans tuned in to the radio.

Boston's choice of a starter was a bit unorthodox as well. Denny Galehouse got the call. Galehouse was a native of Marshallville, in Northeast Ohio's Wayne County. He had been a journeyman pitcher for 14 years, playing with three teams. It was his second time around with the Red Sox, and he was clearly on the downside of his career. His season total of eight wins was only the fifth best on his team. By the following May, he would be finished. But Boston's manager had been looking at the season statistics, and saw that Galehouse had throttled the Indians all season, holding them to only two hits in eight innings of relief.

The strangest managerial move clearly belonged to Boudreau. Baseball purists almost lost their cookies when they heard that left-fielder Allie Clark would start at first base.

Yes, Allie Clark. A guy who never played first base. Biggest game of the year and you change a guy's position?

Boudreau was playing another of his hunches. Looking at the

short left-field fence, he wanted to stack his lineup with right-handed batters. Never mind that Galehouse was a righty. So Boudreau benched the normal first baseman, lefty Eddie Robinson, put Clark at first, and replaced Clark in right field with seldom-used Bob Kennedy. The only lefty in the starting lineup was leadoff batter Dale Mitchell, who had been smoking all year, averaging .336.

The Indians didn't wait long to make an impression. The third batter of the game, Boudreau, drilled a Galehouse fastball over the Green Monster, giving the Indians a 1–0 lead.

In the bottom of the first, the Sox got to Bearden on a double, a groundout, and a single, tying things up.

Nobody made any noise again until the fourth, when Cleveland blew the game open.

Boudreau singles. Gordon singles, and Boudreau stops at second.

Baseball tradition is demanding that Boudreau call for a sacrifice bunt to move two runners into scoring position with one out. Nonsense, says Boudreau. My man, Kenny Keltner, is hitting .297 with 30 homers. Let the man play the game.

Galehouse winds and delivers . . . Keltner swings . . . the ball rises toward the Monster . . . back, back . . . it's gone! Three-run homer. Cleveland takes a 4–1 lead, and Galehouse is off to the showers. Listening back home, Northeast Ohioans are going nuts.

Ellis Kinder replaces Galehouse and looks in at Larry Doby. Doby, hitting .301 for the year, lashes a double. He takes third on a bunt, scores on a groundout, and the Tribe has a 5–1 lead.

One inning later, Boudreau hits *another* homer, his 18th of the season.

But plenty of innings remain. In the bottom of the sixth, Bobby Doerr stands in against Bearden. Doerr is a solid, veteran power-hitter, a smallish second baseman who will eventually be enshrined at Cooperstown. He is known as a clutch hitter, and on this day lives up to his reputation. He jacks a two-run homer, his 27th of the year. Cleveland's lead is cut to 6–3, and things are starting to get interesting again.

But not for long. The Tribe scores in the eighth and again in the ninth. When Bearden strolls to the mound in the bottom of the ninth, he has a cushy 8–3 lead.

Boudreau is looking like a genius. Of course, it's easy to be a good manager when your shortstop goes 4-for-4 with two homers.

Bearden—the rookie who shouldn't be out there—goes the distance with a five-hitter.

After Boston's Birdie Tebbetts grounds out to third to end the game at 3:54 p.m., the players swarm Bearden and carry him off on their shoulders. Bill Veeck, sitting in a box seat by the third-base dugout, scampers across the infield, gimpy leg and all, to embrace the players as they head into the tunnel behind the first-base dugout. In the locker room, he breaks into tears.

In short order, Boudreau receives 200 telegrams. He sits in the clubhouse, smiling, and opens every one.

Back in Cleveland, the city is exploding with joy. Office workers yank open their windows and throw scrap paper into the street. Factory whistles and fire bells ring out. Firecrackers explode. The after-work traffic jam never dissipates as motorists hang around, honking their horns, well into the evening. The newspapers will compare the celebration to V-E Day.

At one point, more than 200 people join a snake dance that started almost accidentally in front of the May Company and built into a python as it made its way up Euclid Avenue to Playhouse Square. The leader is an Air Force sergeant who was simply crossing the street when a happy girl grabbed his shoulders and another girl grabbed *her* shoulders. Next thing you know, an endless human line is weaving back and forth between parked cars, in and out of traffic, shaking and squirming and twisting for all it's worth.

At midnight, people are still packing the downtown, waving signs and pennants. They are about to taste fruit they haven't tasted since 1920—a World Series.

Good thing the 1948 World Series didn't open the day after the playoff game. Most of the Cleveland Indians were severely hung over following a massive blowout at the Kenmore Hotel, half a mile from Fenway.

Because the other Boston team, the Braves, had won the National League pennant, Cleveland didn't even have to leave town. So everyone stayed around and celebrated. The players looked so horrible when they showed up for a 10 a.m. workout the next day that Boudreau called off batting practice, fearing somebody would get hurt.

By Wednesday, though, the Tribe was ready for action.

The Series was almost anticlimactic. After 28 years of standing at the side of the room, Northeast Ohio was happy just to be on the dance floor. Regardless of what was about to unfold, the team had already captured the hardest hearts.

Unlike the Indians, the Braves had cruised into the postseason, finishing 6½ games ahead of the St. Louis Cardinals, 7½ ahead of the Brooklyn Dodgers, and 8½ ahead of the Pittsburgh Pirates.

The Braves were an interesting challenge. They had two aces on their pitching staff: Warren Spahn and Johnny Sain. But they didn't have much of a staff beyond that. Hence the wishful mantra of Braves fans: "Spahn, Sain, and two days of rain."

Sain got the call for Game One. He took a 24–15 record to the mound to face Feller, who had finished the season at a disappointing—for him—19–15. His earned run average was 3.56, the highest since his first full season as a starter, back in 1938.

Sain, by contrast, was at the very height of his career. Over the last three seasons he was averaging 22 wins. Cleveland sent this lineup against him:

1. Mitchell, LF
2. Doby, CF
3. Boudreau, SS
4. Gordon, 2B
5. Keltner, 3B
6. Wally Judnich, RF
7. Robinson, 1B
8. Hegan, C
9. Feller, P

Game One was a pitchers' duel for the ages. During the first four innings, only one batter, Keltner, got so much as a single.

Boston got its first hit off Feller in the fifth, when Marv Rickert singled to left.

Through seven innings, the teams had combined for a grand total of five hits, all singles, and four by Cleveland. But in the eighth, Feller finally made a mistake. It turned out to be a big one—but only because an umpire blew a call.

Feller walked the leadoff batter, Bill Salkeld. A pinch-runner, Phil Masi, replaced him. Masi, a catcher who was nonetheless faster than

Salkheld, was sacrificed to second, and Eddie Stanky came to the plate. Feller walked him intentionally, and Stanky was replaced by another pinch-runner, Sibby Sisti.

With runners on first and second and one out, Sain came to the plate. Unlike his colleague Spahn, Sain was not much of a hitter. But he got the sign to swing away, and flied out to right for the second out.

The third out came on a beautiful pickoff play at second. Boudreau called the signal by putting his glove over his left knee. He alerted the centerfielder, Doby, by raising his right heel. When Boudreau broke to the bag, Feller counted to two, then whirled and threw. Masi was out. The only person in the ballpark who didn't see that was second base ump Bill Stewart, who apparently was caught by surprise. (Years later, Masi would admit he was out.)

Given that reprieve, the Braves sent Tommy Holmes to the plate. Holmes was a .325 hitter, and he ripped a shot down the third-base line to score Masi.

In a game in which even a single was viewed as an offensive gem, this lone run became the Hope Diamond. Boston's 1–0 victory allowed the Braves to keep their home-field advantage.

Next up for the Tribe: 15-game winner Warren Spahn.

Spahn was in his third full major league season but already had 44 wins. He was a lefty, with sweeping motion like Feller's, who would go on to become the winningest lefty in the history of the planet, with 363 W's and a spot in the Hall of Fame.

The Tribe sent out a relatively well-rested Bob Lemon.

Although this game was low-scoring as well, it was not the same thing of beauty, and it didn't carry the same degree of drama. But that was just fine for Indians fans, because it resulted in a victory.

Lemon got in trouble in the first inning, but gave up only one run—thanks, in part, to the same pickoff play used the day before. Apparently, the Braves were not a quick study, because only two innings after Feller's pickoff of Masi the previous afternoon, Lemon turned and nailed first baseman Earl Torgeson on that same, timed play. Boudreau again applied the tag, and this time the umpire made the correct call.

In the top of the fourth, Boudreau doubled, Gordon singled, and Doby singled, giving Cleveland their first runs in 13 innings of World Series play. More importantly, it gave them a 2–1 lead.

The Tribe scored another in the fifth and another in the ninth and coasted to a 4–1 win. Lemon was rock steady, scattering eight hits and striking out five. The Indians had evened the series, and they were heading home.

There was no such thing as a "travel day" in those days, even though travel took considerably longer. Less than 24 hours after finishing Game Two, the Indians and Braves had journeyed back to Cleveland by train and were out on the field again.

Game Three was played on a Friday afternoon in front of 70,306 rowdies at Municipal Stadium. They roared early and often as their first-year pitching sensation, Bearden, kept his knuckleball dancing.

Even more surprising was Bearden's bat. He got two hits, including Cleveland's first hit in the third, a double to right field. He scored on a walk and a fielder's choice.

Boston's starter, Vern Bickford, got into more trouble in the fourth. A walk and consecutive singles by Robinson and Hegan brought home another run, and Boston summoned Bill Voiselle to the mound. Voiselle turned the Indians bats to mush, but the damage was already done.

Bearden was virtually unhittable, giving up only four singles and a double—none in the same inning—and striking out four. The knuckleballer didn't walk a single batter.

October 9, 1948, was a great day to be a Clevelander. The home team held a 2–1 lead in the World Series, it was Saturday, and 81,897 fans were flooding the yellow-brick monster to root their boys on in Game Four.

Boudreau thought about starting Feller on only three days of rest. But the manager played another hunch and went with Steve Gromek. Casual fans were asking, "Steve *who*?" Gromek was not exactly a gate attraction. He had started only nine games the entire season, and never expected to be used in the World Series, even in relief. The manager figured he had some breathing room with a one-game lead, though, and wanted Feller and Lemon to come out later in the series with full tanks of gas.

Warming up in the other bullpen was the nearly unhittable Sain. Hey, Tribe fans, can you say "underdog"?

Surprise, surprise: modest little Steve Gromek pitched six shutout innings. The Braves finally figured him out in the seventh, but not for long. Rickert homered. Period. That was Boston's only run. Gromek retired 9 of the last 10 batters of the game.

Sain was almost as good. But that wasn't good enough. Boudreau's first-inning double accounted for one run, and Doby's solo homer in the third made the difference.

Cleveland won, 2–1. Gromek—*Gromek!*—had out-dueled Johnny Sain. Amazing. And now, with one more home game left, Cleveland needed one win to capture the world championship.

The first four games had been dominated by pitching. The two teams had scored a grand total of 11 runs. And the stage was set for one more great pitching performance.

"Rapid Robert" Feller would take the hill for the Indians. For all his greatness, he had never won a World Series game. And now, at home, in front of a record crowd, he could win the whole deal.

Feller had come on strong toward the end of the season, winning seven games in a row. And he had pitched extremely well in the Series opener. So the 86,288 people who whirled the stadium's turnstiles were expecting big things.

Try to wrap your mind around the figure 86,288. That's 600 people more than the biggest crowd ever to watch a *Browns* game at the stadium. That's close to *twice* the size of the biggest crowd ever to wedge itself into Jacobs Field (45,274 in the 1997 Division Series). The sound cascading down from all points in the gargantuan ballpark was deafening.

And Feller got clobbered.

He had nothing. In the first inning, cleanup hitter Bob Elliott pounded a three-run homer.

The Tribe's Mitchell got one of those back when he led off with a homer, but an inning later Elliott whacked Feller again, this time with nobody on, to give Boston a 4–1 lead.

Cleveland rallied for four in the fourth, tying the game on an RBI single by Judnich and a three-run homer by Hegan. But after ripping the roof off the joint, the fans soon fell quiet.

Feller gave up his third homer in the sixth, this time off the bat of Salkheld. Boudreau yanked Feller in the seventh, but the bullpen imploded. The Braves scored six runs and cruised home with an 11–6 win. It was back to Boston.

Once again, without a break, the teams were suited up on Monday afternoon. Cleveland was still in good shape, needing only one win in two tries, and Bob Lemon was taking the mound. If he couldn't do it, the newest pitching star, Bearden, would be ready for Game Seven.

Boston held out its ace, too. While Sain charted pitches, Voiselle went to the hill in front of 40,103 Sox fans. Packing 40,000 people into tiny Fenway Park, with its narrow aisles and narrower seats, is quite a sporting achievement in itself. And the fans were pumped.

Cleveland struck first. Mitchell doubled leading off the third, and Boudreau doubled him home. Otherwise, Voiselle was holding his own. Through five innings, he had given up only four hits.

The Braves got to Lemon in the fourth on a walk and two singles, and at the top of the sixth, the score was tied at one. Joe Gordon changed that with a home run. A walk, a single, and a fielder's choice added another run. After six, the score was Cleveland 3, Boston 1.

The Indians added a big run in the eighth on three straight singles. Tribe 4, Braves 1. Six outs to go.

Lemon began to wear down. After a single, a line out, a double, and a walk, Boudreau had seen enough. With the bases loaded, he called for No. 30, Gene Bearden.

Yes, the same Gene Bearden who had been scheduled to pitch in Game Seven if necessary. Boudreau figured that Cleveland still had a two-run lead, and that his ace could shut things down and finish the series right now.

But Bearden gave up a sacrifice fly, and Masi ripped a double to left, closing the gap to 4–3. The second-guessers were already warming up their pipes.

Masi was marooned on second, though, as Bearden got Mike Mc-Cormick to ground back to the mound.

Bearden made things interesting again in the ninth, walking the leadoff batter. But the second hitter, Sisti, popped up a bunt attempt, and Hegan caught it and fired to first to get a pinch-runner, Connie Ryan, who was suddenly the least popular guy in New England.

When Tommy Holmes flew out to Kennedy in left field, the 1948 Cleveland Indians were the champions of baseball.

The Indians were elated, but they were so tired from playing 10 pressure-packed games in 11 days that the immediate celebration seemed more muted than the one after the playoff game. That changed on the train ride back to Cleveland, which became a huge party.

The next morning, Tuesday, October 12, the team was greeted by one of the biggest parties in Cleveland history. A tickertape parade was staged from Public Square to Severance Hall at University Circle. That 100-block stretch of Euclid Avenue was swamped with confetti, signs, and cheers. The next day, the *Cleveland Press* unveiled a layout suitable for the announcement of a world war:

"200,000 CHEER THE CHAMPIONS"

Each of the winners eventually took home $6,772—and memories for a lifetime.

And that Boudreau fellow from Illinois was handed yet another award for his massive trophy case: the American League's Most Valuable Player trophy.

Boudreau hit .355, was a double-play machine at shortstop, and seemed to get every clutch hit all year.

His No. 5 jersey was retired by the Indians in 1970—the same year he was inducted into the Hall of Fame.

Best trade the Indians never made.

Rank: #15

RACE OF DOOM

MONDAY, SEPTEMBER 5, 1949

Almost every Labor Day week for two decades, 100,000 people a day would crane their necks skyward to watch airplanes race around at Hopkins Airport. The National Air Races became increasingly dangerous as the years passed, and when a plane crashed into a home in Berea, killing a mother and child, the event was doomed.

ONLY 15 YEARS had passed since Orville Wright climbed onto his odd little contraption and made that first, shaky, 12-second flight. But Cleveland city manager Bill Hopkins realized the boys from Dayton were onto something. Something big. And he wanted to be ready.

In 1918, a special committee headed by Hopkins recommended that Cleveland build a large municipal airport way out in the sticks, south of Brookpark Road, where there was plenty of cheap land— 700 acres, all the land you could possibly need.

Politics in those days was a lot like politics today: ponderous. Three years passed without any action. Only after the city was threatened with losing a spot on the potentially lucrative coast-to-coast airmail route was Hopkins's plan approved. And four more years went by before all the red tape was untangled and construction began.

Soon after its 1925 debut, though, nobody was second-guessing the project. Cleveland-to-Detroit became the first commercial airmail run in the nation. The number of overall flights quadrupled in just three years and, by the late '20s, Cleveland's airport was one of the busiest in the world.

The most fitting way to celebrate that achievement, some thought, was by grabbing the National Air Races.

The races had started in 1920 on Long Island and were moved to a different city each year. In 1929, it was Cleveland's turn. Things went so well that first year that the rotating schedule was all but abandoned. After a stop in Chicago in 1930, the affair would return to Cleveland seven more times in the next nine years.

That was a huge coup. Although the National Air Races did not generate the kind of public clamor associated with today's Super Bowl, it was a blockbuster affair, only a notch behind the legendary Paris air show, and a major publicity bonanza. The 10-day bashes drew the attention of the world and as many as 100,000 daily spectators.

Part of the draw was the sheer audacity of the aviation industry. In barely one generation, airplanes had gone from lightweight, fragile, tentative birds, negotiating with the air currents, to gigantic metal behemoths that ripped through the skies with a supernatural roar at speeds that not long before had been absolutely unthinkable.

The National Air Races offered spectators a glimpse at the cutting edge of aviation. Each year, the pilots and planes would go ever faster, ever higher. For the industry, the races provided a working laboratory. Technological developments spurred by racing inevitably found their way into commercial and military aviation.

The lobbying campaign to bring the races to Cleveland was headed by heavy hitters like Alva Bradley, a shipping tycoon and president of the Indians; Cleveland Trust banker I. F. Freiberger; and M. J. Van Sweringen, a business goliath who, with his brother, developed Terminal Tower and Shaker Heights.

As the debut of the Air Races approached, the town was buzzing. Aviation was still a thrilling concept for most people. It would be three years before Charles Lindbergh's infant son would be abducted in the most famous kidnapping of all time; in eight years, Amelia Earhart would disappear over the Pacific, creating the most enduring aviation mystery of all time. But on Labor Day weekend of 1929, the lives of these famous fliers were rosy. And they were spending them in Cleveland.

Lindbergh, in particular, was in his glory. Just two years after his historic solo flight across the Atlantic, he was a happy, 27-year-old newlywed, having joined forces with Anne Morrow in May. Everywhere the Lindberghs roamed, they were treated like royalty.

Earhart had not yet made her solo voyage across the big pond. That was still three years off. But she had been a passenger on a transatlantic flight the summer before, a female first. At age 32, she was the aviation editor of *Cosmopolitan* magazine and a budding star of the skies.

In addition to the aerial stunts and stationary displays that are the staples of modern air shows, the early shows featured more than 40 races, including half a dozen cross-country battles. In 1929, the major cross-country contest, later known as the Bendix Trophy Race, originated in Los Angeles. Here's how it went, according to the *Akron Beacon Journal*:

> Flying the General Tire & Rubber Company's Lockheed racing plane, Lt. Henry J. Brown Sunday sped from Los Angeles to Cleveland for a new record of 13 hours and 18 minutes. . . . Brown's fuel tanks were nearly empty and his motor was sputtering badly when he shoved his black-and-silver Lockheed monoplane across the finish line. The crowds acclaimed him as he came down. They shouted and applauded uproariously.

After kissing his wife, he talked with the media: "I ran into difficulty when two of my tanks went dry and had to wobble my third to get the gasoline into the motor."

Brown's was one of 1,000 aircraft involved in that first show. Fans—paying $1 a day for general admission or $2.50 for a grandstand seat—were treated to night-flying exhibitions (a radical concept in those days), glider demonstrations (usually towed by automobiles), and blimp formation flying (compliments of Akron's Goodyear-Zeppelin).

Opening day included a four-mile-long parade through the downtown. Also downtown, at Public Auditorium, was a huge display of aircraft and other flight-related exhibits.

Through it all, the headliner was Lindbergh. Although in later years he would encounter some PR problems, mainly over his isolationist stance on the eve of World War II, in '29, "Lindy" was a walking icon.

His immortal *Spirit of St. Louis* had a major Cleveland connection:

its historic flight was powered by 18 valves manufactured by Thompson Products. (Thompson Products, one of a number of Cleveland companies making aircraft parts, would eventually blossom, under the guidance of Frederick Crawford, into aerospace and become known as TRW.)

Lindy didn't participate in any races, but he did climb into the cockpit for a demonstration with a team of Navy pilots known as the High Hats. According to the *Beacon Journal*: "The Colonel and the High Hats put on an extensive show which included the famous tail-on-tail squirrel cage loop, the three-way spread maneuver in which the Colonel loops and the High Hat pair barrel roll at the top, and the accurately timed three-way attack on a target in which the ships miss each other by only a few feet."

The final day of the 1929 show seemed to unfold in slow motion—it featured blimps, flown in from Akron at their ever-leisurely pace.

"Akron Day" began with a car caravan that formed on Exchange Street between South Main and West Market. A miles-long line of autos was led, from above, by three Goodyear blimps, *Puritan, Vigilant,* and the new *Defender*—which would be christened in Cleveland by Earhart. Hundreds more Akron residents made the trip by bus and the "interurban" railroad.

On the *Defender*'s return flight, one of the folks hitching a ride was international celebrity Hugo von Eckener, commander of the *Graf Zeppelin,* the huge dirigible that had just finished circling the globe. Eckener and the gang landed on the 18th fairway at Portage County Club to a roar from 7,000 onlookers. He spent the next day meeting with Goodyear-Zeppelin honchos about potential business deals involving passenger travel.

"I prefer not to be a hero, but simply to be one who demonstrates the safety of airships," Eckener told reporters in his German accent. "If one must be a hero to go on board a dirigible, then airship transportation will never pay and I will be a bankrupt hero.

"Well, now that I have shown that it is safe, I hope that governments and other backers will find confidence to help us establish airship transportation."

Eight years later, the *Hindenburg* exploded, killing 36 people and effectively ending the age of passenger airships.

But in 1929, the prospects for aviation appeared to be unlimited. And every city in America seemed to be catching the fever. Akron would soon stage its own air shows, drawing 100,000 to 125,000 people in the mid- to late 1930s.

None of the smaller shows would develop the high profile of the National Air Races, though. In fact, in 1935, Earhart, then working for a commercial airline, flew into Akron Municipal Airport with a load of mail in the midst of Aviation Day, unaware that anything special was going on. Obviously, she was surprised to see 100,000 people ringing the airfield. And most of them had no idea she was there.

According to the next day's paper, after shaking hands quickly with the governor, "the tall, slender transatlantic flier with the tousled, sun-bleached hair heeded neither frantic pleas . . . to talk over the mike nor the shouted questions of crowding photographers and reporters. 'This plane is on regular schedule,' she said, firmly. 'Nothing must be allowed to hold up the mail. We are already 15 minutes late. I am sorry. But we must go on.'"

In 1929, Earhart was in an even bigger hurry. Although at the time women were not allowed to compete in the more dangerous closed-course races, they had their own cross-country division, an eight-day contest launched in Santa Monica, California. Earhart was leading after the first leg when she came in for a landing in Yuma, Arizona. But her plane nosed forward, smashing the propeller. She was unhurt, and soon obtained a replacement prop. Eventually she finished third, two hours behind the winner, and pocketed $875.

Earhart, referred to in the 1929 program as "America's best-known girl flyer," may have been a trailblazer, but apparently she was not much of a racer. In subsequent years, after the Bendix race had been opened to women, she struggled. While her female colleague, Jackie Cochran, won two Bendix cups, Earhart was shut out.

She wasn't much of a glider pilot, either. A *Plain Dealer* story said she trashed a borrowed glider on the fifth day of the 1929 show while attempting to land in front of the grandstand, which was located roughly where NASA's Glenn Research Center is today. "Although Miss Earhart was badly shaken up," said the report, "she was far more interested in the condition of the glider than in her own welfare."

The problem: pilot error. The public-address announcer told the crowd what had happened: "Miss Earhart had plenty of speed in her landing, but her control was faulty. She permitted it to dip too far to the left and landed on a wing-tip."

It's a wonder Earhart lived long enough to disappear: Though she

never suffered a serious injury, she crashed more times than a demolition derby driver. She crashed upon landing in Ireland. She crashed
upon takeoff in Honolulu. In '35 she got a bug in her eye, couldn't
read her maps, strayed off course, and had to crash-land in a cow pas-
ture in Mexico.

And she didn't only crash planes. She also crashed her "autogyro,"
the name used for a helicopter. In mid-1931, during a—ahem—
"safety demonstration" in Abilene, Texas, Earhart lost control of her
chopper, damaging three parked cars and barely missing a crowd of
onlookers. She was cited by the government for "carelessness and
poor judgment." Three months later, she was at it again, crashing an
autogyro at a fair in Detroit.

Crashes were becoming a growing problem at the air races as well.
And the 1929 show offered a foreshadowing of the disaster that
would strike exactly two decades later.

The '29 races were marred before they even reached Cleveland.
During the cross-country competition from Los Angeles, five pilots
were killed. Then, when the show reached town, another pilot died
only three hours after setting a world record for the longest solo
flight. Thomas Reid crashed into the woods near West 226th Street
and Westwood Road. Another plane plunged through the roof of the
Mills Company at 965 Wayside Drive. And a parachute jumper
nearly died when her chute got tangled and she landed right on
Grayton Road.

There was no letup. Three years later, a man who had just won the
cross-country race died while participating in the Thompson Trophy
race, a dash around pylons that was staged close to the ground. During the eighth lap, the black-and-white monoplane flown by Doug
Davis suddenly veered toward the sky, turned abruptly, and shot
downward at 350 miles per hour. It crashed into a field at Lorain and
Gessner Roads in North Olmsted. The aftermath was not one of
Cleveland's finest moments: Rescue workers were hampered in their
efforts to retrieve Davis's remains by souvenir hunters who were trying to snap up pieces of the wreckage.

In '37, yet another pilot died when his plane began to disintegrate
and smashed into the woods behind a house on Grayton Road.

Another year, another victim: In '38, a plane exploded and roared
into a pear orchard near Wager and Clague roads in Rocky River.
That pilot died after lingering for several days with a fractured skull.

In '39, still another pilot cashed it in, this time in plain view of

65,000 spectators. Flying a Brown Racer, Leland Williams went into a spin and burrowed into a farm field between Grayton Road and Rocky River Drive.

Like many major public events, the air show was suspended at the onset of World War II. But in 1946 it returned to Cleveland, where the fun lasted four more years before coming to an abrupt, fiery halt.

It's one thing when a pilot loses his or her life in a race; pilots know the risks. But when planes start plowing into private homes, the end of the competition can't be far behind.

As the years passed and the airport grew, so did the neighborhoods surrounding it. By the late '30s, the runways that were once in the middle of nowhere were surrounded by Cleveland suburbs.

The mounting death toll should not have been the only warning sign. For every fatality, there were two or three close calls. Engines would blow up, tails would fall off, pilots would simply lose control.

The 1947 affair was a bloody mess. Forget about the three narrow misses—the crash into a cornfield in Brook Park, the crash into an empty lot on Eastland Road, the crash into a boxcar in the railroad yard at West 150th Street. Those resulted in only minor injuries as the pilots bailed out. The most gruesome event was the crash of a Navy surplus Corsair fighter. While 75,000 people watched, Tony Jannazo lost control during a race and his plane exploded. Jannazo's head was lopped off, his body flew into a field, and the plane's engine rocketed across Royalton Road, barely missing a car carrying four civilians.

By comparison, 1948 was almost tame. "Only" one pilot died. His plane crashed into the Rocky River Reservation of the Metropark system north of Brookpark Road.

The inevitable finally happened in 1949. It took place during the highlight of the air races, the Thompson Trophy race, a wild, 50-mile, closed-course dash around seven widely spaced pylons.

Pilots flew incredibly low during pylon races, often at altitudes of less than 100 feet, for two reasons: to make sure they cleared the pylons, and to make sure the judges could see that they cleared the pylons. Shave off one corner and you were penalized a lap, effectively disqualifying you.

The first pylon was at the southern end of Cleveland Municipal Airport, as it was called in those days, near what would become the I-X Center. The second pylon was to the southwest, at Lewis and No Bottom roads in Olmsted Township. From there, it was off to

Sprague and Marks, just south of today's Ohio Turnpike. The fourth post was set up at Albion and Eastland roads in Strongsville, the southernmost point of the race. Next was a northeast turn to Webster and Sprague, then northeast to West 130th, near what is now Southland Shopping Center. The final post was near Snow Road, just east of today's Interstate 71.

Most of the racing was organized by divisions based on engine size. But the Thompson race had no restrictions whatsoever. Want to use dynamite for fuel? Be our guest! Naturally, this free-for-all was a crowd favorite.

For the '49 Thompson race, pilot William P. Odom was behind the controls of a modified P-51 Mustang. The Mustang was a glamour plane, one of the heroes of World War II, a single-engine fighter that was the aviation equivalent of the muscle car. And Odom was a glamour pilot, a man who two years before had set a world record for fastest flight around the globe.

On April 12, 1947, Odom took off in an A-26 Reynolds Bombshell from New York's LaGuardia Airport and returned in three days, six hours, and 55 minutes, clobbering the previous record set in 1939 by Howard Hughes.

Despite that 20,000-mile flight, despite an impressive record as a World War II pilot, Odom was overmatched in the Thompson race. The beast he was flying for the first time—on loan from aforementioned celebrity flier Jackie Cochran—was just too much for him. Moreover, the customized monster was designed for courses with four pylons, not seven. Worst of all, Odom was a novice at closed courses, having never flown in one before this show.

His inexperience was certainly not in evidence four days earlier, when he set a record while winning the Sohio race. But before the Thompson race, he reportedly told one of his colleagues, "I don't belong in this thing. I'm used to flying high off the ground."

At 4:45 p.m. on Labor Day, Odom straps himself into his dark-green machine, named *Beguine*, and roars into the air with nine other pilots. They are racing in a counterclockwise direction in a circle roughly six miles in diameter.

After one lap, Odom is in third place. He blasts around the first pylon at more than 400 miles per hour, and heads toward Pylon 2. The problem begins when he flies too wide and then tries to make up for the lost distance. Instead of banking his plane about 40 degrees, he pulls it to about 60 degrees. The Beguine flips upside down and roars out of control.

It's now 4:48 p.m. Bradley Laird is having a great day, a Labor Day straight out of Norman Rockwell. Less than a week earlier, Laird, 36, had grabbed his piece of the American dream, moving into a new house at 429 West Street in Berea, near Beeler Road, less than half a mile south of Bagley. He paid $16,000 for his dream.

It's just a small, one-story structure, and he's right on top of his neighbors, and there's not much in the way of landscaping. But Laird is thrilled. A stationery salesman from Minnesota, he has a new house in a new neighborhood in a comfortable suburb. The future looks rosy for him, his wife, and their two young boys.

Laird is outside his house, washing windows and getting into water fights with son David, age five. In the front yard, Laird's father-in-law, Ben Hoffman, is keeping an eye on 13-month-old Craig, who is frolicking in his playpen.

Inside the house, Laird's wife, Jeanne, 24, is looking out the bathroom window, enjoying the water fights and occasionally checking out the air races.

Suddenly, a nightmare begins to unfold.

Odom's plane comes streaking into the tranquil neighborhood and crashes directly into the Lairds' attached garage. The Mustang is traveling so fast that its nose goes right through the new concrete floor and digs six feet into the dirt.

Because Odom has completed only one lap of the race, his gas tank is nearly full, and it explodes on impact, sending flames everywhere—including the baby's crib in the front yard. The horrified grandfather grabs the burning baby, runs away from the house, and begins to tear the flaming clothes from his grandson. He is screaming, "Save the children! Save the children!"

The other child is already safe, as is his father. Laird had quickly grabbed young David and pulled him away from the house. But the mother is trapped in the bathroom, unable to escape the inferno stoked by aircraft fuel.

Her husband tries to fight his way into the house, but is turned back by the flames. He tries again and again, but just can't reach his wife.

At least two dozen neighbors rush to the scene, but they are powerless too.

An ambulance arrives quickly, and the baby and the grandfather—

also badly burned—are placed inside. But the grandfather won't stay put. Knowing his daughter is still in the house, he pulls away from rescuers and heads toward the fire. Three times he breaks away before being successfully restrained by medical technicians.

The baby and the grandfather are rushed to Berea Community Hospital. The baby dies within three hours. The grandfather eventually overcomes the burns on his head and his hands. But never the one in his heart

Following Odom's crash, Berea passed a law prohibiting pylon racing over its territory. Other municipalities soon followed suit.

No races were staged anywhere in 1950. And, although various cities held races and air shows in subsequent years (annual races are still flown in Reno, Nevada), things were never the same.

Some observers claimed the flavor had already gone out of the gum. The postwar planes "lost their individuality," according to *The Golden Age of Air Racing*, published in 1963. "They were not the product of a handful of mechanics and pilots who had fathered them from blueprint to reality. They were 'war babies.' Not racing planes any more, but machines—big, powerful, expensive, with no secrets. . . . You measured time and winners by a slide rule and horsepower, not ingenuity and a checkered flag."

Before the war, the pilots had been as quirky as the planes. The 1929 air show was peopled by such renegades as Hollywood's Roscoe Turner, who wore a grandiose handlebar mustache and a matching attitude. He sometimes flew with a lion cub in his cockpit. After the war, the shows were dominated by military types in taxpayer-financed, assembly-line-produced machines.

But there was no denying the appeal of the postwar races to the youngsters and parents who during the late '40s flocked to Cleveland from throughout the Midwest. The show was still a dazzling coming together of the world's finest aircraft. The debut of jets right after the war added even more spice.

Ironically, one of the planes that won the war lost the air races.

Rank: #14

THE CATCH

WEDNESDAY, SEPTEMBER 29, 1954

The 1954 Cleveland Indians won more games than anyone in American League history and fully expected to cruise to a World Series title. Instead, they were swept. The tone was set in Game One, when Willie Mays made a miraculous grab of a smash that would have won the game for Cleveland. That catch is still considered by many to be the most dramatic in baseball history.

CLEVELAND LEARNED a hard lesson in 1954: never put your parade before your championship.

Estimates ran as high as 500,000 people. Of course, that was from the guy in charge of the parade, so we can view that figure with a healthy dose of skepticism. Still, even objective observers estimated that 200,000 to 300,000 people lined the streets of Cleveland on September 21, 1954, as the American League pennant winners paraded from Ivanhoe Road and Euclid Avenue on the East Side all the way to Kamm's Corners on the west.

Sure, we can understand the enthusiasm. It was the best baseball team in Cleveland history—by far. Heck, it was the best baseball team in *American League* history. Still is. One hundred eleven wins in 154 games, a winning percentage of .721. The mighty 1927 Yankees only finished at .714. Even the charmed 2001 Seattle Mariners—winners of 116 games in a 162-game season—fell five points short.

Cleveland's pitching rotation was sent from above: Early Wynn followed by Bob Lemon followed by Mike Garcia followed by Bob Feller. "The Big Four." Throw away the bullpen. Don't need one.

True, the quartet was beginning to show a little wear around the edges. The youngest in the group was "The Big Bear," Garcia, who was 30. Lemon was 33, Wynn was 34, and Feller was 35—downright elderly by the standards of the era. Still, those four guys collectively won 78 games—70 percent of the team's total.

The Indians strutted to the finish line with an eight-game advantage over the Yankees and a 17-game lead over the White Sox. Fans began to believe the World Series would be a mere formality. If the 1948 Indians could win the Series after barely winning the pennant, well, this team would surely march right into the Polo Grounds and show those Giants how the game was meant to be played, more effectively than Abner Doubleday his own semi-fictional self.

That's why hardly anybody, with the possible exception of the players, took issue with the idea of staging a massive victory parade along an 18-mile route through the heart of Cleveland before the World Series began.

Too bad nobody paid much attention to a cranky newspaper columnist named Franklin Lewis. Writing in the September 6 edition of the *Press*, Lewis rued a Cleveland City Council initiative to encourage citizens to flock to Hopkins airport that night to welcome the team back from a three-week road trip. After noting how much he disliked any kind of reception, especially wedding receptions, Franklin wrote:

> I have been swept into many a parade and party for baseball players and I happen to know how they feel about them. They hate the very idea. They shrink from the compulsory personal appearance. And they actively resent having to become Exhibits A, B, C, and Z at an airport platform or while being jockeyed through city streets balancing on the folded lid of an automobile dealer's convertible. . . .
>
> You can't blame them for rebelling at the thought of shoving, clawing, pawing fans, especially when they'd been away from home for three weeks and just over yonder, at the edge of the crowd, awaits the Little Woman.

Well, some of them may have availed themselves of Little Women on the road. But we digress.

If the players did dislike their early-September greeting at Hopkins, where 10,000 people turned out to claw and paw, they must have absolutely detested what was awaiting them two weeks later.

The Big Parade took place on a Tuesday afternoon, with a starting time of 3 p.m. to accommodate school kids. The kids were accommodated even more when the parade began late.

Collinwood High School's band led the way, and the John Marshall band brought up the rear. In between, the Cleveland Indians were paraded two by two in top-down convertibles with their names printed on placards affixed to the doors.

Although the day was bright, a steady wind made things uncomfortable. All of the players sat down in the seats of their cars, hunched against the wind, except for two pitchers, Feller and reliever Ray Narleski, who sat "balancing on the folded lid of an automobile dealer's convertible," trying to soak in every drop of adulation.

The "Cavalcade of Champions," as it was billed, looked like an invasion force. It was led by 29 police motorcycles and contained 28 cars and two trucks.

The procession headed west on Euclid, through Public Square, across the Detroit-Superior Bridge, out to Detroit Avenue, south on West Boulevard, and west on Lorain. Throughout the central city, people were four and five deep along the sidewalks. Thousands more sat on the steps of buildings. Thousands more chose not to venture out into the chill but watched from the other side of windows.

Kids called to the players by name. Confetti was everywhere, blowing sideways in the wind and covering the city like a snow squall.

The traffic commissioner said the turnout was at least as heavy as it had been for war hero Dwight Eisenhower when the general rode from Hopkins airport to Public Square.

Naturally, the politicians weren't about to pass up this kind of attention. Governor Frank Lausche rode in the first open car, and Mayor Anthony J. Celebrezze was in the second.

Maybe the parade was designed to be taken at face value. Maybe it truly was a celebration of throwing off the bonds of Yankee dominance. But to some it seemed more like a premature coronation. And there can be no doubt that it created bad karma. The baseball gods are touchy, and you don't want to make them think you're taking anything for granted.

In the rosy glow of the pre–World Series moment, the hometown fans forgot how streaky their '54 team had been. The Indians actually got off to a rotten start, dropping six of their first nine games.

Then came a six-game winning streak, followed by a week of .500 ball, followed by an 11-game winning streak. In early June, they won nine straight, then dropped five of eight, then won eight straight.

In mid-July, they were horrid, losing four straight. And in late July, they were great, winning 10 of 12. August saw a nine-game win streak and a five-game win streak. Just when they seemed to be on a roll heading into September, they lost four of seven. And then, out of the blue, they won 11 in a row.

Obviously, with 111 wins, the bad moments were few. But the Tribe didn't exactly intimidate the league's top teams. They played only .500 ball against both the Yankees and the White Sox. Cleveland thrived on "beating the hell out of the bums," as was their philosophy at the time. Against Boston, they won 20 of 22. Against Baltimore, then won 19 of 22. And they won 18 of 22 against both the Washington Senators and the Philadelphia A's.

The Tribe's pitching was far more impressive than its hitting. Other than Bobby Avila, who smoked through the season hitting .341, only one other regular hit .300. That was Al Rosen, who hit exactly .300. Rosen was coming off a phenomenal season in which he missed winning the Triple Crown by one hit. He was the American League's Most Valuable Player in the first unanimous vote in history. Forty-three homers, 145 RBIs, and a .336 average.

But in '54, Rosen, only 30, was beginning to suffer from nagging injuries. A broken finger never properly healed, and it would drag down his performance as the months went by.

Larry Doby was the only major power-hitter on the '54 squad, collecting 32 homers and 126 runs batted in. Both totals were best in the league. But he hit only .272.

Fortunately, in early July the Indians picked up a fellow by the name of Vic Wertz. It didn't seem like a big deal at the time. He came from Baltimore in exchange for a young, little-used pitcher named Bob Chakales, and he wasn't even visualized as a starter. "He'll be good insurance," said manager Al Lopez.

Wertz was hitting all of .202, with one lousy homer in two months of baseball. But Lopez knew Wertz had hit .304 in 1949 and .308 in 1950, and figured he might still have a bit of life left in his old bat.

Lopez was a low-key guy who was almost universally liked by players, writers, and fans. In early September, Hal Lebovitz, writing in the *Cleveland News*, declared him "one of the nicest guys in baseball," and said the team had been molded in that image.

There are no bad guys among the Indians, because Lopez won't tolerate them. He's not a taskmaster, nor a tyrant. He simply gets rid of the joy-boys, the rules-breakers and the lazy ones. . . .

He virtually cleaned house this winter, getting rid of several problem cases. He also disposes of the unhappi-ness boys, the gripers, the possible clubhouse lawyers. "A happy club is a team club," he declares.

Lopez knew the players didn't like clubhouse meetings, so he didn't call any. He was so low key, in fact, that the front office had pressured him over the winter to spread around a little more hell. But "I can't do something I don't feel," Lopez told Lebovitz. "I don't be-lieve in that kind of managing. In football, pep talks might be valu-able to key up the players for a certain game. In baseball, we play every day, 154 times a year. You play better when you're relaxed. If I tried to be mean and nasty, it would be an act. . . . If that's what they want, they'd better get somebody else."

Nobody had any thoughts of getting somebody else. Everything about the 1954 season seemed just right—even the happy coinci-dence that Cleveland was hosting the All-Star Game for the first time since 1935.

The National League brought along a young superstar named Willie Mays. Only 23, Mays had already played in a World Series and was universally hailed as one of the best in the business. But he was still somewhat less than completely worldly. As he sat in his room at the Statler hotel on the eve of the game, talking with a reporter from the *Cleveland Press*, he professed to know all about the American League ballpark where the stars would meet, referring to it as "the park with the short right field and the high wall."

His roommate, catcher Roy Campanella, almost fell off his chair laughing. "Not that park!" said Campanella, hearing Mays describe old League Park. "This is the big stadium down by the lake, the biggest baseball park in the country. You could put League Park in-side the Stadium."

Mays liked what he saw the next day, as did most of the rest of the hitters. The contest erupted into a home run derby. The American League whacked four—including a pair by Cleveland's Rosen—and the National League drilled two. All-time records were set for runs and hits—and, quite likely, for excitement. The lead changed hands six times.

The good guys won, 11–9, on the strength of a three-run rally in the eighth. The key hit was the softest of the game—a broken-bat single over second base by White Sox second baseman Nellie Fox with the bases loaded.

In addition to Rosen's explosion, two other hometown boys would have made the ESPN highlights had there been any. Larry Doby and Bobby Avila combined for eight RBIs.

Although ESPN was 25 years away, television coverage was making progress. Seventy-seven of the Tribe's away games were aired on WXEL, Channel 8. Announcers Ken Coleman and Jim Britt called the games. In the radio booth, Jimmy Dudley was back behind the mike for his seventh season, teamed with Ed Edwards on WERE, at 1300 kilocycles, as they used to say. (Nobody referred to the AM dial, because there wasn't an FM dial.)

If the summer of '54 sounds like one big, happy party, well, it wasn't. In some ways, 1954 was a surprisingly rough season. Attendance was barely over half of what it had been in 1948. Granted, most franchises would have been thrilled to put 1.3 million people through the turnstiles. But was this team only half as exciting as the 1948 team?

The dynamic was partly the result of frustration. The Indians had finished in second place three years in a row, trailing the New York Yankees all three years. You can only finish second so many times without wearing down your fans. The Yankees were a baseball version of Michael Jordan and the Cavaliers—a seemingly immovable object standing between Cleveland and a championship.

Moreover, a significant number of fans still harbored some resentment over the departure of Lou Boudreau. The local hero was dumped in 1950 after 13 years with the club, and finished his career in Boston.

Even when the All-Star Game swirled into town, attendance was relatively soft. A gate of 68,751 is not a bad crowd, but certainly lower than expected given the fact that the Midsummer Classic was in town for the first time in 19 years. The 1935 game, played when the Indians were mired in the middle of the pack, actually outdrew the 1954 game by 1,000 fans.

Another drag on the excitement meter was the fact that the Bill Veeck era was over. The wild showman had cashed out in November 1949 in search of new adventure.

Still another problem was the fact that the 1954 Tribe saved its best for the last three months of the season. In July, August, and September, they went 35–7. Who knew they were that good?

Not until a dramatic doubleheader sweep on the second Sunday in September did the Tribe register a TKO over the Yankees and ensure that fannies would remain in the pews the rest of the way.

In an odd bit of scheduling, New York was in town for just one day. The day before, the Tribe had won its fourth straight game, against Boston, behind Art Houtteman. Now, on Sunday, they were back to the top of the rotation. In the first game, Lemon outpitched Whitey Ford, 4–1. In Game Two, Wynn bested Tommy Byrne, 3–2. That gave the Tribe six straight wins and made the pennant look like a sure thing.

Things looked so secure at that point that the big parade was first announced on September 15—three days before they actually clinched the pennant! Yet another example of putting the trophy cart ahead of the horsehide.

Even before that, the team managed to anger scores of businesspeople by tying World Series tickets to advertising commitments. The club said a company would be allowed to buy 40 World Series tickets if it also agreed to pay $800 for a full-page ad in the game program.

The Indians went on to drop three of their last five games, just to make things more interesting, but their lead was never in doubt.

Over the last four months of the season, Wertz had turned himself into a solid starter. He wasn't spectacular, winding up with a .275 average, but he chipped in 14 homers in fewer than 300 at-bats and added a veteran presence.

Game One of the 1954 World Series was scheduled for Wednesday, September 29, at the Polo Grounds in New York.

The Polo Grounds was a funky ballpark. If Cleveland Stadium looked like a horseshoe from the air, the home field for the Giants looked like a bathtub. Because of that shape, the left- and right-field fences were incredibly close to home plate, and centerfield was an endless journey into night.

Left field was 279 feet from home plate—but a 21-foot overhang meant that a fly ball of about 250 could reach the upper deck. Right field was a mere 258. Centerfield was—ahem—483 feet.

Like Cleveland Stadium, the Polo Grounds had two decks surrounding the playing field except in centerfield, where it opened up to roofless bleachers and a scoreboard. The park sat right across the Harlem River from Yankee Stadium.

The *Polo* Grounds? Where were the horses? Well, this was New York's fourth version of the Polo Grounds. The first one, which opened in 1880 as the home of the New York Metropolitans, was indeed a converted polo field. It was at Fifth Avenue and 110th Street, and was used for eight years before being torn down for development.

The second Polo Grounds was built at Eighth Avenue and 155th Street and held 15,000 people. Soon, another ballpark for a rival league went up right next door. One day a player at the Polo Grounds actually hit a homer that crossed the fence at the second ballpark, drawing cheers from both crowds. When the rival team went bankrupt, the old team moved into the second park, which was slightly bigger, and it became yet another "Polo Grounds." That third park burned down in 1911 and was replaced by the concrete-and-steel structure where the Indians would play the first two games of the World Series.

The Giants were entirely comfortable in the place, having won there at a .697 clip while capturing the National League pennant by five games over the Brooklyn Dodgers and eight games over the Milwaukee Braves.

On the eve of the Series, much of the media attention was focused on the Giants' centerfielder, Mays, dubbed "the Say Hey Kid" because of his habit of greeting people by saying, "Say hey." He had a high, squeaky voice, but that was okay, because his bat thundered. He hit for both average and power. Those traits, combined with his blazing speed, brought him more triples than anyone in the game. Mays also was a superb defender with a cannon for a right arm. He led the league in double plays by outfielders.

At one point in late July, Mays was 11 games ahead of Babe Ruth's single-season home-run pace. Although he obviously didn't catch the Bambino (he ended up with "only" 41), New York manager Leo Durocher flatly declared that Mays was "the greatest ballplayer I've ever seen." And Durocher had seen such folks as Ruth, and Stan Musial.

One of the greatest pitchers anyone saw in the late '40s and early '50s was taking the mound to try to stop Mays and his pals. That was Cleveland's Lemon. A converted third baseman, Lemon had won more than 20 games in six of the previous seven seasons, including 23 this season, the most in the American League, with a 2.72 ERA. He was a workhorse, having completed 21 of the 33 games he started, also tops in the AL. *The Sporting News* named him the best pitcher in '48 and '50, and would do so again after the '54 season.

On the mound for New York was Sal "The Barber" Maglie. His nickname came from his habit of giving hitters a close shave. "When I'm pitching," Maglie would say, "I own the plate."

On Wednesday afternoon, shortly before 1 p.m., on a warm, sunny day in the Big Apple, manager Lopez delivered this lineup card to the barber chair:

1. Al Smith, LF
2. Bobby Avila, 2B
3. Larry Doby, CF
4. Al Rosen, 3B
5. Vic Wertz, 1B
6. Dave Philley, RF
7. George Strickland, SS
8. Jim Hegan, C
9. Bob Lemon, P

Durocher started this way:

1. Whitey Lockman, 1B
2. Alvin Dark, SS
3. Don Mueller, RF
4. Willie Mays, CF
5. Hank Thompson, 3B
6. Monte Irvin, LF
7. Davey Williams, 2B
8. Wes Westrum, C
9. Sal Maglie, P

Two of Cleveland's three television stations were airing the game live: WXEL with the local guys and WNBK, Channel 3, with the NBC network announcers. WNBK put a TV in the window of its headquarters at East Ninth and Superior and drew a huge crowd. Same thing happened in front of the window at the Standard Drugstore at East Sixth and Superior.

Those fans, and the thousands of others whose productivity waned at work and at school, saw one of the most memorable games in the history of Cleveland baseball—memorable for all the wrong reasons. It was a study in frustration.

First came the tease. In the first inning, the Indians jumped out to the lead on a hit batter, a single, an error, and a two-out triple by Wertz. They held that lead until the bottom of the third. The Giants scored on a fielder's choice after two singles, then scored again on a single by Thompson.

Lemon and Maglie then settled into a pitcher's duel that kept going through seven innings.

In the top of the eighth, the Tribe began to get to Maglie. Doby worked him for a walk and Rosen singled, moving Doby to second. At that point, Durocher had seen enough. He went to the bullpen for lefty Don Liddle, a spot starter during the season, to face left-handed hitter Wertz.

Liddle comes to the mound, takes his eight warm-up tosses, and glances around at the runners. Doby on second, Rosen on first. Nobody out. Tie game. Eighth inning. World Series opener. The pressure cooker is turned up nearly as far as it will go.

Liddle, No. 37, looks in for the sign. The late-afternoon sun is casting his shadow toward third base, the only one unoccupied. His catcher, Westrum, flashes the sign for a fastball. Liddle stretches, brings his hands together at his waist, and pauses just long enough for a quick glance at second base. He turns and delivers.

As Wertz swings and connects, he experiences a feeling that amateur athletes feel only occasionally: the ball has the weight of a feather. When your mechanics are just right and your timing is perfect, the bat or golf club feels like it has moved through the air without striking anything. As a professional hitter, Wertz has felt this feeling before. But never in his life has he hit a ball this solidly.

The baseball shoots off his bat, heading to the deepest recesses of the bathtub-shaped stadium. The 52,751 Giant fans hold their breath, rapidly doing the physics, trying to calculate whether their hero, Willie Mays, the No. 24 on his back already facing directly away from home plate, will catch up to the ball before it hits the ground. If he doesn't, Cleveland will score at least two runs, and Wertz will be a hero.

Mays reaches back and catches the ball almost directly over his head, two steps from the wall and 450 feet from home plate. In most parks, it's a three-run homer and an Indians victory. At the Polo Grounds, with Willie Mays in center, it's a loud out. The biggest crowd in National League history goes wild.

Mays whirls to throw so quickly that his cap falls off his head. He follows through so forcefully that he crumples to the ground like a run-down top. Even so, Mays is so far from the infield that Doby can tag up and move to third.

Big deal. Instead of a three-run lead, the Tribe has one out and runners at the corners.

Durocher, his heart beginning to beat again, finds the strength to trek to the mound and get Liddle out of there.

The new reliever, Marv Grissom, promptly walks pinch-hitter Dale Mitchell, loading the bases. But another pinch-hitter, Dave Pope, is called out on strikes, and the eighth hitter, Hegan, flies out to left. Two walks . . . a single . . . a 450-foot drive . . . and the Indians have absolutely nothing to show for it.

But Lemon hangs tough, and the Giants have nothing to show for their efforts, either. Cleveland threatens in the ninth after an error and a walk, and threatens again in the top of the 10th when Wertz leads off with a double—his third hit of the game. His pinch-runner is sacrificed to second, but a strikeout and a line drive to first get the Giants out of the inning.

Lemon is still cruising in the bottom of the 10th. He fans the first hitter. Then he walks Mays, and Willie steals second. After an intentional walk to Thompson, the Giants send a pinch-hitter to the plate. It's Jim "Dusty" Rhodes, a seldom-used outfielder who hit .341 in 164 regular-season at-bats.

Lemon throws him a sharp curveball. Rhodes swings and connects, but doesn't make particularly good contact. In fact, the Tribe's second baseman, Avila, starts back after the ball before realizing it will carry to the right-fielder, Pope, who has stayed in the game after pinch-hitting. Pope thinks it's a routine fly ball. He is absolutely certain he will catch it. It just keeps going, though, drifting high in the wind toward the short right-field fence. He leaps at the base of the 11-foot wall, but the ball drops into the first row, a mere 270 feet from home plate.

Ballgame.

The winning homer traveled 180 feet less than Wertz's out.

Is there no justice? Lemon pitches 10 awesome innings and gets beat on a cheap homer? Wertz rips two singles, a double, a triple, and, in any other ballpark, what would have been a homer, swinging with a hand so sore that he has to wear a foam pad, and the Tribe scores two lousy runs?

The Indians ask themselves those questions over and over in their locker room. In the politically incorrect spirit of the day, Lopez calls the game-winner "a Chinese home run." Wertz tells reporters he simply can't hit a ball any better than he did in the eighth inning. "I know this sounds funny," says the balding first baseman, "but I actually thought that thing was going to carry into the bleachers. When I smacked the ball, it felt so good and I was so sure of how hard I tagged it that all the details were erased from my mind. I can't even tell you what I hit."

The next morning's *Plain Dealer* tried to make the hometown fans feel better by running this two-column headline: "Lost first in 1948, too." But Mays's play had set the tone for the series. In Game Two the next day, under overcast skies, the Indians again scored in their first at-bat, a homer by Al Smith onto the left-field roof. But that was the only run they scored all day. New York pitcher Johnny Antonelli gave up twice as many hits as Cleveland's Early Wynn, eight, but his team somehow scraped together three runs. The Tribe, having left 13 men on base for two consecutive games, returned to Cleveland in a 2–0 hole.

Rosen, the cleanup hitter, was hurt and struggling. After going 2-for-8 the first two games, he was benched by Lopez. Doby and Avila weren't doing much with the bats either.

Still, the city was buzzing about hosting a World Series. The airlines added extra flights into Hopkins. The New York Central railroad added 14 sleeper cars on its run from Grand Central. Chartered trains and busses brought fans from throughout the region. Hotel space was at such a premium that the nearest vacancies were in Akron and Mansfield. Dozens of fans had to hole up even farther away, in Pittsburgh.

For Game Three, on Friday, the first day of October, the gates were opened at 9 a.m., and 71,555 made their way to the lakefront. They should have stayed home. Garcia started, and gave up a run in the first and three more in the third. The bullpen coughed up two more runs, giving the Giants a 6–0 cushion after seven. Cleveland scored one meaningless run in both the seventh and eighth.

Now, things were really ugly. The Tribe would have to win the next day to keep from being swept. Here was a team with 111 wins that couldn't seem to do anything right in the postseason.

Manager Lopez considered his options. It was Bob Feller's turn in the rotation, and Feller was well rested.

Feller had won 262 games for the franchise, but he had never won a World Series game. He had been a star for 16 years. Most compelling of all, he had finished the regular season with a 13–3 record and a solid 3.09 ERA—including three wins in his last three outings. Say hey! Pitch the guy!

But Lopez came back with Lemon. The manager decided that, if he was going down, he was going down with his best, the top pitcher in baseball that year, even if that pitcher had gotten only two days of rest.

The decision was not popular—especially when Lemon came out looking like a reject from the Toledo Mudhens. He was pounded for seven hits in four innings. Meanwhile, Liddle, the guy who initiated Wertz's 450-foot fly ball in Game One, started for the Giants, and did a passable impersonation of Cy Young. In the first four innings, he gave up one hit, a single.

The Giants' defense imploded in the fifth. With two out, Liddle dropped a toss while covering first. On the very next play, his second baseman booted a grounder, putting runners on first and second. Hank Majeski pinch-hit for the Tribe and ripped a three-run homer. But the Indians were still down by a grand slam.

After the seventh, when the Giants shut down a Cleveland rally and held a 7–4 lead, the exodus began. By the bottom of the ninth, more than half of the 78,102 fans may have already been on the other side of the turnstiles.

The city was crushed. The glorious season had turned into a heap of ashes in a period of four days.

During the off-season, the fans bristled over the decision to start the weary Lemon over Feller. The greatest pitcher in Indians history never got his one last chance to win a World Series game.

For the next five years, the home team would hear as many boos as cheers, ostensibly because they finished second, second, sixth, fourth, and second. But there was still a deep well of resentment about the Game Four decision on Feller.

The Giants went back home to the embrace of New Yawk. But in three years, they would be gone, moving to windblown Candlestick Park in San Francisco.

The Polo Grounds went dark for five years. In 1962, Casey Stengel's hapless Mets moved in while Shea Stadium was being built. When the Mets moved to Shea in 1964, the Polo Grounds was demolished for a housing development.

Too bad the need for new housing hadn't been more pressing a decade earlier.

THE ROCK IS KNOCKED

SUNDAY, APRIL 17, 1960

The biggest box-office star in the history of Cleveland baseball was Rocky Colavito. But just as he was blossoming into a superstar, he was dealt to Detroit by general manager Frank "Trader" Lane, unleashing an unprecedented torrent of wrath from heartbroken Tribe fans.

EVERY BOY IN NORTHEAST OHIO wanted to be Rocky Colavito. Every girl in Northeast Ohio wanted to marry him.

The boys would head to the playground and imitate Colavito's odd batting ritual. Just before stepping into the box, they'd hold the bat horizontally, across their waist, with one hand near the bottom of the handle and the other out near the end of the barrel. Then they'd lift the bat above and behind the head and pull it down against the back of the shoulders.

Having stretched all of the important batting muscles, they would dig into the box and, with both hands on the handle, point the bat directly at the pitcher. They'd hold that pose until just before the delivery.

The girls of Northeast Ohio couldn't marry Rocky because he was already married. While playing in the minor leagues, he had become smitten with a teenage ballet dancer who didn't know anything about baseball. At the absurdly young age of 21, against the wishes of his parents and her parents, he married her. They became soulmates.

So the girls did the next best thing. They formed fan clubs, wrote him letters, and lined up—with the boys—to get his autograph.

Rocky would sign every last autograph, even if it took an hour. But only if the kids stayed in a line and were polite. Colavito's parents had raised him with a heavy hand, teaching him discipline and manners, and he wasn't about to let his own fans slide. If you didn't thank him for the autograph, he would ask you whether you had forgotten something.

Rocky knew all about the hero–fan equation. He had grown up wanting to be Joe DiMaggio. That should come as no surprise, given the fact that Rocky was an Italian-American kid who lived about seven blocks from Yankee Stadium.

His mother and father both emigrated from the same town in Italy, Bari, on the coast of the Adriatic Sea. His dad served in the Italian army during World War I. In America, he made his living driving a truck in the Bronx while Rocky's mother raised five kids.

Rocky was the youngest, born during the darkest days of the Great Depression. He shared a tiny bedroom with two brothers. The rocket arm he displayed in big league outfields came partly from genetics and partly from their tutelage on the playgrounds. They would constantly challenge him to throw rocks farther than he had thrown them before.

Rocky worked as a delivery boy, and he grew proficient at shooting pool, a fact he did not broadcast to his parents. But his favorite pursuit, by far, was baseball.

Because the Colavito boys belonged to the Police Athletic League, they were able to get seats in the upper deck at Yankee Stadium and watch DiMaggio play three or four times a week. Rocky absorbed every DiMaggio quirk. When Rocky started playing in amateur leagues, he would swing three bats in the on-deck circle, just like Joe, and wear uniform Number 5, just like Joe. Unfortunately, Rocky also grew up copying his hero's funky batting stance.

DiMaggio stood with his legs far apart, toes pointed outward, left leg open. It worked for him, but it didn't work for many others. Consciously or subconsciously, Rocky continued to imitate Joe D even after he turned pro—and it nearly cost him his career.

In 1953, in the low minors, Colavito was hitting .200 when a manager finally convinced him that the open stance was too much Joe and not enough Rocky. Colavito had heard that plenty of times before, from plenty of different baseball people, but now that he was mired in a seemingly endless slump, he agreed to make a major effort to readjust. Almost immediately after closing his stance, bringing his feet together and bending slightly at the knees, he watched his batting average soar. His awesome power only increased.

The revamped swing led to steady progress, and he received a late-season call-up to the bigs in 1955. He hit well in limited duty and figured he was on his way.

Still, there were plenty of skeptics. After watching Colavito struggle during spring training of 1956, *Akron Beacon Journal* columnist Jim Schlemmer wrote, "It is difficult to see big league caliber in Colavito." Rocky managed to break camp with the big club, but was sent back down in June by manager Al Lopez.

While playing with the team's minor league affiliate in San Diego, Colavito entered a pregame distance-throwing contest and unleashed a heave that measured 436 feet. His arm was so good that he had to constantly fight off management attempts to convert him from an outfielder to a pitcher. Colavito didn't want to pitch because starting pitchers sat out three of every four games. He wanted to play—every day.

Colavito returned to the bigs in late July and hit .305 the rest of the way. That earned him second place in the Rookie of the Year balloting, behind Luis Aparicio.

The next year, 1957, his first full season in the bigs, he generated 25 homers and 84 RBIs. Still, as late as 1958, he was far from a fixture in the Tribe outfield. After a series of fielding woes, manager Bobby Bragan moved him to first base. Initially he played well there, despite an almost total lack of first-base experience. But then he blew a game with an error and was benched.

Colavito, nearly distraught at this point, went into the manager's office and offered a brash guarantee: *If you play me every day, I'll hit you 35 homers.*

Believe it or not, Bragan told Colavito he had a deal. Rocky tried to amend the figure to 30, saying he had missed a lot of games already, but Bragan held him to it. Colavito was in the lineup regularly, and his homer total began to mount.

But the team was faltering and, in mid-July, Bragan was fired.

The new manager was Joe Gordon, a fan favorite from his days of playing second base next to shortstop Lou Boudreau. Gordon appreciated Rocky's power but thought he hit into way too many double plays, struck out way too many times, and swung way too hard.

Gordon persuaded him to cut down on his swing and go to all fields. The lightbulb went on in Rocky's head. He went on a tear. By the end of the year, he had 41 homers—six above his guarantee and only two short of the Indians' all-time record, set five years earlier by Al Rosen. He also led the team in RBIs (113), batting average (.303), and doubles (26). His homers accounted for 25 percent of the team's total.

Like so many other baseball people, Gordon was enthralled with Rocky's arm. During a charity game against Cincinnati that summer, he put Rocky on the mound for two innings—and Colavito struck out five batters. A second exhibition appearance wasn't as impressive, but he had displayed enough potential that Gordon soon waved him to the mound in a real game.

The shocking move took place in mid-August, during the second half of a doubleheader against Detroit. Colavito took a while getting to the mound because he thought Gordon was pointing to the bullpen, rather than at him. But eventually he figured it out, managed to keep his jaw from dropping completely off his head, jogged to the mound, threw eight warm-up pitches, and held the Tigers scoreless over three innings.

Gordon claimed Rocky's fastball was faster than Bob Feller's in his prime—the ultimate compliment. Cleveland's front office was worried about an injury, though, and Colavito's pitching career ended abruptly—with an ERA of .000.

Still, watching him throw from right field was worth the price of admission. He threw so hard that the ball had practically no trajectory. A catcher for the San Diego farm club told the *Plain Dealer*'s Gordon Cobbledick about a laser shot Colavito had unleashed from right field to the plate. "He turned it loose about chest-high, it passed the cutoff man chest-high, and I caught it chest-high," he said. "You don't believe it? I wouldn't, either, if I hadn't seen it."

In 1959, Rocky confirmed the notion that he had developed into one of the game's elite power-hitters. He finished the year with 42 clouts, tying the Senators' Harmon Killebrew for the American League crown.

No one would have predicted it during the first half of the season. On June 10, Colavito was suffering through a 4-for-30 slump. Trade rumors were beginning to circulate. And the Tribe was playing that night at Baltimore's Memorial Stadium, the toughest park in the majors for a home-run hitter. Oddly enough, that dismal setting produced one of the most memorable games in Cleveland baseball history.

In his first at-bat, Colavito drew a walk, then jogged home on a round-tripper by Minnie Minoso. In the second inning, with Baltimore at bat, as he ran into the right-field corner to track down a fly ball, a fan threw a beer on him. The Rock summoned every bit of self-control and managed to refrain from going into the stands after the guy. He didn't even say anything. He simply, silently, vowed revenge.

A half-inning later, he got it, hitting a 365-foot homer just inside the left-field foul pole.

In the fifth inning, he got it again, hitting a 400-foot shot into the bleachers in left-center.

In the sixth, he got it again, driving a low fastball 420 feet into the centerfield seats.

In the ninth, he got it again. This time he jacked one high into the power alley in left. It landed 425 feet from the plate. And Rocky landed in the record books.

Only two other batters in baseball history had hit four consecutive homers in one game. The first guy did it in 1894; the second, Lou Gehrig, in 1932. Pretty fast company for a guy from the Bronx.

Even the Baltimore fans gave Rocky his due. They erupted in a standing ovation after Number Four, and it was still going when he trotted out to right field.

Colavito was the epitome of the streak hitter. When he was on, he was deadly. When he was off, he was dead. Unfortunately, he died that season just when the Indians needed him the most.

For the first time in eons, the Indians were embroiled in a pennant race. They and the Chicago White Sox—think Aparicio, Nellie Fox, Sherm Lollar, Billy Pierce, and staff ace Early Wynn (ouch)—had been duking it out all summer. In the month of September, during the heat of the pennant race, Rocky hit .207. The Tribe lost by five games.

The skid actually began on the last weekend in August, when Chicago came to town to play four games in three days. The weekend series would likely set the tone for the rest of the season. More than 70,000 people attended each game. And the Tribe tanked every one of them. Zip for four.

For the year, the Indians were 7–15 against the White Sox, a miserable .318. It cost them the pennant.

Still, Cleveland baseball was enjoying a renaissance. From 1958 to 1959, attendance more than doubled, to 1.5 million. On September 12, 1959, against the dreaded Yankees, the Indians set a major league record for attendance at a doubleheader—84,587.

And the team's best player was only 26 years old.

Colavito posted 111 RBI, second-best in the league, and was chosen for the All-Star team. His two-year total of 83 homers and 224 RBIs surpassed the two-year totals of both Mickey Mantle and Willie Mays.

The only person who could stop Rocky Colavito was a nasty little man in a coat and tie who spent every waking moment on the telephone.

Unfortunately for Rocky and the Indians—and, for that matter, the city of Cleveland—on November 12, 1957, the team had hired a general manager named Frank Lane.

Lane didn't give a damn about the popularity of Colavito or DiMaggio or anyone else. While he was the GM in St. Louis, he didn't think twice about trading star second baseman Red Schoendienst, who had grown up nearby and was immensely popular. In fact, Lane wanted to trade the city's biggest icon, Stan Musial, but the owner vetoed that one.

Heck, at one point Lane wanted to trade the entire St. Louis roster for another team's roster. Later in his career, he did succeed in trading managers.

Are you detecting a theme here? "Trader Lane" would trade his mother and father if he thought it would get him a newspaper headline. He had an almost pathological need to deal. During a two-year period beginning in December 1957, Lane made 60 trades. Some of them were good. Many of them were bad.

Among his brainstorms was the one that sent Roger Maris out of town for Vic Power and Woodie Held. That would be the same Roger Maris who broke Babe Ruth's single-season home run record, the same Roger Maris who was voted the American League's Most Valuable Player, the same Roger Maris who was an outstanding outfielder and team player and appeared in more World Series during the 1960s than any other ballplayer.

Granted, Power and Held were decent talents, especially Power, whose Gold Glove at first base erased plenty of blunders by infielders like Held. But neither player had anywhere near the impact of Maris.

Famous names . . . hot young prospects . . . pitchers . . . position players . . . none of that mattered to Frank Lane.

Clearly, Lane and Colavito were on a collision course. Their relationship wasn't helped by Rocky's determination to get a big raise after his breakout 1958 season.

In '58, Colavito made about $14,000. Lane grudgingly agreed to double that figure in 1959, but their relationship was deteriorating. In fact, during the off-season, Lane offered Colavito to the Senators for Pedro Ramos and Jim Lemon. That didn't fly, so he tried to send Rocky to Detroit, with Maris, for Al Kaline.

Colavito's prowess at the plate was only part of the reason to keep him in an Indians uniform. He was a huge local favorite, the most popular Indian since Lou Boudreau—and quite possibly the most popular Indian ever.

He fit the classic description of tall (six-three), dark (olive skin, thick facial hair), and handsome (in a boyish kind of way). His patience with fans was impressive, as was his zealous loyalty to his family. He didn't smoke, hardly ever swore, and was a devoted Catholic who went to church every Sunday. He would have an occasional beer or red wine with dinner, but never came close to making the papers for tangling with some punk in a bar. He was a relentless optimist, and that attitude shone through.

To be sure, Rocco Domenico Colavito was not a Hall of Famer. He was agonizingly slow. He couldn't beat a mule from home to first if you spotted him half the distance. His feet were so flat that they earned him a pass from the draft board during the Korean War.

Statistically, he looked like a great outfielder. One year he played in 162 games without making an error. But you can't drop a ball that you can't get to.

Although Colavito had one of the strongest throwing arms in baseball history, in his early days you never knew where the ball was going. If Rocky wasn't throwing to the wrong base, which he did often, or throwing a rainbow over the head of the cutoff man, which he did routinely, he was uncorking a wild heave into the grandstands.

He also tended to be a slow starter, a guy who struggled in April before blooming during the late spring and summer.

It was during one of those down times, in 1957, that legendary Cleveland sportswriter Hal Lebovitz responded to criticism of Colavito with a column headed, "Don't knock the Rock!" The phrase instantly won a spot in the local lexicon.

The message was clear: Rocky was flawed, but he was ours. He didn't hit for an astronomical average, but he could pound the ball 400 feet with incredible regularity. He couldn't run like Jesse Owens, but he didn't butcher too many plays with his glove. He might have been a bit erratic with his throws, but he could gun down a runner trying to go from first to third as well as anyone who ever played. So don't knock the Rock.

To Frank Lane, all of that was trivia.

Lane's first move after being hired by the Indians was to dump local hero Early Wynn. Wynn went to the White Sox and two years later led the league in victories and innings pitched.

A week before the 1960 season opener, Lane was in his usual frenetic state. First he unloaded first baseman Norm Cash, sending him to Detroit for third baseman Steve Demeter. Demeter would play four games for the Indians. Cash would start for the next 14 seasons and hit 373 home runs.

Then, on Easter, two days before the home opener, Lane engineered a trade that rocked Cleveland, a trade that would haunt the franchise for the rest of the century.

On April 17, 1960, the Indians are playing their last exhibition game of the spring, a tune-up against the White Sox in Memphis. Colavito hits a three-run homer in the second inning, then grounds into a force play in the fourth. He is replaced by a pinch-runner. As he runs off the field—he never walks, always runs—the manager calls him over.

"That's all, Rock," says Gordon. "That was your last time at bat for this ballclub. Frank Lane just told me you've been traded."

Colavito smiles. "Sure I have," he replies. "So what else is new?"

"No," replies Gordon, grim-faced. "This is for real. You're going to Detroit for Harvey Kuenn."

Kuenn is a fellow outfielder, but he's on the opposite end of the offensive spectrum: no power, great average.

Realizing the manager isn't joking, Colavito retreats to the bench and buries his head in his hands. He is devastated.

When the inning is over, he looks around the ballpark for his best pal, pitcher Herb Score. He recounts the conversation to Score, but Score blows him off, assuming it's a joke. Score refuses to believe the news until he hears it directly from Gordon.

The same scenario is played out in dugouts and press boxes around the league. In Northeast Ohio, it is replayed in homes, schools, churches, and bars. In some cases, the reaction verges on violent.

Little wonder. Trading the league's leading home-run hitter for the league's leading singles hitter is like buying a front-row ticket to a rock concert to watch the bass player. Or bidding on a masterpiece at Sotheby's because you love the frame. It just isn't done. Or, at least, it shouldn't be.

Homers are the juice, the fire, the money shot, the single biggest thing that has propelled the game into its second century. In a sport whose pace borders on listless, the homer is the ultimate payoff, the reward for all the patience. It is a usually unexpected lightning bolt reaching across innings of gray.

Fans so love the home run that a parade of baseball commissioners spent the last third of the 20th century seeing to it that the pitchers didn't get too far ahead of the sluggers. As a result, home-run totals that once seemed Ruthian became affiliated with aging journeymen.

Back in the 1950s, when power was still power and only the manly were "going yard," the Cleveland Indians had uncovered one of the premier sluggers in the game. And the fans absolutely worshipped the guy. Then, with one phone call, Frank Lane burned down the house.

Colavito flew on to Cleveland with the team, but checked into the visiting team's hotel, the Sheraton-Cleveland. Remarkably enough, the Tigers were coming to town two days later for the home opener.

The following day, Rocky's pal, Score, a sentimental fan favorite trying to come back from a horrid eye injury suffered when a line drive came back through the box, was dealt away too. Fans were saddened by the departure of Score, but the reaction was nothing in comparison to the furor over the Colavito trade.

At the home opener, the crowd was surly. People hung effigies of Lane from the upper deck. They burned pictures of him. They chanted, "Bring back the Rock . . . Bring back the Rock." The newspapers uncorked barrels o' bile.

The *Plain Dealer* and the *Press* conducted surveys, and the pro-Rocky voters outnumbered the pro-Lane faction nine to one.

Although the calendar said 1960, the Sixties had not yet arrived. The assassination of John F. Kennedy was still three years away. The first major race riot was five years off. Most people couldn't tell you the general location of Vietnam. April of 1960 was, in the overall scheme of things, a time of innocence. In baseball, it was an era well ahead of free agency. Successful players tended to stay with their clubs—especially if the players were popular among the fans. The people wearing Indians uniforms were not just mercenaries passing through town. They were our guys. So we were mortified when Lane dealt Colavito.

For Lane, it was just another day at the office. In 1958 and 1959, he made trades that involved 140 players. Check out the changes from one year to the next, even with a successful team. On Opening Day of 1959, the Tribe fielded this formidable lineup:

1. Jimmy Piersall, CF
2. Billy Martin, 2B
3. Minnie Minoso, LF
4. Rocky Colavito, RF
5. Russ Nixon, C
6. Vic Power, 1B
7. Woody Held, SS
8. Bubba Phillips, 3B
9. Gary Bell, P

The next year, despite winning 89 games the previous season, the first four spots were completely different:

1. Johnny Temple, 2B
2. Harvey Kuenn, CF
3. Walter Bond, RF
4. Tito Francona, LF
5. Russ Nixon, C
6. Vic Power, 1B
7. Woody Held, SS
8. Bubba Phillips, 3B
9. Gary Bell, P

When Rocky walked onto the Cleveland Stadium turf wearing a Tigers hat on April 19, 1960, the world seemed completely out of kilter. His certainly was. Trying far too hard to prove his worth in front of 52,576 riled-up spectators on a brutally cold day, he went zip for six and fanned four times.

Lane was able to gloat. But not for long. At Detroit's home opener, Rocky hit a home run in his first at-bat to lead the Tigers to their third straight win in front of a record opening-day throng of

53,563. Meanwhile, Kuenn was nowhere near the player who hit .353 the previous year.

Poor Harvey. He wasn't a bad guy, but he wasn't Colavito. And he would have had to hit .800 to make people forget the Rock. Despite batting .308 in Cleveland, he was constantly booed, and after one year, he was gone, traded to San Francisco. It was, fittingly, the last deal Trader Lane made in Cleveland.

The Colavito deal unleashed the worst baseball vibes since the 1899 Cleveland Spiders lost 134 games, finished 84 games out of first, and were so bad they were kicked out of the National League.

Clearly, the gods of baseball were offended. They voted to unleash a hex to rival the Curse of the Bambino in Boston. The 1960 Indians finished fourth. The 1961 Indians finished fifth. The 1962 Indians finished sixth. The 1963 Indians finished fifth. In 1964, the Indians finished sixth.

Finally, on February 10, 1965, a new general manager tried to right the wrong. Gabe Paul brought Rocky Colavito back home. The GM twisted himself into a pretzel pulling off the deal, a three-team shuffle that involved eight players.

But timing is everything, and Cleveland's was bad. Rocky was nearly toast. Although he drove in 108 runs his first year back and hit .287, the following year his average dropped 50 points, his RBIs dropped by 36, and midway through the following season he was gone again, traded for virtually nobody.

Even worse, the two players the Tribe gave up to bring him back—pitcher Tommy John and outfielder Tommie Agee—went on to become stars.

The franchise was a mess. From 1956 to 1986, the Indians had seven ownership groups. But that was the least of it. As Terry Pluto pointed out in his book *The Curse of Rocky Colavito*, an almost unbelievable string of horrible things happened to the ballclub during the next three decades. A partial list:

- Third baseman Max Alvis comes down with spinal meningitis and is never the same.
- Shortstop Larry Brown and outfielder Leon Wagner crash into each other chasing a popup, leaving Brown with a broken nose, a broken cheek and a fractured skull. He is unconscious for three days.
- The Indians are forced to forfeit a game to Texas when

drunken fans flood the field on Beer Night, attacking players.

- With the advent of free agency, the Indians cough up megabucks for a guaranteed, 10-year contract with pitcher Wayne Garland, who ruins his arm in the first game of spring training.

- The Indians are awarded the All-Star Game in 1981, but a players' strike pushes it back to August and causes widespread fan resentment.

- "Super Joe" Charboneau makes a dramatic debut, winning the 1980 Rookie of the Year honors. Within a year, he hurts his back and heads back into the minors.

- *Sports Illustrated* predicts the 1987 Indians will be the best team in baseball. The 1987 Indians lose 101 games.

- Two pitchers die in a 1993 spring-training boating accident and a third is severely injured, and another pitcher dies in a car crash eight months later.

From 1960 to 1993, the final year at Cleveland Stadium, the Indians played 5,419 baseball games. Not one of them was a postseason game. Little wonder. The Indians lost 387 more games than they won.

In fact, it's hard to believe a team could be that bad and remain in business. In 33 years of baseball, the *best* thing the Cleveland club could offer its customers was a third-place finish, 16 games back.

Only the opening of a new, $169 million stadium in 1994 canceled out Rocky's curse. Most of it, anyway.

Truth be told, the jury is still out.

Rank: #1

UPSET!

SUNDAY, DECEMBER 27, 1964

Despite boasting the best runner in all of football—Jim Brown—the Cleveland Browns were huge underdogs against the powerful Baltimore Colts when the NFL Championship Game kicked off on a snowy Sunday in Cleveland. But the Browns played a nearly perfect game and throttled the Colts, 27–0.

IF, AS JOHN DONNE famously asserted, no man is an island, this man would turn out to be as close as you can come—largely self-contained, seemingly immune to the powerful forces that sweep across the mainland and erode our contours. So it is entirely fitting that the greatest athlete in Cleveland history was born on an island.

Nathaniel Brown spent the first eight years of his life living on a sliver of land called Saint Simons, just off the coast of Georgia. Only 13 miles long, it is among a slew of barrier islands that parallel and protect Georgia's coast.

Saint Simons was slow to develop compared to its better-known siblings, Jekyll Island to the south and Sea Island to the east. But by the end of the 20th century, it was the most populated of all of Georgia's "Golden Isles," crammed with 14,000 residents.

The place was radically different during Nate Brown's childhood. Only a few hundred people lived there. He had the run of the place. Nobody bothered him when he jogged down the dirt roads and dove into the clear ponds or picked grapes off the vines or lay on the beach to watch the sand crabs.

Brown was blissfully ignorant of Saint Simons's bloody history. The Indians who lived there as early as 2500 A.D. eventually tangled with the Spanish, who arrived in the 1500s. The Indians managed to toss out the Spanish by 1680—only to be overrun by the British in the 1700s. In 1739, the Brits, although outnumbered five to one, fought off the Spanish in a major conflict that became known as the Battle of Bloody Marsh. Once the British were dispatched during the American Revolution, the island was carved into 14 cotton plantations. It is likely Brown's forefathers labored in those fields before the Civil War.

But for Nate, as his buddies called him, Saint Simons was a childhood paradise. He was free to roam the big, white beach that ran seven miles along the southeast coast. He had any number of natural jungle gyms—banana trees and fig trees and grapefruit trees and orange trees and pecan trees and palm trees. Some varieties weren't so hot for climbing, such as the moss-covered oaks. But they were certainly pleasant to look at.

Good thing the boy had some diversions, because life at home wasn't pretty. His daddy was a boy named Sue. Literally. Pop's proper name was Swinton Brown, but he was known to acquaintances as "Sweet Sue" and to friends as simply "Sue." By any name, he was a gambler. He loved dice and cards. That's why he and his wife, Theresa, broke up shortly after little Nate was born.

Theresa wanted a fresh start. So when Nate was two years old, she moved to New York City, leaving her only child with his great-grandmother. Great-grandma had a modest but comfortable four-bedroom ranch house that she shared with the boy's grandmother and aunt.

Their island was among the least inhabited in the region. But that began to change in 1942, when Nate was six. With a war on, the U.S. Navy arrived and converted the small airport to a base for torpedo bombers.

Two years after that, Nate's mother finally sent for him, as she had promised to do when she landed in the right situation. Her job as a live-in maid on Long Island fit the bill, and Great-grandma sent the boy packing.

From one island to another. But nothing about this new island was the same, and Brown was forced to make big adjustments. Even his name changed. "Nate" disappeared after he signed up for school using his full name, "James Nathaniel Brown." The teachers glanced at the name and automatically called him James. The kids, called him Jim or Jimmy. He was too shy to correct them.

That sounds unthinkable today. But in those days, his assertiveness lagged far behind his physical development.

Physically, Jimmy Brown was supernatural. When he first encountered organized sports after rejoining his mother, he found he could do just about anything. As a high school running back (wearing Number 33), he averaged 15 yards per carry both his junior and senior years. His senior basketball season, he averaged 38 points and lit up one team for 55. In track, he high-jumped six feet, three inches. In golf, he shot in the 70s. His best sport, and his favorite, was lacrosse, which he dominated even more thoroughly.

Brown's *worst* sport was baseball, and he was so good at baseball that the Yankees and Braves wanted to sign him out of high school. As late as 1958, a year into his pro football career, Indians general manager Frank Lane invited him to spring training.

As an adult, Brown weighed 232 pounds and had a 32-inch waist. He was strong, fast, and durable—and unbelievably versatile. One summer in college, with no real coaching, he entered a decathlon at an AAU track meet in Atlantic City and finished 10th in a field that included Rafer Johnson. A couple of years into his football career, the man who managed middleweight boxing champ Gene Fullmer offered Brown $150,000 to become a pro boxer.

But all of that was a long way off. Back on Long Island, little Jim had more bumps to get over. When he was 11, only three years after coming north, his mom decided he was too old to live with her in their one-room apartment, so she farmed him out again, this time to a white family in Manhasset. Two years later, when her employment situation changed, they reunited again.

Brown got into plenty of fights growing up, on both of his islands. In New York he fell in with a gang. He and his mates carried switchblades, but never actually used them. Fortunately, Brown's athleticism attracted the attention of some adults, who guided him onto a better path.

By the time he was a senior in high school, 45 colleges wanted him. He chose one that didn't—Syracuse—because one of his mentors pushed him there.

At Syracuse, where he was the only black football player, he struggled to win favor from the coaches. He got off to a rotten start, fumbling on his very first carry. As late as his junior year, he was on the second team. But finally he began to do what you'd expect—run wild. He ran through, around, and over people. Heck, he even did the place-kicking.

When the NFL draft arrived, the guy who would turn out to be the best football player of all time was selected *sixth*. Granted, the first five guys could play a bit. Paul Horning, Jon Arnett, John Brodie, Ron Kramer, and Len Dawson all went on to become professional stars. But no star was brighter than Jimmy Brown.

JB didn't even look like other running backs. He carried the ball away from his body, like a quarterback rolling out for a pass. He ran erect, rather than hunched over. It was riskier than the standard style, of course. If you're running around palming the football, you'd better know exactly where the defenders are. Fans and coaches carped about it, but what could you say when the guy was racking up monstrous yardage totals and rarely fumbling?

"If you're going to be a great runner," Brown said in his 1963 autobiography, *Off My Chest*, "you can't just tuck the ball away and fold yourself over it all the time. You can do that and be a good runner, a safe runner, but not a great runner."

Every time he was tackled, he got up exactly the same way—*veeeeery* slowly. He acted like he'd never walk again. That was by design. He didn't want the guy who tackled him to know whether the hit had shaken him up or not.

The only part of Brown's game that didn't reek of greatness was the part that took place when he wasn't getting the ball. JB was an atrocious blocker. Half the time, he didn't even seem to try. And he wasn't much for running fakes, either.

In fact, at the start of the 1964 season, former star quarterback Otto Graham lambasted Brown. "If I were the coach," he told a gathering in Canton, "I would tell the fullback that I would trade him if he didn't block and fake. The Browns will not win anything as long as Brown is there."

Well, Otto was a great quarterback, but much of a prognosticator. He did, however, have a point: Brown simply didn't block very well.

Over the years, Number 32 tried to explain away that shortcoming by saying he simply hadn't learned good blocking techniques because he had spent his whole life learning to run with the ball. That sounded lame. Hey, the guy was a world-class athlete! How could he not figure out how to get in somebody's way? Most fans figured he was just dogging it to save energy—and we usually forgave him because of what he did when he did have the ball.

Jim Brown ran like no man before or since. Forget the stats, even though they were impressive—say, eight rushing titles in nine years. To really appreciate the guy, you had to see the way he got those yards. A burst of speed here . . . a straight-arm there . . . guys bouncing off his thighs . . . guys tugging futilely at his ankles . . . attempted gang-tackles ripping apart like soggy paper bags.

Brown gave Cleveland fans another form of entertainment too—watching him grow up as a man.

When he first arrived in Cleveland, he hardly opened his mouth. Part of the reason was that Browns veterans advised him that the head coach, Paul Brown, didn't appreciate suggestions. "Jim is a quiet fellow," wrote the *Plain Dealer*'s Chuck Heaton in 1958. "He seldom initiates conversation and he thinks before he answers." Brown was so quiet that his teammates nicknamed him "Gabby."

But as the years passed and the yardage totals continued to mount, he climbed farther and farther out of his shell. He began to speak with confidence and, finally, became known for his outspokenness.

Players usually negotiated their own contracts in those days, and JB proved to be as rugged at the bargaining table as he was on the football field. Part of his strategy was to negotiate in the newspapers. The NFL had no rival league during his first three years, so Brown wisely came up with a series of alternatives to playing football. At various times he used baseball offers, boxing offers, movie offers, and his own beefs about the team to squeeze more money out of the Browns. He also had a good off-season job with Pepsi, and he implied that he was ready to turn that into a full-time job at a moment's notice. After only four years in the league, Brown was the second-highest-paid player behind Baltimore's Johnny Unitas, at $31,000. In his sixth year, he became the highest-paid player in football, at $37,000.

Brown never smoked or drank. He was a sharp dresser who drove Cadillacs.

Everything about his demeanor demanded respect. He looked you in the eye when he spoke to you, and he never blinked. He spoke logically but with passion. He had no time for small talk. And he was brutally honest. Above all, he had a powerful dignity.

As Brown matured, he began to speak out about race relations. "I do not crave the white man's approval," he wrote in his book. "I crave only the rights I'm entitled to as a human being." Hardly a controversial statement by today's standards; pretty provocative by the standards of 1963.

An article in *Look* magazine in the fall of 1964 also raised eyebrows. In it, Brown said, "it boils my blood" that white America believed black stars should in some special way be grateful for their success.

> I needn't thank my lucky stars for being successful, because I worked hard to achieve success. I was taught that America is the land of free enterprise, the land of the individual, and that every man can have a chance to be president; that if a kid worked hard and went to college and got educated, he would have a chance to make decent living. So today, I cannot say to myself, "Considering your ancestors were slaves, you're lucky to be where you are."

Brown was well on his way to national prominence as a black spokesman. According to former *Sports Illustrated* writer Ralph Wiley, in 1964, when Cassius Clay changed his name to Muhammad Ali and declared himself a conscientious objector, other black superstars wanted to find out whether the boxer was sincere or this was just another piece of showmanship. Ali had become a national lightning rod. The public either loved or hated him, and the nation's top black athletes wanted to discover what made the man tick. So Bill Russell, Lew Alcindor, and a handful of others summoned the brash young boxer to a summit meeting—in Cleveland, at the business office of Jim Brown.

"Muhammad came to the Mountain," wrote Wiley. "The Mountain was Jim Brown. . . . It was Jim Brown who authenticated even The Greatest."

The first time Brown ventured onto a limb locally came when he spoke out against the man the team had been named after. Paul Brown was the unchallenged czar of the Browns when JB arrived in 1957. JB liked him at first, but began to chafe against the rigid structure of his coaching style and took to calling him "Little Caesar" behind his back. The relationship suffered a fatal blow during halftime of a game in 1959 when PB questioned the severity of an injury that was keeping JB out of a game.

JB thought PB treated the players like robots. Although JB believed the coach was a brilliant play-caller, he also believed the team suffered because the coach wouldn't let the quarterback change a play at the line of scrimmage.

"I had no relationship with Paul Brown," he said in his autobiography. "I wanted to have a relationship with him, but his aloofness put him beyond approach."

When the fullback got his wish and Paul Brown was fired after the 1962 season by new owner Art Modell, JB really came to life. In 1963, he set an NFL record with 1,863 yards in a 14-game schedule—an average of 133 yards every game.

Brown had the benefit of a fine supporting cast. In the late '50s and early '60s, the front office put together some incredibly productive drafts. They didn't blow a first-round pick from 1956 through 1964, in a string that produced, in addition to Brown, halfback Preston Carpenter, defensive back Jim Shofner, receiver Rich Kreitling, defensive end and linebacker Jim Houston, receiver Gary Collins, and 1964 rookie Paul Warfield.

They found cornerback Bernie Parrish in the ninth round of the 1958 draft, safety Bobby Franklin in the 11th round of the 1960 draft, and Leroy Kelly in the eighth round in '64. They heisted a quarterback named Frank Ryan from Los Angeles before the '63 season for a couple of mid-round picks, then stole Ernie Green from Green Bay for a seventh-round pick.

And they still had Lou Groza, who simply wouldn't quit. A member of Paul Brown's first team in 1946, "Lou the Toe" was a former All-Pro offensive tackle who in his dotage was restricted to placekicking. But even in his early 40s, he could still kick with the best of them.

With Paul gone, JB had a new lease on football life. The new coach, fatherly Blanton Collier, was personable and imaginative—and willing to consider suggestions from the players. The game was fun again. Jim Brown wasn't the only player who felt that way, and Cleveland came out of the chute with six straight wins.

Did the fans notice? For Game Four against the Steelers, 84,684 tickets were sold. In Week Seven, a riot broke out on a Wednesday afternoon at the Stadium, where 5,000 people were trying to get tickets for that week's Browns–Giants game. Fans had been waiting in lines, some for as long as seven hours. When the windows finally opened, people toward the back broke ranks and pushed ahead, mashing hundreds of people at the front against the brick walls and causing at least two serious injuries.

But the frenzy was premature. The '63 Browns were relatively young. They had five new starters on offense and four on defense. After that great beginning, the players tightened up. The mentality changed from "Let's win" to "Let's try not to blow it." Over the last eight games, they played only .500 ball and had to settle for the post-season consolation game.

In those days, the NFL was split into two divisions. The runners-up in the East and West would play each other for third place in Miami in what was called "the Playoff Bowl." Whoopee. The Browns were bombed by the Packers, 40–23. Meanwhile, in the real game, the Bears edged the Giants for the championship.

Optimism ran rampant at the start of the '64 season. The team sold out a preseason doubleheader, drawing more than 83,000 on a Labor Day weekend to watch back-to-back practice games involving the Browns–Packers and the Giants–Lions. During the regular season, the Browns averaged 78,476 fans, the best in all of football.

The rise of the Browns coincided with one of the worst periods for the Indians. At every opportunity, the Cleveland papers used the high attendance at Browns games to try to counter a growing national buzz that the Indians' days were numbered simply because Cleveland wasn't a good sports town.

The Browns also provided a welcome diversion in a world that was tense and changing. Vietnam was heating up, as were the ghettos of the nation's big cities. The assassination of John F. Kennedy in 1963 and the strange report of the Warren Commission in 1964 had the public on edge. The Browns were an oasis.

As attendance soared, so did the value of the franchise. Midway through the 1964 season, *Fortune* magazine estimated the team's worth at $10 million—not a bad return for Art Modell, who had paid $4 million just three years earlier (a sum other owners thought was outrageously high). One of the keys was a new TV contract with CBS that called for each NFL team to receive $325,000 per season.

The 1964 Cleveland Browns didn't come out nearly as hot as the '63 model. The Brownies beat a weak Washington team by two TDs on the road, and then settled for a tie at home against the St. Louis Cardinals. They barely edged a lousy Philadelphia team on the road, then drilled the Cowboys at home, 27–6. In the season's fifth game, they laid a huge egg, losing 32–7 to the struggling Steelers in front of a disgusted Saturday-night Stadium crowd of 80,530.

That shocking upset got their attention. The Browns went on a five-game winning streak, nailing the Cowboys, Giants, Steelers, Redskins, and Lions. Four of those wins were by 10 points or more. In the Steelers game, Jim Brown gained 149 yards—including the yard he needed to push him over 10,000 for his career, the most in NFL history. Against the Lions, JB added 147 more. By mid-November, the Browns were strutting around with an 8–1–1 record.

Then they ran into Vince Lombardi's Packers. Playing at Milwaukee's County Stadium, where the Packers played twice a year, the Browns blew a first-half lead—and looked absolutely horrid doing it. After the intermission, JB gained a grand total of eight yards and fumbled twice. The crushing blow was a 55-yard pass from the Packers' Bart Starr to Max McGee on a fourth-and-one.

The Browns ripped up the Eagles the following week, cashing in on a bunch of Philly turnovers and 133 yards from Brown. But then, with a chance to clinch their first division title in seven years, they went into Busch Stadium to face a tough Cardinal team and came up short. The Cards were second in the division and played like it. Groza kicked four field goals, but Cleveland managed only one TD in a 28–19 defeat.

The season came down to the final game. The bad news: It would be in New York, against a team that had won three consecutive Eastern Division championships. The good news: New York certainly wasn't going to win any titles this year. In a single season, the Giants, directed by old, bald, aching Y. A. Tittle, had fallen from 11–3 to 2–9–2. But they still had plenty of pride and certainly weren't going to roll over.

The Browns–Giants rivalry was at its peak. Both teams had been in contention many times and feelings on both sides were strong—strong enough that, despite the standings, 63,007 Giants fans turned out on a damp, overcast day.

A year earlier, Cleveland had come into the second Giants game as a 5½-point favorite and came out with a 27-point loss. So the Browns were anything but overconfident when they walked onto the turf of Yankee Stadium wearing their white jerseys and white pants, with brown numbers and brown-and-orange trim around their sleeves and down the sides of their pants.

No one could know that the guy with Number 13 on his back, Ryan, was about to have the best day of his career.

It didn't look that way at the beginning. The Cleveland QB was tentative, the offense stalled, and the Giants took a four-point lead into the second quarter. But on this amazing afternoon in the Bronx, 38 percent of Frank Ryan's passes would go for touchdowns. Seriously. He threw only 13 times, but completed 12—and five of those took the Browns across the goal line. A game that was tight in the second quarter turned into a 52–20 Cleveland blowout.

The tide turned when Parrish intercepted a second-quarter Tittle pass meant for Frank Gifford. He returned it 31 yards, well into Giants territory, and a few plays later Ryan found Collins on a slant over the middle.

Jim Brown provided the balance, smashing his way to 99 yards on the ground against a defense that always cherished the chance to beat him up. When Brown caught a short pass from Ryan in the third quarter and faked his way into the end zone, he tied the all-time NFL scoring mark held by Don Hutson of the Packers.

The good guys were so far ahead that backup Jim Ninowski was at the controls the entire fourth quarter. And even he completed four of six passes, including yet another TD.

The Browns had their first division championship since 1957. In two weeks, they would have a shot at their first NFL title since 1955. Browns fever was raging off the charts. After the game, between 5,000 and 7,500 people showed up at the airport to welcome the team back, even though the plane was two hours late, delayed by fog.

The city was split, however, on who deserved credit for the football team's resurgence. Fans of Paul Brown said the '64 team succeeded only because PB had assembled the personnel. Critics of Paul Brown said Collier's coaching was responsible for pushing the team over the top because he had loosened the reins.

In truth, this team was the best of both worlds. It still had much of the discipline and respect for detail demanded by PB, but it also had the creativity and emotion encouraged by Collier.

Collier had the look and demeanor of a math teacher, which he was before joining the original Browns as an assistant. He left in '54 to coach the University of Kentucky, rejoining PB as an assistant in 1962. Collier always wore a hat, a tie, and thick black glasses. He was hard of hearing, which made him seem even more grandfatherly. But the switch to Collier didn't just help the Browns psychologically. He also instituted a completely new blocking scheme that called for the offensive line to fire hard off the ball and block in a way that gave JB the option to cut back when things got clogged up. JB loved it, and so did his linemen.

The starting offense in '64 contained two Browns and three Johns (four when John Brown started at right tackle, as he sometimes did):

WR: Paul Warfield, 42
LT: Dick Schafrath, 77
LG: John Wooten, 60
C: John Morrow, 56
RG: Gene Hickerson, 66
RT: Monte Clark, 73
TE: Johnny Brewer, 83
WR: Gary Collins, 86
QB: Frank Ryan, 13
HB: Ernie Green, 48
FB: Jim Brown, 32

The defense lined up like this:
LE: Paul Wiggin, 84
LT: Dick Modzelewski, 74
RT: Jim Kanicki, 69
RE: Bill Glass, 80
LLB: Jim Houston, 82
MLB: Vince Costello, 50
RLB: Galen Fiss, 35
LCB: Bernie Parrish, 30
RCB: Walter Beach, 49
LS: Larry Benz, 23
RS: Bobby Franklin, 24

The Baltimore Colts gave the impression they couldn't care less who was wearing those uniforms. They swaggered into town with a high-powered offense, a nasty defense, and a Gibraltar-size chip on their shoulder.

In Vegas, the initial line had the Colts as 18-point favorites. Two touchdowns, a field goal, and then some? Take the points, even if the underdog is Andrews School for Girls.

Heavy betting on the Browns drove the spread down to seven by game time, but many "experts" insisted it should have been much higher. After all, Baltimore had everything: six future Hall of Famers, including the league's Most Valuable Player, quarterback Johnny Unitas; a trio of superb receivers; a shifty halfback, Lenny Moore, who had set a league record with 19 touchdowns; and a defense that led the league in sacks. While the Browns needed a victory in their final game to qualify, the Colts had run off a 12–2 record to win their division by three games.

The two teams hadn't played each other for three years, though, so neither knew exactly what it was getting into. Remarkably, their coaches agreed to address that lack of knowledge with a mutual assistance plan.

By the end of the century, every team would have a video department that could put together a package showing every move by every opponent from 500 different angles. But in 1964, scouting was far less sophisticated. In an unusual display of sportsmanship, the Browns and Colts agreed to give each other unlimited access to each other's game films. Baltimore's second-year coach, Don Shula, even advised Blanton Collier that a higher-quality film of a fog-draped Colts–Redskins game was available from the Redskins. The Redskins' camera position had been closer to the field than Baltimore's, so that film was better.

Give Cleveland two thumbs up. The Browns spotted something that would help them shut down Baltimore's high-falutin' offense, an offense that not only led the NFL in points but set an all-time record with 54 touchdowns.

The adjustment would require the Browns to alter their entire defensive philosophy. All year long, they had played "soft" coverage in the secondary. Their credo was "bend but don't break." The cornerbacks and safeties would gladly give up dozens of short passes than get burned on a couple of long ones. The media dubbed them the "Rubber Band Defense."

But the Colts' superb wide receivers, Raymond Berry and Jimmy Orr, were not particularly fast. They had great hands and ran great routes, but they rarely beat anyone by blazing past them. So the Browns decided to play the 1964 equivalent of a "bump and run." They'd play mostly man-to-man, jam Berry and Orr at the line of scrimmage, and force Unitas to look for a secondary receiver. Cornerback Walter Beach would guard Berry, cornerback Bernie Parrish would guard Orr, and big linebacker Jim Houston would cover big tight end John Mackey.

Unitas, forced to look for a second or third option, would need more time to get rid of the ball and give the defensive line more time to get him. Ideally, Unitas would be forced to scramble, which was not exactly his forte. His black, high-top spikes seemed to be soled with 25-pound horseshoes.

Of course, the Browns didn't have a lot to lose by taking a defensive gamble. The 1964 defense allowed more first downs than any team in the entire league, gave up more rushing yards than anyone, and surrendered the second-most pass receptions. Talk about bending.

The media looked at the stats and declared "no contest." Some of the national writers were even referring to the Browns as "the Laugh Champs." Every time the Browns picked up a newspaper or magazine, they read about how badly the Colts were going to beat them. And they were getting a sick of it.

It's not as if the Browns were helpless. In addition to the best running back in the game, they had a halfback, Ernie Green, who had rushed for nearly 500 yards. Quarterback Ryan, who was studying for a Ph.D. in mathematics at Rice, was smooth, accurate, and savvy. He had some lovely targets, including a sensational rookie receiver in Warfield, who had caught 52 balls and averaged 18 yards per catch. The other wideout, Collins, had 35 catches and a 16-yard average. Even the tight end, Brewer, was averaging 13 yards on 25 receptions. Nor could Baltimore's secondary ignore the running backs: Brown had 35 catches and Green had 25.

Cleveland's defense was far stronger than it looked at first glance. Despite giving up vast chunks of yardage, it had given up fewer points than every other team in the East except Dallas.

The Cleveland Browns practiced the week after the Giants game, took the weekend off, then resumed their workouts at League Park. The field looked like wild horses had been feasting on it; little remained but dirt. When the weather worsened later in the week and the dirt turned to muck, practice was shifted to Western Reserve University's Clarke Field.

Meanwhile, at Cleveland Municipal Stadium, Modell was doing everything possible to keep the playing surface in decent shape. One week before the big game, he flew in equipment to defrost the field. Huge heaters blew hot air under the tarp. Straw was used to keep heat in the ground.

The Colts flew into town on Christmas Day and holed up at the Sheraton-Cleveland Hotel.

Back on the East Coast, in midtown Manhattan, the editors at

Sports Illustrated were trying to work ahead. They were losing a day because of the Christmas holiday, but the presses would roll at the usual time, not long after Sunday's game. The editors knew the NFL Championship Game would be their cover story. And when they analyzed the match-up, they saw only one logical result: Baltimore would win handily. So they laid out their cover with a nice color photograph of Coach Shula and his ace quarterback, Johnny U.

Northeast Ohio had a little different mindset. The Browns were far and away the chief topic of conversation. A contest announced on the weekly *Quarterback Club* TV highlight show turned chaotic. More than 150,000 entries flooded into the team's offices—followed by loud complaining that the contest rules had been changed in midstream and that the promise of duplicate prizes had not been kept.

Fans had been asked to identify seven historic Browns plays shown on the program. The tiebreaker was guessing the attendance for the last home game. Well, figuring out the seven plays was relatively easy. And just in case you couldn't do it on your own, the Cleveland Public Library, which had been inundated with requests for access to old sports clippings, was handing out mimeographed sheets with answers. So it came down to the best guess on the attendance. The stakes were high—a new Ford Mustang was among the prizes—and some folks got together and went full bore. One group mailed in 21,000 entries spanning a 21,000-person attendance range.

The team denied the contest had been changed and pointed out that two Mustangs were given out, along with four console TVs for second-place ties, rather than the one TV that had been promised.

Not that those TVs would be of much help on game day. The NFL had a 75-mile blackout rule. Whether or not the contest was sold out, no TV station within that radius was permitted to carry a home game. Because of that, Northeast Ohio electronics stores did a brisk business in directional TV antennas. Homeowners would rotate their dials toward places like Erie, Pennsylvania, and try to pick up some football action among the fuzz on the screen.

In the euphoria that followed the win over the Giants, Cleveland City Council had unanimously passed a resolution urging the NFL and the Browns to waive the TV ban. Fat chance. However, Cleveland television was permitted to air a tape of the game the night after.

Having a ticket for the title game didn't mean you'd live happily ever after. Any game held in late December on the shores of Lake Erie has the potential to be fatal. And that's the way things sounded as the game drew near. The medical writer for the *Cleveland Press* quoted the city's health commissioner as saying the consumption of alcoholic beverages in the frigid conditions could lead directly to "pneumonia." The official also advised women to take blankets they could wrap around their bare legs. "In fact," he added, "this might be one time when women would be better off wearing slacks in public." How adventurous.

On Saturday after practice, Frank Ryan predicted an 18-point Browns win. Local reporters thought he was nuts.

That night, the Browns stayed together downtown at the Pick-Carter Hotel (which would be the scene of a fatal fire six years later). When they awoke the next morning—two days after Christmas, with Mr. Jing-a-ling's keys still ting-a-linging on Halle's seventh floor and the huge Sterling Lindner Christmas tree still twinkling like the aurora borealis—they must have cringed. The temperature wasn't bad for late December—30 degrees—but the wind was whipping in from Lake Erie in 20- and 30-mile-per-hour bursts. Some of those bursts were filled with snowflakes.

The Browns defense may have been freezing on the outside, but they were on fire inside, seething from lack of respect and single-minded in their effort to revamp public opinion. They forced Unitas to scramble the first four times he tried to pass. Before the day was over, they would force the Colts into two fumbles and two interceptions.

The Colts botched their best chance to score in the first half when the holder dropped the ball on a 19-yard field goal attempt.

But the Browns weren't doing much on offense either. By halftime, neither team had scored. *New York Times* columnist Red Smith summed up the first half by writing, "Never have so many paid so dearly—$10, $8, and $6—and suffered so sorely to see so little."

The halftime show didn't warm anybody up either. Modell had hired the huge Florida A&M marching band, known for its 320-step-per-minute cadence, to race around the field at nearly three times the speed of a normal band and create rapidly changing words and designs. That was the band's claim to fame. But on this afternoon, the director decided he wanted his troops to be taken seriously as musicians. So they moved onto the field and nearly stood at attention as they played. Modell was livid.

In the second half, the Colts elected to receive. Blanton Collier agonized about his own choice: whether to take the wind in the fourth quarter—the normal strategy, in case you need to rally at the end of the game—or the third quarter, because scoring first would be important and nobody knew whether the stiff breeze would continue all afternoon. He took the wind right away, and it paid immediate dividends.

A Baltimore punt into the gale went only 29 yards, setting up a 43-yard, wind-aided field goal by The Toe. Given the lack of offensive action in the first half, those three points seemed huge, and the fans roared with delight.

Defensively, the Colts were focusing on Warfield, double-teaming him on nearly every play. They were giving him so much attention that the Browns began to use him as a decoy, which eventually opened up big gaps for the other wide receiver, Collins.

Collins and Ryan, both in their third season with the Browns, had been clicking all year. They first started working together as rookies, when both of them rode the pine. After every practice, Collins, a tall guy from Maryland who doubled as the punter, would hook up with Ryan, and they would work on their timing. They worked particularly hard on the "post" pattern, where Collins would start out straight and then slant on a 45-degree angle toward the goalpost. Over and over they ran it until they could run it in their sleep.

By the middle of 1964, they were running post patterns in the biggest of games. They hit one during the division-winning game against the Giants to give the Browns their second TD and set the tone for the rest of the day. So when Baltimore became obsessed with Warfield, Ryan certainly didn't panic.

Even though the Browns weren't scoring, they were setting up the Colts for future damage. At first, Baltimore's secondary was taking away sideline passes. So Ryan began calling for hook patterns. When the defense came to expect the hook, the Browns starting going deep. They were going so deep that Ryan's first TD pass—18 yards—was by far his shortest of the day.

On that first scoring pass, Collins was supposed to run a down-and-out into the corner of the end zone. But he couldn't get there, so he improvised, cutting over the middle. Ryan, who was preparing to scramble, saw what Collins was doing and heaved the ball right down the middle. At first, both he and Collins feared the ball might hit the crossbar of the goalpost, which in those days was planted right on the goal line and held up with two support posts. Hitting the goalpost wouldn't have been unprecedented; Ryan did it five times during the regular season. But this ball passed just below the post, into Collins's outstretched arms. Browns 10, Colts zip.

The Colts were stretched even thinner because they were devoting so much attention to the running back from Saint Simons Island. That, of course, was standard procedure. Nobody ignored Jim Brown. Even when defenses were geared to stop him, hardly anybody could, even a team with Gino Marchetti and Ordell Braase at defensive end. Brown was his usual workhorse self, cranking out 114 yards on 27 carries as Cleveland dominated the time of possession.

One of Brown's carries was responsible for setting up the first TD. Early in the third quarter, the only score having been Groza's, Brown started left on a sweep, cut back to the middle, and roared 46 yards to the Baltimore 18. It was vintage JB, and it made everything else work.

The Ryan-to-Collins pass was just the beginning. Not long afterward, with the Browns on the Baltimore 42, Collins ran a long post pattern that split defenders Bobby Boyd and Jerry Logan. Ryan hit him at the 15, and he could have crawled in from there.

The Colts still didn't learn their lesson. After a second Groza field goal, they let Collins slip away again in the middle of the field. This time the play went for 51 yards.

Collins's three TD catches set an NFL record. He was named MVP of the game and given a Corvette. Ryan hit on 11 of 18 passes.

Still, it was the Cleveland defense that set the tone. When you think of the 1964 championship game, you should think of 11 defenders who had been poor-mouthed for weeks, 11 guys who combined animalistic passion with thoughtful Xs and Os and played an almost perfect football game. They held the Colts' Big Three receivers to six catches. They held Moore to 40 yards. They drove Unitas crazy.

Tall, blubbery, 22-year-old defensive tackle Jim Kanicki, who had been consistently mauled early in the season, played his best game ever, manhandling Baltimore's All-Pro lineman, Jim Parker. Short, stocky, 33-year-old Dick "Little Mo" Modzelewski, playing beside Kanicki and talking him through things, also spent much of the day in Unitas's face. But when Browns fans think of the 1964 title game, many of them think of one play by one linebacker:

Second quarter. Scoreless game. Colts with the ball. Browns fans uneasy, waiting for Baltimore's offense to explode.

Unitas throws a little flair pass to Lenny Moore. Moore appears to have plenty of running room. Nobody within 10 yards of him. Suddenly, a guy in a white uniform with Number 35 on his back, a cast on one hand, roars into Moore's space as if he had been shot out of a torpedo tube.

It's Galen Fiss. Fiss makes no attempt to tackle Moore. He doesn't try to wrap him up with his arms or jerk him down by his jersey or throw a forearm at his neck. He simply runs into him at full speed. It's the football equivalent of a kamikaze attack. Direct hit. Moore goes flying across the frigid surface right onto his butt. The Colts lose six yards. For the first time, the 79,544 fans—and maybe the Browns themselves—begin to think Cleveland's defense is the real deal.

With the clock running down and the game long ago decided, fans streamed onto the cold turf and tore down the goalpost in front of the bleachers. It was hardly a vicious mob. It was an exuberant group that was thrilled with the city's first championship of any kind in nine years. But the celebrants drew a strong rebuke from the *Cleveland Press*. "If Cleveland wants to gain in national prestige, it cannot afford the gross behavior by those uncontrollable people who swarmed all over the field before the game was even over," sniffed the lead editorial.

The people at *Sports Illustrated* were even grumpier. The editors had to scramble to come up with a new cover. Their color photo of Unitas and Shula certainly wasn't going to cut it, not when Unitas was held to less than 100 yards passing, picked off twice, and beaten to a pulp. The editors needed somebody from the winning team. Because of the tight production schedule, they were forced to go with a black-and-white shot, an action photo of Frank Ryan.

But you know what? That cover turned out just fine. We'll take two.

Rank: #19

BEER NIGHT

TUESDAY, JUNE 4, 1974

―――――――――――――

Struggling at the gate, the Cleveland Indians staged a promotion in which fans could buy unlimited quantities of beer for only 10 cents a cup. Some of the imbibers started a riot that forced the Indians to forfeit the game and left another stain on the city's already soiled reputation.

NOTHING ABOUT IT should have been surprising, not from the first moment the lightbulb blinked on in the left frontal lobe of a Cleveland Indians marketing maven.

"Hey, I know! Let's sell beer for 10 cents a cup!"

Sure. And for our next promotion, how about Brass Knuckles Night?

Or maybe free spray paint to the first 5,000 fans?

And perhaps an enticing Little League promotion—all kids under 13 get Chief Wahoo switchblades!

The Tribe's front office has put together some ridiculous promotions over the years—we can start with the Mother's Day giveaway in which every woman at the ballpark was handed a free can of deodorant—but the concept of distributing virtually unlimited quantities of an intoxicating beverage is one for the ages.

The media didn't seem the least bit put off by the prospect. In his pregame story in the *Cleveland Press*, baseball writer Jim Braham gleefully proclaimed, "Rinse your stein and get in line. Billy the Kid and his Texas gang are in town and it's 10-cent beer night at the ballpark."

Granted, the culture was significantly different in 1974. The drinking age was 18. There was no such thing as Mothers Against Drunk Driving. The Breathalyzer itself was only 20 years old, and people who exceeded the legal limit were frequently able to plea-bargain the charge down to reckless operation.

Adding fuel to the festivities was an anything-goes attitude that reigned over much of the local populace. The fabled Sixties didn't actually arrive in the Midwest until the 1970s. But when they got here, they got here in a big way. During that post-Pill, pre-herpes, pre-AIDS era, large pockets of Northeast Ohio became a perpetual wild party. And the party usually was well lubricated with alcohol.

At a downtown nightclub called the Mad Hatter, draught beer was dispensed for a penny a cup every Wednesday night. The two-story club drew enormous crowds, but was saddled with tiny bathroom facilities upstairs. Therefore, week after week, guys sitting on stools at the circular tables on the main level would simply unzip and relieve themselves under the table. Newcomers couldn't figure out why the carpet was so spongy. *Ick.*

The baseball team mirrored the times. During the '70s in particular, many players drank heavily. Once, in Detroit, on a bus ride from the airport to the team hotel, Tribe pitcher Don Hood lit up a joint. (After much debate in the front of the bus about which member of the coaching staff was going to go back and tell him to put it out, Rocky Colavito drew the assignment.)

Rick Manning and Dennis Eckersley didn't swap wives and families, as Yankee pitchers Mike Kekich and Fritz Peterson had, but Manning was living at Eckersley's house for a while and ended up walking away with Eckersley's wife.

So perhaps, given the context, it should not be a complete shock that Cleveland's professional baseball team, struggling mightily at the gate, would park some big beer trucks behind the outfield fence, plug in the taps, and pour beer as if June 4 were the last day on Earth.

The team hadn't drawn a million fans in 14 seasons, and in recent times hadn't even come close. The average attendance the previous three seasons was 611,000.

No wonder the marketing department was pulling out all the stops. (The identity of the guy or gal who came up with the dime beer concept—my money's on a guy—has somehow managed to elude historians.) And, in a sense, the ploy worked perfectly. About 25,000 tickets were sold—more than triple the average gate—for a weekday game against the Texas Rangers.

Mind you, for decades baseball had had a long, chummy relationship with beer, just as tight as its relationship with peanuts and Cracker Jack. Baby boomers who grew up watching the Indians grew up chirping, "Mabel, Black Label," the advertising tagline of a locally produced beer. Milwaukee fielded a team of Brewers, and Anheuser-Busch made no secret of its ownership of the St. Louis Cardinals.

At Municipal Stadium on that warm June evening, the beer of choice was Stroh's. At concession stands or from vendors, you could get a 12-ounce cup of the "fire-brewed" nectar for one thin dime. You could buy six at a time, and then return for more.

About 65,000 cups were consumed. This by a crowd of 25,134. If you do the math, don't forget to subtract all the people who likely didn't drink a drop. Let's say half the crowd consisted of teetotalers, juveniles, and the elderly. In that case, the average consumption would have been more than five cups per person. And let's not forget the considerable number of fans who reportedly had been imbibing before they even got to the ballpark.

Another element was adding tension to the evening. Just six days earlier, in Arlington, Texas, the Tribe and the Rangers had gone at each other in a bench-clearing brawl.

The trouble in Texas began in the fourth inning. Ranger Tom Grieve walked. Lenny Randle singled to center, and Grieve stopped at second. The next batter hit a double-play grounder to third. Tribe third baseman John Lowenstein stepped on the bag for the first out, then rifled the ball to second. As second baseman Jack Brohamer crossed the bag to force the second runner, Randle nailed him with a hard slide.

The payback came in the eighth inning. With two outs and nobody on base, Tribe relief pitcher Milt Wilcox threw a pitch behind Randle's head. Let's just say Wilcox wasn't suffering from a sudden lack of control.

Randle didn't charge the mound. He was more subtle. On the next pitch, he laid a bunt down the first-base line. And when Wilcox came over to pick it up and make the tag, Randle threw a forearm into him. The Tribe's hulking first baseman, John Ellis, was standing nearby. And as Randle took a few strides past Wilcox, Ellis leveled him.

Ellis was six-three, 225 pounds. Randle was five-ten, 170 pounds. It wasn't pretty.

The benches emptied, and the Texas crowd grew rowdy. Dozens of cups of beer were thrown onto the visiting Tribesmen.

After the game, Rangers shortstop Toby Harrah expressed concern that the Texas fans were becoming "more and more like the ones in Venezuela." American players had experienced Venezuelan crowds during Winter League play, and those crowds were several notches less civilized than even the worst ones in the U.S.

At least until June 4, 1974.

When Texas arrived for its first Cleveland appearance of the year, the brawl at Arlington was still fresh in the minds of Indians fans. Many people expected more fireworks on the field. But nobody expected the kind of eruption that would take place during what would become a three-hour nightmare.

The evening's honored guests started the game this way:

1. Cesar Tovar, CF
2. Lenny Randle, 2B
3. Alex Johnson, LF
4. Jeff Burroughs, RF
5. Tom Grieve, DH
6. Jim Fregosi, 1B
7. Toby Harrah, SS
8. Leo Cardenas, 3B
9. Jim Sundberg, C
P: Ferguson Jenkins

The Rangers' usual first baseman, Mike Hargrove, a sensational rookie who would hit .323 for the season, wasn't in the starting lineup with a lefty on the mound. But he would take the field midway through the game and figure prominently in the game-within-the-game.

As Texas manager Billy Martin ran out to deliver the lineup card to the umpires, he was booed heavily, a reaction to the Texas fight. Martin sarcastically tipped his cap and blew kisses.

Cleveland manager Ken Aspromonte carried out this lineup:

1. John Lowenstein, 3B
2. Jack Brohamer, 2B
3. Leron Lee, LF
4. Charlie Spikes, RF
5. Oscar Gamble, DH
6. George Hendrick, CF

7. Ossie Blanco, 1B
8. Dave Duncan, C
9. Frank Duffy, SS
P: Fritz Peterson

Yes, Fritz Peterson, the wife-swapping guy. He had been traded to the Indians to get him away from Kekich and the social mess in New York.

The first sign of trouble came even before the playing of the "Star-Spangled Banner." In the box seats near home plate, a vendor and a fan got into a heated argument about spilled beer. The argument turned into a fistfight.

More hints of trouble came shortly after Peterson completed his warm-ups. Small explosions were heard in various parts of the ballpark. An incredibly large number of fans had stocked up on firecrackers, some as big as M-80s.

The fact that the Rangers took the lead in their second at-bat didn't help the atmosphere. But the score probably had little to do with the reason a beefy woman climbed out of the stands in the second inning, scampered into the Tribe's on-deck circle, and gleefully lifted her shirt.

The woman single-handedly—or perhaps we should say double-breastedly—touched off a three-hour parade of interlopers.

In the fourth inning, when the Rangers' DH, Grieve, hit his second homer of the game, a male fan sprinted naked to second base and slid into the bag—as Grieve was still circling the bases.

A father-and-son team got into the act one inning later, running together into the outfield and mooning their brethren.

When the Indians' Leron Lee rifled a pitch right back into the gut of the Rangers' Jenkins, dropping the hurler to the ground, fans in the upper deck cheered, then chanted, "Hit 'em again, hit 'em again, harder, harder."

Things really heated up in the bottom of the sixth when Lee was called safe on a close play at third and the Rangers argued the call. Spectators began tossing things onto the field.

One fan ran out on the grass, picked up a tennis ball, and threw it back into the stands. When a cop started to chase him, he ran to left field, where another fan gave him a hug. A cop nabbed the tennis-ball thrower and was soundly booed. Meanwhile, another fan raced toward right field, climbed the fence, and escaped.

Public address announcer Bob Keefer warned the crowd to stop throwing objects—which, of course, brought a renewed barrage. Some of it was directed his way.

The beer kept flowing. Customers were allowed to go right down behind the outfield fence, where the beer trucks were stationed, and stand in line, waiting to refill their cups.

In the top of the seventh, three more spectators took the field. As one of them was climbing back into the stands, a cop grabbed him. But people in the stands pulled the man free.

Down on the first-base line, a woman waved grandly to all corners of the ballpark. When a cop arrived, she fought him, and he pushed her. The cop was booed.

In the visitors' bullpen along the left-field line, the Texas relief pitchers were being pelted with firecrackers. Home plate umpire Nestor Chylak sent the pitchers to the dugout to protect them, vowing he'd give them as much time as they needed to warm up.

Meanwhile, fans in the left-field stands were trying to pull the padding off the left-field wall for a souvenir. The grounds crew sprinted to the wall to try to hold it in place. A tug of war developed.

Soon, groups of two or three fans were running across the field. Then groups of 10. Then 20. Some people stopped just long enough to do a somersault. Others took the time to disrobe and streak through the outfield. The vast majority were male, and the vast majority were completely smashed.

Hargrove, who had gone in to play first base in the fifth, was targeted with hot dogs and spit. At one point he was nearly hit with a gallon jug of Thunderbird wine.

During the sixth inning, radio announcer Joe Tait, calling the game with Herb Score, looked down from his perch in the front row of the upper deck and saw fathers gathering their families and ushering them out of the ballpark. In the seventh, Tait watched most of the Indians' front-office people walk by the back of his booth on their way out. Among them was vice president Ted Bonda.

In those days, the Cleveland Police Department left most of the baseball policing to the team's ushers, many of whom had long ago retired from other jobs. As a result, the trespassers met little resistance.

By now it was clear that something else was lurking inside the stadium on this 68-degree, full-moon night. The game was taking place only four years after the shootings at Kent State. The Vietnam War

was a seemingly bottomless quagmire. Richard Nixon was still in the
White House, despite mounting evidence that he was, indeed, a
crook. Many people in their late teens and early 20s had grown a
deep distrust, even a hatred, for any kind of authority. They lived in
an almost constant state of unfocused anger. And apparently, after 10
beers, umpires, cops, and even the players began to look like enemies.

Gradually, the streaking, showboating, and taunting gave way to
sheer violence. Fights raged in the stands all evening, but direct com-
bat didn't spread to the field until the ninth, when one guy climbed
over the outfield wall, ran up behind Texas right-fielder Jeff Burroughs, and grabbed his cap.

The playing field had been constructed with a severe crown to as-
sist in water runoff, and from the Cleveland Stadium dugouts, you
couldn't see below an outfielder's knees. So when Burroughs whirled
to retrieve his cap, slipped, and fell, Texas manager Martin, standing
in the third base dugout, knew only that Burroughs had gone down.
Martin couldn't tell whether his player was hurt, but he certainly
wasn't going to wait around to find out.

Martin grabs a fungo bat and tells his team to follow. The players
quickly run to right field to help Burroughs. As soon as they arrive,
they are surrounded by 300 wild-eyed drunks, some carrying chains,
knives, and pieces of stadium seats they have broken apart.

In the Cleveland dugout, manager Ken Aspromonte sees how far
the situation has deteriorated and realizes the Texas players might literally be fighting for their lives. He tells his own players to grab bats
and help out the Rangers.

Suddenly, two teams that were throwing punches at each other a
week ago are fighting back-to-back against a maniacal horde of
drunks.

People tuning in the radio broadcast at home could be excused for
thinking they had accidentally dialed up professional wrestling.

TAIT: "Tom Hilgendorf has been hit on the head. Hilgy is in def-
inite pain. He's bent over, holding his head. Somebody hit Hilgendorf on the head, and he is going to be assisted back into the dugout.
Aw, this is absolute tragedy. Absolute tragedy . . . I've been in this
business for over 20 years and I have never seen anything as disgusting as this."

SCORE: "I haven't either."

TAIT: "And I'll be perfectly honest with you: I just don't know what to say."

SCORE: "I don't think this game will continue, Joe . . . The unbelievable thing is people keep jumping out of the stands after they see what's going on!"

TAIT: "Well, that shows you the complete lack of brainpower on the parts of some people. There's no way I'm going to run out onto the field if I see some baseball player waving a bat out there looking for somebody. This is tragic. . . . The whole thing has degenerated now into just—now we've got another fight going with fans and ballplayers. Hargrove has got some kid on the ground and he is really administering a beating."

SCORE: "Well, that fellow came up and hit him from behind is what happened."

TAIT: "Boy, Hargrove really wants a piece of him—and I don't blame him."

SCORE: "Look at [Texas backup catcher and former Indian] Duke Sims down there going at it."

TAIT: "Yeah, Duke is in on it. Here we go again."

SCORE: "I'm surprised that the police from the city of Cleveland haven't been called here, because we have the makings of a pretty good riot. We *have* a pretty good riot."

TAIT: "Well, the game, I really believe, Herb, now will be called. Slowly but surely the teams are getting back to their dugouts. The field, though, is just mobbed with people. And mob rule has taken over."

SCORE: "They've stolen the bases."

TAIT: "The security people they have here just are totally incapable of handling this crowd. They just—well, short of the National Guard, I'm not sure what would handle this crowd right now. It's just unbelievable. Unbelievable . . . "

SCORE: "[As soon as] people go back in the seats, others jump down and take their place."

TAIT: "The bases are gone. Both teams are back in their respective dugouts . . ."

The public address announcer informs the crowd that the game has been declared a forfeit. The decision is booed.

TAIT: "It will go into the books as a 9–0 forfeit to the Texas Rangers. So the Indians battle back, tie the game in the ninth [an explosion rings out], and then the game is ruled forfeit. That's it. It's all over. Well, there's no sense wrapping it up because it goes into the book as a 9–0 forfeit. Now what about records in a game like this? I'm not up on this because I've not been in on one before."

SCORE: "I have never seen this before. I suppose we will just have to await a ruling from the American League office . . . "

TAIT: "Well, that's it . . . [Another cherry bomb goes off.] The final score, in a forfeit, ruled by the umpires after a riot broke out here in the ninth inning after the Indians had tied the game 5–5, final score in the books then will be Texas 9, Cleveland nothing."

As Tait and Score are talking, you can hear the stadium's organist playing merrily away, like something out of a Kafka novel.

People are still milling about the field. Some are shooting firecrackers. Some are throwing objects toward the radio booth and the press box.

The official box score: nine arrests, seven hospitalizations, and one major error by Indians management.

Only after Score mentioned the lack of police protection did Cleveland's finest arrive in force. Later, Score was told that a cop listening to the game in his squad car had heard his comment and radioed headquarters.

When the teams and the umpires were safely back in their dressing quarters, they were still livid. "That was the closest you're ever gonna be to seeing someone get killed in this game of baseball," said Billy Martin. "They had knives and every damn thing. We're lucky we didn't get stabbed. I've played 25 years and I've run over guys and been run over and given no ground. But to have people act like idiots, that's ridiculous."

The home plate umpire, Chylak, was even more vocal. Bleeding from the head, where he had been hit with part of a chair, he yelled, "[Bleeping] animals. You just can't pull back a pack of animals. . . . When uncontrolled beasts are out there, you gotta do something. I saw two guys with knives and I got hit with a chair. My guys [Joe Brinkman, Nick Bremigan, and Larry McCoy] were getting roughed up. I'm not out there to see anyone get killed. They almost killed the four of us. But we're expendable. We're umpires."

With a bleeding hand, Chylak held up a beer bottle that had been wrapped inside two paper cups and hurled at him. "This is how cheap they were."

The only place he had ever seen anything like this, he said, was "in a [bleeping] zoo. If the [bleeping] war is on tomorrow, I'm gonna join the other side to get a shot at them."

Several months later, when Chylak encountered Score and Tait at an Indians game in Oakland, he confided that he really wanted to complete the game because the Indians were in the midst of a remarkable comeback and deserved a chance to win. He finally decided to give up when he was standing at home plate and felt something pressing against the back of his left shoe. He turned around and saw a hunting knife sticking out of the ground.

For what it's worth, the game itself, as Chylak noted, had turned into one the most dramatic of the season. The Tribe had been down 5-1 in the sixth but rallied for two runs on double, an error and a George Hendrick single.

Then, in the bottom of the ninth, with one out, Hendrick doubled. Pinch-hitter Ed Crosby singled. Pinch-hitter Rusty Torres singled. Pinch-hitter Alan Ashby singled. When Lowenstein lifted a sacrifice fly to centerfield, scoring Crosby, the game was tied. But that was the very moment the fans chose to attack Burroughs.

For the Indians, this was far worse than a loss. If the rowdy fans thought they were showing their loyalty and standing up for the home team after it was abused in Texas, their actions had the opposite effect. The players were disgusted. Their manager implied that the riot had effectively killed any good feelings between players and fans. "Cleveland may have lost a ballclub tonight," said Aspromonte.

Just like the 10-cent drunks, the Indians' management had no plans to stop at one. Three more beer nights were scheduled for later in the season, and, incredibly, vice president Bonda said he had no intention of canceling them. American League president Lee MacPhail was forced to step in and order the team to turn off the taps.

The fallout was immediate. Five years after the burning river, two years after Mayor Ralph Perk caught his hair on fire while demonstrating his prowess with a blowtorch, and two years after that same mayor's wife turned down an invitation to the White House because it was her bowling night, the lead story on the network news shows, and the top story in the nation's newspapers, was about a drunken brawl in Cleveland.

"Since the Indians haven't been worth much more than 10 cents in 20 years, the beer was obviously the attraction, not the game," wrote Dave Anderson in the *New York Times*. In the *New York Daily News*, Dick Young ripped the management, not the fans. "Hungry for customers, they decide to sell beer, not baseball. They lure people into the park by offering a beer giveaway, 10 cents a cup. So, crowds go there to tank up, not to watch baseball. What do the Lords of Baseball expect to happen?"

Bonda seemed intent on killing the messenger. He was so angry with Tait for proclaiming the incident a "riot" on the air that he wanted to fire him. According to Tait, Bonda said the term "riot" was an exaggeration, that the affair was merely a "disturbance." Bonda added: "Herb Score never would have referred to it as a riot."

Well, Score actually broadcast the term before Tait did.

Team owner Nick Mileti was out of town, and Bonda couldn't ax Tait by himself. When Mileti returned and Bonda began to rant about Tait's coverage, Mileti contacted the police and ballpark employees to get the scoop on exactly what had happened. After getting an earful, Mileti told Bonda, "I think Joe was kind. He could have been a lot harder on us."

The second game in the three-game series was held the next night, without incident. This affair wasn't advertised as Beer Night; this one was on the opposite end of the spectrum. It was called "Strike Out Cancer Night." It was held in honor of two local media personalities who had succumbed during 1973, Marty Ross and Jim Runyon. A chunk of the gate receipts would benefit cancer victims.

The attendance: 8,101.

ONE SWING OF THE BAT

TUESDAY, APRIL 8, 1975

With the eyes of the nation upon him, Cleveland's Frank Robinson—the first black manager in baseball history—stepped up to the plate on Opening Day and drilled a home run in his first at-bat.

THE HIRING OF Frank Robinson as the first African-American manager in baseball history was the worst-kept secret in sports.

The speculation began as early as August 1971, when *New York Daily News* columnist Dick Young predicted that Robinson would get the Cleveland job the following season. He didn't. Instead, the Tribe hired yet another white guy, Ken Aspromonte. But the concept wouldn't die.

Rumors began flying again on September 12, 1974, the day the Indians acquired Robinson as a player from the Angels. In its story announcing the deal, the *Plain Dealer* waited only three paragraphs to predict that Robinson would become a player-manager. The *Akron Beacon Journal* waited two, and the *Cleveland Press* waited all of one.

Nothing wrong with that, as long as you weren't the current manager, Aspromonte, who had instantly become the lamest duck since Daffy.

Sure, everybody said the right things. General Manager Phil Seghi announced that Robby was on board simply to help the Indians make a run at the pennant with his bat. Robinson dutifully proclaimed, "I'm here as a player to do whatever the manager asks me to do to help him and us win the division."

But then Robinson went on to talk at length about how the two-

year-old designated-hitter rule would make it far easier to be a
player-manager, and how the hiring of a black manager was long
overdue, and how plenty of blacks had the "know-how" to do the job.
Adding to the speculation was the fact that Robinson had plenty of
offshore managerial experience on his resume: five seasons at the
helm of the Santurce Crabbers in the Puerto Rican Winter League.

Let's just say Aspromonte wasn't about to take on any new home-
remodeling projects.

Another problem was brewing that would undermine the '74
squad. The day before the trade, Gaylord Perry had won his 19th
game. Two years earlier, Perry had taken the Cy Young Award with
24 wins, the most by a Cleveland pitcher in 26 years. A salty six-foot-
four veteran of 13 major league seasons, Perry was the undisputed
leader in the Indians clubhouse.

That was a problem because Robinson had been the undisputed
leader in every clubhouse he had ever set foot in. He had been
around even longer than Perry—19 seasons—and had been even
more successful, winning the Most Valuable Player award in both
leagues. Only three players in baseball history had hit more homers,
a trio of gentlemen by the names of Aaron, Ruth, and Mays.

The relationship between Robinson and Perry didn't get any
smoother when Perry immediately popped off about their salary dis-
parity. Perry was making about $100,000. Robinson was widely
reported to be making $172,000. Robby's agent, Ed Keating of Cleve-
land, also had negotiated a clause that said Robby could not be traded
without his permission and even then couldn't be traded until a sat-
isfactory contract was worked out for the year after the trade.

So the king of Cleveland's pitching mound told reporters, "I want
what he's getting and a dollar more." Perry had won more than 60
games in the previous three years and thought he deserved to be the
top dog. He was also worried—quite justifiably—about the team's
ability to pay two whopper salaries. Everybody knew the Indians
were in financial trouble.

That soon led to a full-volume clubhouse confrontation. Perry
was sitting on the stool in front of his locker when Robinson suddenly loomed over him, holding a newspaper, and asked whether the
quotes were accurate. Perry said they were. Robinson barked, "Keep
me out of your negotiations and out of the paper." Perry barked right
back, saying he had a right to say anything he wanted. Robinson
challenged Perry to stand up and vowed to "knock you on your ass."

We're not sure whether Perry would have reacted differently had he already been standing up, but he certainly wasn't going to take a chance that Robinson would unload on him as he rose from his stool. So he just sat there.

Aspromonte heard the commotion and came out of his office. But at that point, he couldn't have cared less. He wanted everyone to quiet down so he could announce that he was no longer managing. Ah, the joys of Cleveland baseball.

When the Tribe landed Robby, the team was 71–71 and had an outside shot at making a pennant run. After he arrived, they lost three straight—and 13 of their first 17. Even after winning the final series of the year, the post-Robby record was a hideous 6–14. But now the coast was clear for a new manager.

The formal announcement was a horribly kept secret, too. A full two weeks before the October 3 news conference, the *Cleveland Press* already was reporting it as gospel.

The official unveiling was, as more than one writer described it, not so much an announcement as a coronation. Baseball commissioner Bowie Kuhn was on hand, along with American League president Lee MacPhail. How often do you see the commissioner hanging around at a press conference to announce the hiring of manager?

One of the more dramatic moments came when Robinson was handed a telegram and asked to read it to the gathering.

HEARTIEST CONGRATULATIONS ON BEING NAMED THE NEW MANAGER OF THE CLEVELAND INDIANS. YOUR SELECTION AS A PLAYER-MANAGER IS WELCOME NEWS NOT ONLY FOR THE INDIANS, THE AMERICAN LEAGUE AND ALL OF BASEBALL, BUT ALSO FOR BASEBALL FANS ACROSS THE NATION. MORE THAN THIS, IT IS A TRIBUTE TO YOU PERSONALLY, TO YOUR ATHLETIC SKILLS, AND TO YOUR UNSURPASSED LEADERSHIP IN THE SPORT.

I KNOW MILLIONS OF AMERICANS JOIN ME IN SENDING YOU WARMEST GOOD WISHES FOR EVERY SUCCESS IN FUTURE SEASONS. AGAIN, CONGRATULATIONS AND WARM PERSONAL REGARDS.

SINCERELY,

[PRESIDENT] GERALD R. FORD

Nearly 100 members of the media from all over the eastern United States were at the Stadium Club for the announcement, so many that the juice drawn by their lights and cameras knocked out the electricity twice before the news conference began. Just another day in the life of a fourth-place team.

Cleveland Press columnist Bob August gave Robinson high marks the following day. After noting that such affairs are always more about general impressions than the banalities a new manager is obligated to utter, August wrote, "Robinson appeared relaxed and totally in command of himself. He seemed strong without being arrogant, shrewd in analyzing his situation, and a pleasant thread of humor was woven through his remarks."

"My wife says I can't even manage my children," Robby quipped.

"I don't want [the players] to stay away from me. I want to be close to them. If I come into a cocktail lounge, I don't want them to think they have to gulp their drink and get out. I might even buy them a drink—now that I have an expense account."

When asked by a reporter about his horrible relationship with Perry, though, Robby played it straight: "Gaylord's a real pro and so am I. I don't see any reason why we can't get along."

Interest in all things Robinson was so high that the *Cleveland Press* actually published the following paragraph: "At the conclusion [of the event, he] was offered a choice of 'good luck' desserts . . . coconut cream loaf cake or pecan pie. Robinson chose the cake—his first managerial decision."

Because of the historical import of the hiring, conspiracy theories began to bubble up. According to the buzz, Major League Baseball, embarrassed by how long it was taking for anyone to hire the first black manager, had browbeaten the Indians into naming Robby as their manager and promised to pay part of his salary.

Nonsense, said the Tribe. "A joke," responded general manager Phil Seghi. "As for the league picking up part of his salary, that's the funniest line of the year. Can you imagine other clubs paying our manager? It's pure, unadulterated bunk."

It seemed even bunkier in view of the fact that Indians president Ted Bonda was well known for his civil rights activism. One of his close pals was ultra-liberal politico Howard Metzenbaum.

Robby insisted until two days before his hiring that he had never been given any official assurance that he would become the team's manager. When the offer was first tendered, Robby didn't like it.

Keating, his agent, who was part of Mark McCormack's powerful and growing IMG operation, had negotiated a healthy annual wage of $200,000. But that represented only $20,000 more than he would have gotten simply to play. Keating persuaded Robinson that he might never get another chance to manage if he didn't take the Tribe's offer. So Robby "settled" for 200K.

Somewhere, Gaylord Perry was going ballistic. Again.

By the time Frank Robinson finally trotted out to home plate to hand his lineup card to home-plate umpire Nestor Chylak, the act had been discussed and anticipated for four years. Still, it was dramatic. The crowd gave him a lengthy standing ovation.

They also roared when former Tribe pitcher Mudcat Grant came out to sing the national anthem.

Fittingly, the opponent for the big debut was the Indians' all-time biggest rival, the New York Yankees, wearing their classic gray road uniforms.

The Tribe unveiled new uniforms for the occasion, uniforms that would come to be known as the loudest and gaudiest in team history. They were bright red jerseys over bright red pants, with "Indians" across the chest in a font best described as "Caveman." New acquisition Boog Powell, looking significantly beefier than the 250 pounds attributed to him in the program, would soon be dubbed "the World's Largest Bloody Mary."

When it came to uniform styles, Robinson had been a trendsetter. He was the first, or at least among the first, to wear the high stirrups that left a ribbon of colored sock over the white sanitary hose worn beneath. Now, he was strolling out to home plate wearing a heavy red jacket over his red-over-red uniform, covering the big, white Number 20 on his back. In the style of the day, he wore a moderately long Afro and sideburns two-thirds of the way down his ears.

Here is what was written on his historic card:

1. Oscar Gamble, LF
2. Frank Robinson, DH
3. George Hendrick, CF
4. Charlie Spikes, RF
5. Boog Powell, 1B
6. John Ellis, C
7. Buddy Bell, 3B

8. Jack Brohamer, 2B
9. Ed Crosby, SS
P: Gaylord Perry

For the record, the first four batters were black; the next five and the pitcher were white.

Robby's debut coincided with the debut of loges at the aging stadium. Clinging to the bottom of the upper deck were 84 new, two-story boxes. Stadium boss and Browns owner Art Modell had long dreamed of adding that amenity, and had finally found the cash to do it. His wife, Pat, coordinated the interior decorating and was at the stadium until midnight the night before the game to oversee the finishing touches.

A writer on the *Cleveland Press*'s women's page quoted one occupant of Modell's own loge as declaring, "There are not even better seats at the opera." Indeed.

The reporter went on to note that "the loges are packed with conveniences and extra flourishes such as color closed-circuit TV for instant replay and other programs, a spiral staircase leading to a lavatory on the second floor, heat and air conditioning, a supplementary public address system, maid service, refrigerator and food services."

The heating system would come in handy. At 2 p.m., when the first pitch was thrown, the temperature was 36 degrees. The Tribe's John Lowenstein was among those wearing a stocking cap. The horn players in marching bands from Collinwood, Mentor, and Lincoln West nearly froze their lips to their mouthpieces.

Robinson's clubhouse nightmare, Perry, came out hot. He set down the first three batters without anyone hitting a fair ball. The Yankees' leadoff hitter, Sandy Alomar, Sr., drew a walk but was thrown out trying to steal second. Perry then fanned Lou Pinella and Bobby Bonds.

When Perry walked off, Robinson walked out to the on-deck circle carrying a weighted bat—and the weight of the world.

He had long been accustomed to performing in a bright spotlight. Growing up in Oakland, he was on a high school basketball team with Bill Russell. His high school baseball teammates included future Indians Vada Pinson and Willie Tasby. He had been in World Series and All-Star games.

Still, this was unprecedented. Not even the World Series could put as much pressure on a player or manager as Robinson was now facing. Months earlier, a black Cleveland utility player named Tim

McCraw had proclaimed: "Frank is not just managing a ballclub. He isn't managing for himself, either. He is managing for all black people. And the future of all blacks as managers depends on how good a job he does. If he succeeds, the door will be open for other qualified black managers. If he fails, it may set back this thing for a number of years." No pressure there, eh?

The build-up to this single at-bat had lasted six months and five days. Not only the city of Cleveland but much of the nation had been speculating about how Frank Robinson would fare.

In a broader sense, and a more important sense, the wait had been even longer. The wait had been hundreds of years.

This black man was not just playing alongside the white folks; he was their boss. He was the guy who determined which players sat and which players played, what time they would go to bed, and how much they would be fined if they were late to a meeting. Things just hadn't worked that way in America. And to overturn the long-standing order of things in this very public business was truly groundbreaking.

The pressure facing the aging superstar was far subtler than the crush that enveloped Jackie Robinson 28 years and 51 weeks earlier, when he became the first African American to play in a major league game. Since then, all but the most racist elements of society had toned down the rhetoric, if not the ill feelings. Signs in public facilities no longer announced where a person could eat, drink, or sit. No longer could a university ban a person because of race. But those times were still fresh in the memories of many—including Robby, who entered the big leagues in 1956.

Here's how backward professional sports had been on the eve of his major league debut: In 1954, one of the Indians' minor league teams, the Spartanburg [South Carolina] Peaches, dropped out of their league to protest the use of a black player by an opposing team. When the player appeared in the first game of a four-game series against Knoxville, Spartanburg completed the game but quit the series—and the league—a few hours later. If they had to play against a "Negro," the team president declared, they'd rather not play at all.

Because minor league franchises in most cases are not owned by the major league clubs, Cleveland's front office was helpless. All GM Hank Greenberg could do was take the players themselves, who *are* owned directly by the teams, and move them elsewhere in the Cleveland system.

Mind you, this was going on at the time Robinson was in the minors himself, albeit in Ogden, Utah. Now, barely two decades later, baseball was preparing to take a quantum leap forward, and Clevelanders were justifiably proud.

Although Cleveland's professional sports teams have been disproportionately bad in terms of winning championships, they have a remarkably good record in terms of race. When Indians owner Bill Veeck signed Larry Doby in 1947, the skinny outfielder became the first black in the American League—and second only to Jackie in all of baseball. By contrast, the New York Yankees, playing in supposedly the most cosmopolitan of U.S. markets, didn't hand a uniform to their first black player until 1955, when catcher Elston Howard pulled on the pinstripes. Detroit and Boston lagged even further behind.

Paul Brown was a pioneer in integrating pro sports as well. When he was coaching the Browns in the All-American Football Conference in 1946, not a single team had a black player before he hired Marion Motley and Bill Willis. Brown thought nothing of it. Motley had played on the team Brown coached at the Great Lakes Naval Training Station. Motley was a good player and a good person, so Brown wanted him. End of story. Remember, this was one year *before* Jackie broke baseball's color line.

When the Browns won the NFL title in 1950, their first year in the league, newspaper photos taken in the euphoric winners' locker room showed four black faces among those surrounding Brown. At the time, that was still eye-opening.

Color lines were broken in basketball before Cleveland fielded an NBA franchise, but the Cleveland Cavaliers of 1986 pushed the envelope by employing African Americans as both coach (Lenny Wilkens) and general manager. The GM, Wayne Embry, also served as the executive vice president.

And now the Indians were doing it again, taking a step that was overdue but nevertheless cutting edge.

Ironically, one of the coaches fired when Robinson took over was Doby. Robinson had been watching the dynamics of the team in the dugout at the end of 1974, and he didn't think Doby had shown enough loyalty to the manager. He didn't want to take a chance that Doby would second-guess him, too. (Doby would later become the second black manager in all of baseball, replacing former Indian Bob Lemon at the helm of the White Sox in 1978.)

Commissioner Kuhn was in the stands for Robinson's debut, as was Rachel Robinson, Jackie's widow. Both of them addressed the crowd and drew cheers.

During the game, Mrs. Robinson sat next to Robby's wife of 13 years, Barbara. Barbara and the kids were still living in the tony L.A. suburb of Bel Air, and they had flown in the night before and stayed with Frank at his downtown hotel.

Barbara Robinson had accompanied her husband to the original press conference and had been an immediate hit. She was a glamour girl, friendly and pretty, whom reporters were consistently fawning over in print. Coverage of the manager's wife landed in both the sports and society sections. One male sports reporter breathlessly announced to his readers that her dress size ranged from 8 to 10. Well, baseball *is* a game of stats.

Shampoo was playing at the Great Lakes Mall, *Murder on the Orient Express* was showing at the Cedar-Lee, *Tommy* was on the big screen at the Colony at Shaker Square—in quadraphonic sound, no less—and *Godfather II* was at the Parma. But all anyone seemed to be reading and talking about was the upcoming action at the stadium.

The Tribe's leadoff hitter, Oscar Gamble, was retired on a pop fly to third baseman Greg Nettles in foul territory. The crowd buzzed as Robinson made his way to the righthand batter's box and dug in against Doc Medich, a six-foot-five righty in his fourth year with the Yankees. Although Medich was coming off a 19-win season, New York's decision to hand him the ball on Opening Day was a surprise, seeing as how the team had paid $3.7 million over the winter for Catfish Hunter. But Medich had looked better in spring training, so manager Bill Virdon called on the guy who was hot.

Listen in as Joe Tait makes the call on flagship station WWWE (1100 AM):

"Robinson's combined stats with California and Cleveland last year, a .245 batting average with 22 homers and 68 runs batted in.

"He used himself sparingly this spring, going 3-for-9 with four runs batted in. Pitch—a strike on the inside corner, Strike One. And Frank Robinson looks back quickly to Nestor Chylak. It will not be the last such look of the 1975 season.

"Medich delivers. Robby takes fastball, 0-and-2 . . .

"Last night, it was Nolan Ryan with 12 strikeouts over Kansas City, 3–2, at California.

"Bouncing foul, over the third-base dugout. The count is 0-and-2.

"Windup and the 0–2 pitch . . . Robby drills it back into the upper deck, and the count is Strike Two.

" . . . Carlton for the Phillies and Seaver for the Mets . . .

"Pitch to Robinson, a fastball low and outside, one ball and two strikes . . .

"It's a popup foul, coming back off to the left of the screen. That will drift to the seats. Out of the upper deck, downstairs, and the count remains at 1–2."

Herb Score: "Somebody gets their first souvenir of Frank Robinson the manager and Frank Robinson the hitter . . . "

Tait: "Fastball inside to Robinson. The count is 2 and 2 . . .

"Two balls, two strikes, one out, first inning at the stadium. No score. Pitch to Robinson . . . line drive to left field, well back . . . it is gone!"

Fireworks explode above the scoreboard as the crowd roars in amazement and delight.

Tait: "Frank Robinson just hit a home run in his first at-bat as a playing manager of the Indians! How about that! Boy, that goes down in the baseball storybooks right now."

Neither Tait nor Score mentioned anything about race. Perhaps they didn't have to. But race was everything, at least on this day. Race is why the attention of the nation was focused on Cleveland. Race is why tales of this otherwise-routine homer would be told and retold for decades.

"The most dramatic home run in the history of the Indians," wrote Bob Sudyk of the *Press*, clearly caught up in the heat of the moment. Writer Dick Young, the guy who had prematurely predicted Robby's elevation to manager, was in the press box too, and was nearly as effusive. He called it "the most dramatic home run I've seen probably ever in an opener." This from a guy who had covered the Yankees for 30 years.

"It parallels Henry Aaron's record 715th home run of a year ago," Young added.

The pitch had been a fastball, low and away, and it got out as fast as it went in. As Robinson rounded the bases, the crowd thundered and waved most of the 25,000 pennants that had been handed out at the gates. Chills ran up and down the spines of both fans and players, including Robinson.

Perhaps because of the emotion of the moment, Perry was out of synch in the top of the second. The Yankees ripped three singles and a double to take a 3–1 lead. But they couldn't touch Perry after that. Meanwhile, the Indians began chipping away. They got one in the second, one in the fourth, and two more in the sixth.

Perry gave up only five hits outside of his one bad inning, so the possibility of a nasty exchange with the manager during a pitching change never materialized. In fact, if you hadn't known about their personal animosity, you never would have guessed how much they disliked each other. Perry was the first to congratulate Robby after his homer, giving him a hug as he crossed home plate. At the end of the game, Perry handed Robby the game ball.

Robby nearly repeated his feat his third time up, hitting another shot to left that was caught on the warning track. Truth be told, though, the offensive player of the game was not Robby but Boog. Boog hit a long homer, doubled, singled, and walked. He scored twice and got three of the five RBIs. But in the packed postgame clubhouse, hardly anybody headed toward Boog's locker. They went directly to the first black manager, the manager whose career record was perfect.

"Right now," Robby said, mashed into a corner of his tiny office by 50 members of the media, "I feel better than I have after anything I've done in this game. Take all the pennants, the personal awards, the World Series, the All-Star games together, and this moment is the greatest. The greatest.

"The crowd—unbelievable. I've [never heard] a crowd like this. It sent chills up my spine. . . . If I could have asked God for a good kind of day, I never would have asked for something like this and expected it to happen."

The racial component would never go away, but it began to recede. The primary issue for all involved became winning and losing. And, unfortunately, Cleveland was doing nearly equal amounts of both.

Robby hated to lose. "He wants to win so badly we can't even play cards together," said his wife. "He won't even let the kids win." Writers often compared him to the notorious Ty Cobb or the nasty, win-at-all-costs Gashouse Gang.

The fact that the fourth-leading home-run hitter of all time had been traded with ever-increasing frequency should have told us something. After 10 years in Cincinnati, he spent 6 years with Baltimore, a year with Los Angeles, and a year and a half with California. After each stop, his departure was accompanied by sniping from both sides.

Clearly, Cleveland had not hired another warm-and-fuzzy Al Lopez type. Robinson was confrontational and tough. Perry wasn't the only player who hated him. Rico Carty and Robby despised each other and almost came to blows one time in the dugout.

Robinson's relationships with players didn't fall along racial lines, and race truly did not seem to be nearly as much of an issue as personality type. Rick Manning and Duane Kuiper, both white guys, swore by Robinson both during and after his reign, saying he was easy to play for as long as you hustled and did your job.

But Robby clearly had an attitude. Always did. As Doug Clarke once noted in the *Press*, "box scores won't show that F. Robby, as he is referred to, had a batting stance [that] dared pitchers to throw at his head—front foot close to the plate, head bent over—an obligation they willingly fulfilled on numerous occasions."

That's for sure. He was hit 110 times during his decade with the Reds, including 20 times during his rookie season, a major league record. It's difficult to tell how many of those bruises were inflicted because of the color of his skin, but surely more than a few.

Robinson fought on the field only once, and lost badly. That happened in 1960 for reasons that had nothing to do with race. On a play at third base, Robinson came in standing up and smashed into Eddie Mathews of the Braves, trying to get Mathews to drop a throw. Mathews barked at him and Robby threw a punch. He missed. Mathews then drilled him with a right hand, knocking him onto his back, and jumped on top of him, pummeling him until other players broke it up.

The action took place in the first game of a doubleheader. In the second game, Robby—right eye swollen nearly shut—retaliated with a homer and a double to lead the Reds to a 4–2 win. After that, he figured he'd let his bat do the talking, at least on the field.

Well, okay, there was that one incident during an exhibition game. The Indians were playing their own AAA farm team, Toledo, and Robby and his famous coach, Rocky Colavito, agreed to take one at-bat each for PR purposes. Robby's came in the fifth inning against Bob Reynolds, who had been cut during spring training. Reynolds threw the first pitch way behind Robby's head. Robinson called him "gutless" for not throwing close enough to actually knock him down. After Robinson flied out a couple of pitches later, he passed by the mound and again called Reynolds "gutless." Reynolds, who was miffed by the fact that Robinson never told him personally that he was being demoted, said, "At least you're talking to me now. I should just take care of you."

Instead, Robinson took care of him. A right-left combination and the Indians manager had flattened an Indians farmhand. Nice PR.

Within months of Robby's glorious Opening Day debut, the starting battery from that game was gone. Gaylord Perry was traded in May. He helped write his ticket out of town when he refused to run in spring training in Tucson, telling the manager he didn't need to be told how to get in shape. A confrontation in July sealed the fate of catcher John Ellis. He mouthed off in the dugout after Robby sent in a pinch-hitter. Robinson fired right back: "You're batting .217. You're lucky you're here."

Ellis escalated the stakes by dropping a verbal nuke: "You're lucky you're here too."

Before the year was out, Ellis was traded to Texas.

The Indians finished Robby's first season at 79–80, in fourth place, 15½ games out. The following year, they were two games better, but finished fourth again—marking the 22nd consecutive season without a pennant.

Part of the growing unhappiness in the front office was due to the fact that Robinson didn't use himself in games very often. Management knew that more Robinson at-bats would draw more people, and attendance was dropping. But he was struggling with a bad shoulder, didn't have the same stroke, and thought he had enough to worry about with managing.

The team's malaise continued into Year Three, and after 57 games, the Tribe's deep thinkers had seen enough. Robby was replaced by Jeff Torborg.

By that point, Frank Robinson had become exactly like every other manager in baseball history: hired to be fired.

THE MIRACLE OF RICHFIELD

THURSDAY, APRIL 29, 1976

Only five seasons after fielding one of the worst teams in NBA history, the Cleveland Cavaliers made a strong run at the league championship. They put together a string of last-second playoff victories and captured the hearts of Northeast Ohio's basketball fans. Perhaps never before or since have local sports fans made more noise per capita.

A MYTHIC BARRAGE of sound thundered through the building even before the team came out to warm up.

"WE WANT THE CAVS! WE WANT THE CAVS!"

The refrain quite literally shook the building. The Coliseum was a solid facility, only a year old, built with enough steel to crush the Eiffel Tower. But the place was vibrating, just as surely as if it were sitting atop a fault line that had swung into geological action.

"WE WANT THE CAVS! WE WANT THE CAVS!"

In the visiting locker room, coach K. C. Jones asked his assistant to walk over and hold the blackboard against the wall to keep it from shaking. Jones was having a hard time drawing the plays. And this was half an hour before the tip.

"WE WANT THE CAVS! WE WANT THE CAVS!"

Only someone who was hearing impaired could have avoided a prolonged case of the chills. No, scratch that. You didn't even need ears. The noise was so intense you could feel it in your chest.

"WE WANT THE CAVS! WE WANT THE CAVS!"

Perhaps never before or since has Northeast Ohio fallen harder for a sports team. During the 1975–76 playoffs, the love seemed absolutely unconditional. It was such an unlikely affair, and one so passionate, that the fling became known as "The Miracle of Richfield."

Outsiders look at that moniker and scratch their heads. A team that failed to win the Eastern Conference championship, much less the NBA championship, is regarded as miraculous?

You betcha. For those of us who knew where the Cavaliers had been during the previous five years, this was something on the order of loaves and fishes.

The Cleveland Cavaliers were born in 1970 at 3717 Euclid Avenue, in a 33-year-old structure known as the Cleveland Arena. By that time, the place seemed less like an "arena" and more like a glorified gymnasium.

The place had been built primarily for hockey, and hockey—minor league hockey, at that—was still the driving force. The Barons were in their 35th season and had a decent following. Basketball was just another sideshow, along with wrestling, boxing, the circus, the Globetrotters, roller derby, Disney on Parade, and ice shows. You want ice shows? Both the Ice Capades and the Ice Follies were booked for extended runs. And don't forget the TRW Christmas party, also dutifully listed on the facility's printed schedules.

The Arena's game program—the same one was sold for both basketball and hockey—touted "a bigger and better variety of refreshments," such as "pizzas and hamburgers." How adventurous.

You could buy a souvenir Cavaliers cap for $2, a T-shirt for $3, and a Cavaliers winter jacket for $15.

All else being equal, you wanted to park at the Midtown Sheraton across the street, not in the parking lot behind the Arena, because you stood a better chance of recovering your car when you came back out.

Just to the right of the main entrance was a place called the Wine & Roses. It was a strip joint. On the other side of the Arena's entrance was Richie Vojtesek's Sporting Goods. One door past that was a greasy spoon called the Tick-Tock.

Inside the Arena, patrons circled a ground-level concourse to get to their seats below. The place sat about 10,000, but you could jam in 11,000 on the rare occasion when that many people were interested.

The Arena's locker rooms were only somewhat more luxurious than the facilities at a forced labor camp. They were about 12 by 20 feet, with concrete-block walls and three showerheads that dripped and rarely delivered warm water. Team owner Nick Mileti tried to spruce up the place by hanging banners over the concrete, but he wasn't fooling anyone. Around the league, the Arena was known as the Black Hole of Calcutta.

The moldy facilities were so bad that the visiting players changed into their uniforms in their hotel rooms and walked across the street. After the games, they'd return to the hotel for their postgame showers.

Visiting players didn't always take the most direct route to the game. Before their first game against the Cavaliers, for instance, three of the Los Angeles Lakers paid a brief visit to the Wine & Roses—wearing their warm-ups.

If that doesn't sound very professional, well, it was difficult to take the Cavaliers seriously in those days. In fact, it is hard to exaggerate how truly horrible that first team was.

The first game was ugly—a 15-point loss to a fellow expansion team, Buffalo—and things went straight downhill from there. Cleveland began its maiden season with 15 consecutive losses. And most of those weren't even close.

By the night of the home opener, they were already 0–7. Still, their debut drew a respectable crowd of 6,144. The first starting lineup looked like this:

F: McCoy McLemore, 18
F: Bingo Smith, 7
C: Luther Rackley, 45
G: Johnny Egan, 21
G: John Warren, 11

Naturally, the home team was blown out by San Diego. The next night, against the Cincinnati Royals, the crowd dropped 48 percent, to a mere 3,199.

After finally winning their first game—against another expansion team, Portland—they lost 12 more in a row. Their second win came against Buffalo, and was followed by seven more losses. On Christmas morning, Cleveland's new team woke up sporting a record of 3–36.

Want to talk about ineptitude? For the season, the best free-throw shooter on the team was Walter Wesley, who posted a percentage of—get this—.687. That's only marginally competent for a high school player. The big center, taken from Chicago in the expansion draft, also owned the team's best field-goal percentage, an almost-as-lame .455.

What the young Cavs lacked in shooting they made up for with terrible defense. In two home games over a three-day period in November, they gave up 53 points to Milwaukee's Kareem Abdul-Jabbar and 43 points to Atlanta's Lou Hudson.

By the way, Jabbar recorded his first double-bird during that game. Not a double-double, mind you, a double-bird. As his point total grew, the fans started booing him with increasing enthusiasm. Why? Hard to tell. Maybe just because he was good and our guys weren't. Milwaukee was on track to win 51 games more than the Cavs. Anyway, near the end of the game, as Jabbar stood at the free-throw line and boos cascaded down upon him, he raised both hands above his head and unfurled both middle fingers.

You could get away with that kind of thing in those days, before ESPN was replaying every cough, every itch, every trickle of sweat. Heck, only 60 percent of the Cavaliers games were even on the radio.

The flagship station—okay, the *only* station—was WERE (1300 AM). Unfortunately for the Cavs, WERE was carrying every sport in town. Some nights, the new basketball team had to compete for airtime with both the Indians and the Barons. And it was no contest. Even the Barons outdrew the Cavs, and they were competing for an AHL championship. Tape-delay broadcasts weren't happening, either. If it wasn't on live, it wasn't on.

The lowly Cavaliers were not Cleveland's first crack at professional basketball, not by a long shot. Pro ball in Cleveland was already at least 0-for-5. A team called the Cleveland Rosenblums, named after owner Max Rosenblum, a department store magnate, had come and gone, despite winning the ABL title in 1928–29. So, too, had the Allmen Transfers, the Chase Brassmen, the Rebels, and, most recently, the Pipers, who won an ABL title in 1962.

Now came the attempt by Mileti, an entrepreneur who had shelled out $3.7 million to gain entry in the 25-year-old National Basketball Association. Three other teams were supposed to be added that first year—Portland, Buffalo, and Houston—but Houston dropped out because of a lack of money.

At times, the Cavaliers seemed destined for the same fate. A mere 1,737 people paid for tickets to a January 4 game against Portland. Four times that first season, the crowd numbered 2,000 or fewer. The average was a pitiful 3,518.

On November 2, the Cavs journeyed to Philadelphia and put on one of the worst performances in NBA history. They lost by 54 points. In other words, all five starters could have scored 10 more points each, and it wouldn't have made any difference.

The new play-by-play announcer, Joe Tait, didn't make the trip because of a broadcast schedule conflict. So he went back to Terre Haute, Indiana, to move more of his belongings to Cleveland. While he was packing, he was listening to the game over a Philadelphia station. In the middle of the second quarter, he heard one of the announcers say, "This is the worst basketball team I have ever seen. No one will want to see this. If people see them once, they will never come back. This franchise won't make it beyond the All-Star break."

Mind you, Tait had just quit his job as a station manager in Terre Haute to take the Cavs job alongside his old acquaintance, coach Bill Fitch, for half the pay—$100 per game. Now even that meager salary seemed to be in jeopardy.

But the Cavs managed to draw just enough attention and revenue to hang on. How they did is an enduring mystery. We're talking about a bunch of guys who were so bad that they actually shot at the wrong basket, like little kids in a Saturday-morning peewee league.

That bizarre scene took place on a Thursday evening, December 9, during one of 12 games against Portland. Picture this: The teams come out for the fourth-quarter jump ball, and Walt Wesley taps it to Johnny Warren. Warren takes off the wrong way. He has plenty of company. Rookie John Johnson is on one side, and expansion pickup Bobby Lewis is on the other. Both of them are calling for the ball, thinking they have a better shot. But Warren takes it to the rack and scores—for *Portland*.

Think that's bad? Portland's center, Leroy Ellis, tried to block the shot!

As if grade-school teams needed any more bad examples, the Blazers found themselves a few minutes later with six men on the floor, drawing a technical. Once back in a traditional basketball alignment, they still had enough manpower to overpower the Cavs, 109–102. That dropped Cleveland's home record to 1–12.

Tickets anyone?

Even with the expansion draft on top of the normal collegiate draft, Cleveland's roster wasn't exactly deep. One of the bench players was a fellow by the name of Gary Suiter, a six-foot-nine, 240-pound forward from that basketball powerhouse, Midwestern University, in Downer's Grove, Illinois.

Suiter may well have been the worst player in Cavaliers history.

He also had some quirks. Among his odd habits was a tendency to spend quite a bit of time in the restroom shortly before game time. Most of the time, he would emerge from his stall right before the trainer locked the clubhouse for the first half. But more than once, when the trainer called out for stragglers, nobody answered, and Suiter was locked inside. Because he never played, nobody noticed until the team returned to the locker room at halftime.

Suiter's big chance finally came late in the season at a road game against Buffalo. He was truly an awful player, shooting 35 percent from the field and 44 percent from the line, but the Cavaliers had sustained so many injuries that the coach finally wrote in his name as a starter. Just before tip-off, Fitch gathered the starters around to finalize their defensive assignments. He noticed that Suiter was missing. The trainer was dispatched to the locker room to see whether he was locked inside again. He wasn't. The team's starting forward was finally discovered standing in front of a concession stand, in full uniform, with a hot dog in one hand and a beer in the other.

After the game, Suiter was cut. (Even the Cavs had *some* pride.) When he came downtown the next morning to collect his travel pay, he stopped first at the Wine & Roses, which, during daylight hours, was a frequent hangout for ladies of the evening. Suiter looked around the house and asked one of them whether she wanted to make $50—not in the traditional manner, but by accompanying him to the Cavaliers offices and posing as his wife. That way he could collect extra per-diem travel money for the previous road trip.

Fitch came out of his second-floor office, looked at Suiter, looked at the woman, and promptly shoved Suiter down the stairs and back out onto Euclid Avenue.

Suiter's replacements, though perhaps more businesslike, weren't much better, and the team finished the season at 15–67. That's fewer than two wins every 10 games.

As painful as the 1970–71 season was, it was not totally unexpected. Fitch and Mileti had decided—unlike the other two expansion teams, which picked up established but aging veterans in an attempt to be competitive right away—that they would assemble a collection of youngsters, give them experience, then add a couple of vets when the kids began to jell.

Most of the guys on that first team really did try. The adversity brought them together, gave them a camaraderie that most teams don't have, and made them play even harder. And, with the exception

of Suiter, they usually did what they were told. In fact, after Fitch retired three decades later, he said the maiden Cavaliers ran his offense
better than any team he ever had. The problem was they simply
weren't good enough to make the shots.

During their second season, the Cavs won only eight more games
but moved solidly into the realm of respectability, thanks in large
measure to a first-round draft pick from Notre Dame. Austin Carr
was a scoring machine, averaging nearly 35 points per game during
his three years with the Irish, and he came out firing in the pros. Carr
was humming along at 21.2 points per game when he blew out a knee
in the season's 43rd game.

The second-year team also benefited from the services of guard
Butch Beard, who had been taken in the expansion draft but missed
a year because of military duty. The frontcourt was bolstered by the
draft of UCLA's Steve Patterson and a trade for Lakers center Rick
Roberson. Roberson was a beast on the backboards, averaging 12.7
rebounds per game. In addition, second-year-man Johnson really
began to produce, averaging 17 points.

Carr's midseason injury was too much to overcome, though, and
the team never made a serious run at the playoffs.

Meanwhile, Mileti was creating an instant empire. First, he put
together a group of investors and bought powerful WKYC radio, re-
naming it WWWE (1100 AM), or "3WE." Fewer than a dozen stations in the entire nation could match its 50,000 watts. A month later,
he assembled another group that bought the Cleveland Indians. A
few months after that, he bought a Cleveland franchise for the World
Hockey Association.

Who *was* this guy? Most Clevelanders had never heard of him before he headed a group that bought the Arena and launched the Cavaliers. He had practiced law and, while working on a project for the
Lakewood Jaycees, found a business niche in putting together funding for housing projects for the elderly. He became nationally known
as an expert on the funding and maintenance of elderly housing, and
worked as a well-paid consultant. Still, most of the money he was
throwing around was coming from other people's pockets. This flashy,
pendant-wearing son of Sicilian immigrants could put together a deal
like few others.

Mileti's basketball team improved again during its third year,
adding another nine victories, to finish at 32–50. That season Fitch
began to import some experience, trading Beard for an All-Star point

guard, Lenny Wilkens, and a veteran forward with a great shooting touch, Barry Clemens. The Cavs also added two more youngsters, swapping a future draft pick for a second-year Lakers guard named Jim Cleamons, and using their own first-round pick on big Dwight Davis.

Carr was healthy again, and both he and Wilkens averaged 21 points a game. For the first time, even the best teams in basketball had to pay attention or pay the price. Just ask the Celtics, Bucks, or Lakers, each of whom won 60 or more games but dropped at least one contest to the Cavaliers. The young Cavs beat Los Angeles by 15, Milwaukee by 14, and Boston by 5. Only a lousy February kept Cleveland from amassing enough wins for a late-season playoff run.

The master plan developed a rip in Year Four. In a notable regression, Cleveland won three fewer games. Part of the problem was a major personnel shakeup at the start of the season. Roberson and Johnson were sent to Portland for the rights to University of Minnesota star Jim Brewer. The new group, unaccustomed to playing with each other, began with four straight losses and dumped 15 of their first 19. Given the shaky start, the 29-win season was not a total disaster. And hope was on the horizon. On the southern horizon, to be precise.

Out in the wilds of northern Summit County, amid 33,000 untouched acres that in another few years would become a national park, Mileti—borrowing heavily—was creating his own personal dream, a massive, state-of-the-art arena in which his basketball team could finally blossom.

Just off Interstate 271, and just up the pike from Interstate 77, the location was, Mileti said, easily accessible from throughout the region. He initially envisioned hotels, restaurants, and other amenities springing up around it. Others had a harder time with his vision—namely, Cleveland's biggest bankers. Most of them thought the plan too risky, and Mileti was forced to go out of state for the bulk of his money.

Lawsuits slowed him down too. The project not only teed off Cleveland's power brokers, who wanted the team downtown, but plenty of people in Richfield, who had no interest in importing an additional 5,000 automobiles every night of the week.

Legal wars raged, some of them going all the way to the U.S. Supreme Court. But Mileti persevered, and eventually—two years behind schedule and almost twice the projected $17 million cost—

the Cavaliers had a glorious place to play. Looking back, in 1979, a *Sports Illustrated* article remarked, "No arena was more beautiful than the Coliseum, a magnificent structure in Richfield, Ohio."

Not that basketball was the only game in town. The Coliseum would provide an even bigger list of entertainment offerings than the Arena.

Never one to underplay an opening, Mileti arranged for Frank Sinatra to christen the new palace with a black-tie concert. Other than a nightmare traffic jam that resulted in dozens of people simply abandoning their cars and walking the final half-mile or so in tuxedos and evening gowns, the affair won rave reviews.

Everybody called it "the Richfield Coliseum" except for the people who worked in the corporate offices there. They were adamant: it was "the Coliseum in Richfield." In other words, the Coliseum was gracing Richfield, not the other way around. Newspaper reporters were chastised for reversing the order—which led, of course, to even more reversals.

No matter what the place was called, emotions of the potential customers were decidedly mixed. Fans in Akron, Canton, and southeastern Cuyahoga County loved the place because it was a more convenient destination than downtown Cleveland. Folks in other areas were far less enthralled. The most vocal criticism may have come from Cleveland sportswriters, who were forced to drive out of town every night in the dark, in all kinds of weather, and no longer had the luxury of returning to their newsrooms to write their stories.

Once inside the building, though, few people had any complaints. The sightlines were marvelous. The Coliseum had a wonderful communal feel. Unlike the future Gund Arena, whose design shepherds patrons into their one little seating area and traps them there, the Coliseum had a wide inner concourse about halfway between the floor and the top row. You could enter anywhere you pleased and truck around to your section without taking your eyes off the court. If you spotted a pal, you could walk right over and talk.

The Coliseum was one of the first arenas to offer loges, but the loges were way up out of the way, ringing the top row of seats, and took absolutely nothing away from the hardcore fans in the regular seats. Quite a contrast to the Gund, where the loges dominate the lower bowl, starting only 15 rows above the playing floor.

The first year at the Coliseum, inspired by the new digs and reinforcements from the now-defunct American Basketball Association, the Cavs won 40 games, 11 more than the previous season and only one below the once-impossible dream of a .500 season.

The key acquisition for 1974–75 was center Jim Chones, who had been playing in the rival ABA. Los Angeles held his rights, but the Cavs sent the Lakers a first-round draft choice to change that. It was a choice well spent. Chones, only 24, averaged 14.5 points a game and led the team in rebounding.

Fitch traded draft positions with Seattle to get ahold of guard Dick Snyder, and on draft day called the name of an unknown point guard from West Georgia, Foots Walker.

As the 1975–76 season opened, though, the Cavs gave every indication that they were backsliding. Losing their home opener was no big deal—hell, they'd done that six years in a row. The problem was that nothing much changed as the schedule unfolded. After 17 games, Fitch's boys were 6–11. They had broken 100 points only four times. They were averaging barely 9,500 fans in the fancy new building, less than half the capacity. Then, something magical happened.

The Miracle of Richfield was, in many ways, the Miracle of Nate Thurmond.

Thurmond, an inch shy of seven feet tall, was a seemingly un-workable collection of spindly legs, huge hands, and massive biceps. But he somehow managed to move with uncommon elegance.

He had grown up less than 20 miles south of the Coliseum, on the rough-and-tumble streets of inner-city Akron. Among his high school teammates was Gus Johnson, who would go on to a brilliant career with the Washington Bullets.

They went to Central High (now Central-Hower) together. Afterward, Johnson, who was three years older, went off to the NBA while Thurmond was tearing up the Mid-American Conference at Bowling Green. When the two returned home during the summertime and hit the playgrounds, Thurmond couldn't believe how rough Johnson had become. The message was unspoken but clear. *That's the way we do it in the big time, son. The NBA is a war. You gotta be tough. If you let them push you around, you won't be there long.*

Thurmond learned the message—learned it so well that he blossomed into one of the most feared defenders in NBA history, a man who made the Hall of Fame primarily on the strength of his defense and rebounding.

He was drafted by San Francisco, which many people considered

On a steamy Los Angeles day in 1912, the pride of Cleveland's West Side, Johnny Kilbane, mixes it up with reigning featherweight champion Abe Attell in front of 9,000 fight fans. Another 3,000 to 5,000 were turned away. But those crowds were tiny compared to the 200,000 people who would turn out for the victory parade through downtown Cleveland. (Cleveland Press Collection, Cleveland State University Archive)

New featherweight champ Johnny Kilbane is exhausted but thrilled after his convincing 20-round victory over the legendary Abe Attell. In the early 1900s, boxing was a way out of the ghetto. And Kilbane didn't waste any time cashing in: he spent the next month on the vaudeville circuit. (Cleveland Press Collection, Cleveland State University Archive)

CLEVELAND AMERICAN LEAGUE BASE BALL CLUB
CHAMPIONS 1920

The gloves were little but the hearts were big. The 1920 Cleveland Indians delivered the first World Series championship in the city's history. Their achievement was even more notable given the fact that one of their leaders and best players, shortstop Ray Chapman, had been killed by a pitch only a couple of months earlier. (National Baseball Hall of Fame Library, Cooperstown, NY.)

Ray Chapman's tombstone can be seen in Section 42 of Lake View Cemetery, where he was buried after one of the biggest funerals in Cleveland's history. But you can't see much film of him in action, so you may not appreciate just how good he was. Although he is known primarily as a historical footnote—the only player ever killed in a major league game—he was an excellent athlete, a .300 hitter and perhaps the fastest man in the American League. (National Baseball Hall of Fame Library, Cooperstown, NY.)

Little-known Akron golfer Herman Keiser displays a nice swing during the 1946 Masters. But it wasn't Ben Hogan's swing, and that bothered the folks who ran Augusta National. They desperately wanted the superstar to win the first Masters after World War II, and they did everything in their power to unnerve the pro from Northeast Ohio. (AP/Wide World Photos)

Shortstop Lou Boudreau leaps over a sliding runner on a double-play attempt during the single most exciting Cleveland Indians game in 100 years of competition. This was about the only play where Boudreau came up short during the one-game playoff to determine who would represent the American League in the 1948 World Series. He carried the team on the field, at the plate, and in the dugout. (Cleveland Press Collection, Cleveland State University Archive)

When the 1948 season began, nobody on the planet expected to see this scene: rookie knuckleballer Gene Bearden being carried off the field after pitching the Tribe into the World Series with a five-hitter against the Red Sox. This was just the start of a celebration that lasted far into the night. The players were in such bad shape the morning after their victory party that manager Lou Boudreau called off practice, fearing someone would get hurt. (Cleveland Press Collection, Cleveland State University Archive)

This is all that was left of the modified P-51 Mustang that pilot John P. Odom was flying when he lost control during the 1949 National Air Races. With a full tank of gas, he nosed into a house in Berea, killing a mother and her baby and putting an end to the races, a 20-year Cleveland tradition. (Cleveland Press Collection, Cleveland State University Archive)

One of the most popular players in Indians history stretches out his slow legs and his powerful arms. Rocky Colavito had pounded 83 homers in the two previous seasons when general manager Frank Lane dealt him to the Tigers for Harvey Kuenn, thereby earning Lane a permanent spot on every Cleveland sports fan's enemies list. (Cleveland Press Collection, Cleveland State University Archive)

Perhaps the greatest catch in major league history. Runners on first and second, Tribe down by one run in the eighth inning of Game One of the 1954 World Series in New York. Vic Wertz hits a monumental drive to center field that seems destined to give the Indians the lead. But a young outfielder named Willie Mays sprints to a spot 450 feet away from home plate, catches the ball over his shoulder, whirls and fires it back to the infield so fast that only one runner can advance. (New York Daily News)

Jim Brown pounds the ball into the line against the Baltimore Colts during the 1964 championship game at Cleveland Stadium. His third-quarter romp of 46 yards set up Cleveland's first score, triggering one of the biggest upsets in NFL history. At right is receiver Gary Collins, who would catch three touchdown passes on that cold, glorious December day. (Diamond Images)

Even Frank Ryan, a Ph.D. in mathematics, couldn't add up all the people who swarmed around to congratulate him after he fired three touchdown passes in the Browns' stunning 27-0 win over the powerful Baltimore Colts in the 1964 title game. (Cleveland Press Collection, Cleveland State University Archive)

The Texas Rangers administer a little frontier justice on an inebriated fan who thought it would be a great idea to run onto the baseball field during a game and punch some players. Ironically, the Rangers had the full support of the Indians during the Beer Night fiasco—despite the fact that the two teams had fought each other only a week earlier in Texas. (Paul Tepley)

Given the amount of weight on his shoulders at this moment, it's a wonder the guy could even lift a bat. But with this one swing, Frank Robinson blasted his way into the history books. First black manager in baseball . . . first at-bat of his first season . . . a line-drive home run over the left-field fence at Cleveland Stadium. (Akron Beacon Journal, Ron Kuner)

The temperature of Len Barker's postgame ice bath must have been perfect, because everything else was on the night of May 15, 1981. Forget the drizzly weather. Forget the fact that Barker was supposed to pick up his brother at the airport but the plane was late and they missed connections. Everything worked out perfectly. The big righty tossed the first flawless game anywhere in the big leagues in 13 seasons. (Cleveland Press Collection, Cleveland State University Archive/Paul Tepley)

The noise seemed loud enough to break the glass of the backboards. But, fortunately, North Canton's Dick Snyder still had a target as the action wound down in Game Seven of the 1976 playoff series between the Cavaliers and the Washington Bullets. With four seconds left, Snyder arches the ball over Phil Chenier, kisses it off the glass, and drops it in the net. Such is the stuff of miracle—in this case, the Miracle of Richfield. (AP/Wide World Photos)

They didn't call this the "Ice Bowl" for nothing. When the Cleveland Browns took the field for their 1981 playoff game against the Oakland Raiders, the temperature was 1 degree and the wind chill was minus-37. But that year's Browns, dubbed the Kardiac Kids, had been so hot that everyone expected them to cut through the chill and provide another miracle finish. (Akron Beacon Journal)

Defensive back Mike Davis (in white) had the worst hands of any player in the Oakland secondary. Who would have thought that after three hours on a frigid, wind-whipped field, those hands would turn into warm, supple suction cups? Davis' interception of this Brian Sipe pass, intended for Ozzie Newsome, shut down the heartbeat of the Kardiac Kids and brought the phrase "Red Right 88" into the local lexicon. (Akron Beacon Journal)

Defensive end Reggie Camp (in white) shouldn't feel bad about failing to catch John Elway on this scramble, because nobody else could stop the guy, either. In one of the most amazing drives in NFL history, Elway carried his Broncos on a 98-yard march to force the game into overtime and kill the Browns chances of going to the 1987 Super Bowl. (Akron Beacon Journal, Susan Kirkman)

As the Browns drove down the field late in the fourth quarter of the 1988 AFC championship game in Denver, Earnest Byner was either the ballcarrier or the pass receiver on four of the final six plays. He clearly was the driving force in the Browns amazing second-half rally. But all anyone will remember is his crushing, game-losing fumble. (AP/Wide World Photos)

This photograph provides a new angle on "The Shot," Michael Jordan's 1989 dagger into the hearts of Cleveland Cavaliers fans. Good thing. If we have to see that replay one more time—the one taken from behind Jordan as he hangs in the air for an eternity before sinking a jumper over Craig Ehlo—we're going to scream. (Paul Tepley)

Yes, the place was built on a landfill. Yes, the sightlines were atrocious. And, yes, during its golden years, the playing field was a disaster and the plumbing was a joke. But the yellow-brick monster known as Cleveland Stadium was ours—rotting fangs and all. When the Indians played their final game there on October 3, 1993, tears flowed in the stands and on the field. (Akron Beacon Journal, Phil Masturzo)

Given the speed with which Kenny Lofton raced home from second base on a passed ball in the final game of the 1995 ALCS, it's a wonder he didn't sheer off some body parts along with his helmet. He stunned everyone in the ballpark by traversing 180 feet before catcher Dan Wilson could throw the ball to Seattle's Randy Johnson, who was covering home plate.
(Akron Beacon Journal, Phil Masturzo)

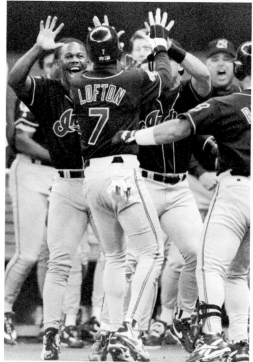

The instant Lofton crossed the plate with the run that put Cleveland ahead by three, all 58,489 people in the Seattle Kingdome—and the 815,000 households watching in Northeast Ohio —knew the American League pennant would be coming back to Cleveland. Here, the Tribe's leadoff hitter gets a joyous round of high fives from his teammates in front of the visitors' dugout. (Akron Beacon Journal, Phil Masturzo)

How does it feel to go from a Cleveland icon to Public Enemy Number One? Only Art Modell knows for sure. As he tried repeatedly to justify his move to Baltimore (top), the fans weren't buying any of it. At the final home game, on December 17, 1995, some fans vented their anger with signs, while others got physical, ripping out entire rows of seats and passing them down to the field. Modell didn't get much help from his pals in the television industry, either: During this game, NBC's Bob Costas called the move "one of the outrages of the century in the world of sports."

(Top: AP/Wide World Photos, Bottom: Akron Beacon Journal, Phil Masturzo)

How many Cleveland Indians can you get on one pitching mound? The Tribe seemed determined to find out in the waning moments of Game Seven of the 1997 World Series. The pitcher, catcher and infielders are all ears as manager Mike Hargrove tries to talk them into their first championship in 49 years. Whatever he said, it didn't work—thanks in large part to the failure of ace relief pitcher Jose Mesa (below), who sits forlornly in the dugout after coughing up the lead.
(Top: AP/Wide World Photos, Bottom: Akron Beacon Journal, Ed Suba)

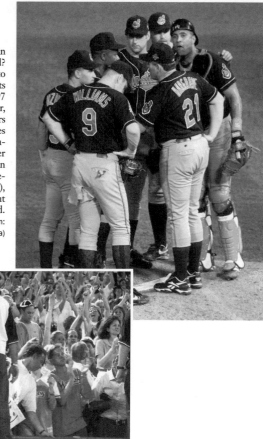

an odd move, given the fact that the Warriors already had a center by the name of Wilt Chamberlain. Chamberlain could play a bit. And, at seven-foot-one, 275 pounds, he gave Thurmond all he could handle in practice.

Thurmond learned plenty from Wilt—both on and off the court. Like Chamberlain, Thurmond developed a little black book the size of a Michener novel.

Unlike Wilt, Thurmond didn't keep stats on his off-the-field successes. Nor did he brag about his basketball talent. But he quickly showed he could hold his own in the pivot against anyone. He made the all-rookie team, and looked so strong that the Warriors traded Chamberlain back to Philadelphia the following season. Big Nate would spend the next decade as the unchallenged king of the paint in the City by the Bay.

But things went sour with the Warriors, as things almost always do with any team in any professional sport, and after 11 years Thurmond was sent packing. He was traded to Chicago for Clifford Ray and a tall stack of bills. The trade shocked and hurt Thurmond. The next psychological stage is anger, and by opening day of 1974, when Thurmond walked onto the home court in his new Bulls uniform, he was plenty angry. He channeled that anger into a manic performance that led to a quadruple double, a feat that has been done only four times in the history of the NBA. And it wasn't even close: give him 22 points, 14 rebounds, 13 assists, and 12 blocked shots.

The rest of his season was far less glitzy. The big man was beginning to show his mileage. His scoring average plunged to 13 per game, on horrendous 36 percent shooting, and the Bulls had seen enough. The following year, they wanted to dump him, and the Cavs were delighted to accept him. On November 27, 1975, Cleveland sent Steve Patterson and Eric Fernsten to the Bulls for Thurmond and Rowland Garrett

The Miracle of Richfield began two days later. That was the day Nate Thurmond pulled on the wine-and-gold for the first time.

Gradually, Thurmond had worked his way back home, from the ancient Cow Palace in San Francisco, 2,200 miles from his childhood playgrounds, to the aging Chicago Stadium, 325 miles from home, to the new Richfield Coliseum—a mere 18 miles from where his parents now lived in West Akron.

The hometown fans knew the hometown team was not getting the original equipment. The new guy wearing No. 42 had lost most of his hair and wore a big pad on his aching right knee. He was 34 years old. A generation of basketball players later, Michael Jordan would average 20 points at the age of 40. But this was the mid-1970s, when training methods and equipment were nowhere near as good. Few people trained year round. In those days, it was not unheard of for a professional player to light up a cigarette at halftime.

Thurmond didn't smoke, but he was no longer the same physical specimen who could fly up and down the court for as long as it took to get the job done. He had undergone two knee operations in an era when there was no such thing as arthroscopic surgery. Before the 'scope, a surgeon would have to slice open the whole knee to repair the damage, then close it with 30 stitches.

Now, as Thurmond's career was winding down, his coach had to keep an eye on the clock. But that was fine. The Cavaliers didn't need a young buck in the post. They already had one—Jim Chones, six feet, eleven inches of energy and flash. What the Cavaliers needed was somebody to spell Chones, preferably a big, intimidating boulder in the middle of the lane.

They came to the right place. Nobody got an offensive rebound over the back of Nate Thurmond. Nobody cruised down the lane for an easy layup. Bring that weak stuff into the paint and Big Nate would swat it away like a horse shooing insects with his tail.

The Cavs needed about 18 minutes of intimidation per night, just enough to keep Chones well rested—and just enough to rub off on the guy who was resting.

After initially being threatened by Thurmond's arrival, Chones soon realized that Thurmond wanted nothing more than victories. Fitch appreciated Thurmond's incredible work ethic, as well as his full-fledged support, something that was not always present early in the season.

Thurmond knew all about hard work. His father, Andrew, had labored for 31 years at Firestone. If Dad could put up with that, Nate figured, he could certainly give it everything he had when he was playing a game.

In addition to his toughness, Thurmond brought a hunger that had been lacking. He knew his days were numbered, and after 12 seasons of banging against monsters from Boston to Los Angeles, he had never gotten a championship ring. He felt like a winner, he burned to be a winner, but the basketball world had not officially acknowledged that designation with jewelry.

Thurmond thought he was good enough to play for a champion, and he was troubled that the rest of the Cavaliers didn't seem as certain of themselves. A couple of games after he arrived, he called them together in the locker room and told them they were good enough to win it all, but they had to start believing in themselves.

Off the court, Thurmond was a good example too. He had developed into a mannerly, refined, well-spoken man. He liked the good things in life—in San Francisco he had tooled around in a classic Rolls, and he knew his way around a menu and a wine list—but he was far more than just show. He was bright, and he treated people with respect. He was an easy guy for a basketball fan to love.

Thurmond completely transformed the team. Probably never before or since has a man playing only 18 minutes a night had such a huge impact.

Before he arrived, the Cavaliers were 6–11. As soon as Nate came on board, they went on a 12–4 run. They had a .352 winning percentage without him; the rest of the season, they were .662.

Thurmond didn't blow holes in the record books, scoring 4.6 points per game, but he was a monster in the middle. Opponents had grown accustomed to having their way in the paint once Chones took a breather; they were quickly forced to reassess that situation.

During one particularly physical game against Detroit, the Pistons' massive center, six-foot-eleven, 260-pound Bob Lanier, got so angry that he threw a left hook at Thurmond. Big Nate caught Lanier's arm and tugged it forward so hard that he dislocated Lanier's shoulder.

Most opponents knew better than to tangle with the backup center. Some would simply refrain from driving the lane; others would alter their shot when he was nearby.

Thurmond was not, however, the only reason for the breakthrough. The 1975–76 Cavs were 10 players deep, and both units managed to carve out their own personalities.

The first team was more structured. It would nurse the ball and control the tempo. The starters:

F: Jim Brewer, 52
F: Bingo Smith, 7
C: Jim Chones, 22
G: Dick Snyder, 10
G: Jimmy Cleamons, 35

The second group was the "run and gun" unit. With the exception of Thurmond, these guys started shooting almost before they took the floor:

F: Campy Russell, 21
F: Rowland Garrett, 23
C: Nate Thurmond, 42
G: Austin Carr, 34
G: Foots Walker, 14

Carr was coming off knee surgery, but there was nothing wrong with his shooting arm. He averaged nearly a shot every two minutes of playing time. Russell pulled the trigger even more often.

Opponents couldn't match the Cavs' depth. The wine-and-gold not only was tough at home, but the second-best road team in the game.

On March 31, with seven games left in the season, they marched into the New Orleans Superdome and beat the Jazz, 110–101, to clinch the first playoff berth in the history of the franchise.

On April 10, they beat the Knicks to clinch the Central Division crown, a feat inconceivable only six months earlier.

These playoff novices then found themselves facing the playoff-hardened Washington Bullets, winners of the previous five Central Division titles.

The Bullets featured superstar Elvin Hayes, who had averaged 20 points a game for eight seasons. They had hotshot guards Phil Chenier, coming off his fifth straight 20-point-per-game season, and Dave Bing, who had moved over from Detroit after nine seasons of stardom. Bing was in the twilight of his career, and his scoring average had dropped from the high 20s to 16, put he could still make the scoreboard flicker. Washington had plenty of beef in the middle, too, with six-foot-eight, 250-pound Wes Unseld, averaging 13 boards per game.

By the time the playoffs arrived, the new Coliseum was beginning to look too small. The place was packed more tightly with each succeeding game. The second home game drew 21,061, an NBA playoff record. Another 251 squeezed in for the next game, and 252 more for the game after that. Finally, the fire marshal put up his hand when the figure reached 21,564, the attendance for Game Seven.

Simply getting inside the building had turned into a social coup. None of the games was on local television that season—for the simple reason that no local television station had wanted to buy the rights. Why would any station manager knock down the door to sign a TV contract with a team that averaged 28 wins during its first five seasons?

Now, suddenly, the whole region had contracted Cavs fever, and Mileti was relishing the turnabout. He permitted local TV stations to air only one 30-second cut-in from the Coliseum each hour.

As a result, the playoffs were a coming-out party for Joe Tait, the radio announcer personally imported by Fitch. Cleveland radio in those days was dominated by WMMS (100.7), a rock station on the FM band. Bruce Springsteen's hit *Born to Run* had become a local anthem, airing every Friday at 6 p.m. to kick off the weekend. But tens of thousands of Greater Clevelanders were suddenly switching over to the AM dial to hear Tait's vivid blow-by-blow descriptions of the town's basketball Cinderella.

Tait's playlist included a peppy fight song written the year before by Cleveland radio announcer Larry Morrow—"Come on Cavs/got to make it happen." And they did.

The most amazing thing about the crowds at the Coliseum was not their size but their enthusiasm. You'd think every last spectator had a blood relative on the team.

Some of them did. Thurmond's older brother, Ben, a special-education teacher in inner-city Cleveland, brought a cassette tape recorder to the games, held it in his lap, and captured the incredible crowd noise as a souvenir for Nate.

You wouldn't know they were brothers. Ben was only six-one. (For that matter, Nate's father and mother were a relatively normal six-three and five-eleven.) No matter. In those days, every hoops fan in Northeast Ohio felt a little bit like Nate Thurmond's brother.

Game One of Cleveland's first-ever playoff series took place on a Tuesday night. The Cavs owned the home-court advantage, and the Coliseum's parking lot filled up early.

A crowd of 19,974 was on hand. Unfortunately, the Cavaliers were either nervous or intimidated by Washington's playoff experience, or both, because they fell behind 8–0 and never made much of a game of it, eventually losing by five and dumping their hard-earned home-court edge.

Still, there was plenty of time left in the best-of-seven series. Nobody was panicking. Cleveland had beaten Washington four times in six regular-season games, so the first-game defeat was viewed by the newly confident Cavs as little more than a bump. The players saw no good reason why they couldn't go into Landover, Maryland, two days later and even things up.

Reaching the playoffs was particularly sweet for Bobby "Bingo" Smith, the only player left from that first dismal Cavaliers team. He stood six-six, plus a few more inches with his big Afro, and he never saw a jump shot he didn't think he could make.

That's why nobody was particularly surprised when, in Game Two, with the contest on the line—and quite possibly the direction of the whole series—Smith rose off the floor with two seconds left, 25 feet from the basket, well back from the top of the circle, and drilled a jumper to give Cleveland a thrilling 80–79 win.

The shot capped a remarkable comeback; Cleveland had trailed by five points with only 1:27 left. Buckets by Chones and Cleamons set the stage.

For Game Three, on a Saturday, back home, the Cavs were on national television. Remember, this was a team that had been so weak it didn't even have a local TV contract. So this was another milestone for the franchise, and 21,061 showed up to lend support.

This time the Cavs showed no sign of stage fright. Carr stroked 15 first-half points as the Cavs drilled the Bullets, 88–76.

The action shifted back to D.C. for Game Four, which turned out to be one of the oddest games of the series. As the stars pounded away at each other all night, a seldom-used bench player, Clem Haskins, who had averaged all of six points during the regular season, sneaked out of the pack and led the Bullets to a 109–98 win. He hit 10 of 14 shots to blow open a game that had been tied at halftime.

Now the series was tied again.

For Game Five at the Coliseum, another record crowd arrived early and cheered often. The game was tied after one quarter, and the Bullets led by one at the half. Cleveland came out strong in the third quarter, and the game took a six-point swing.

The fourth quarter was a war. The game was tied 78 . . . then tied at 86 . . . then tied at 88.

With 36 seconds left, Chenier hit a jumper over Snyder to give the Bullets a one-point lead. Then Unseld knocked away a pass, and Washington began to run out the clock. Campy Russell whacked

Hayes to stop it. "The Big E" would get two foul shots with only seven seconds left. "Hayes can give the Cavaliers an almost insurmountable task," intoned Tait.

But Hayes missed his first free-throw. Then he missed the second. Brewer grabbed the rebound. Time out, Cleveland, with six seconds to go. Now it's simple: If the Cavs score, they win. If they miss, they lose.

Snyder inbounded the ball near the middle of the floor. He passed to Chones at the top of the key, and Unseld, knowing the Bullets had a foul to waste, immediately slapped him.

Snyder inbounded again with five seconds left. The pass went to Smith, who dribbled and threw up a runner that fell short. But Cleamons grabbed the ball under the basket and, in one motion, flipped a reverse layup behind him.

"GOOD!" shrieked Tait. "Cleamons got it! Cleamons got a rebound! And the game's over! Cleveland wins, 92–91! Unbelievable! Jimmy Cleamons rebounded a missed shot with one second to go! And the Cavaliers have won it! And the place is going crazy!"

That marked the second miraculous finish in five games.

Now it was back to Landover, with the Cavs needing only one more win. Washington's veteran team was not about to roll over, though. Hayes was on a mission, having blown Game Four, and the Bullets came out smoking, quickly building a 17-point first-half lead. But Carr got hot, and the Cavs cut it to 49–44 at the intermission.

Washington bumped its lead to six after three quarters, but the Cavs fought back again and tied the score with two minutes left. That's where it stayed, thanks to vicious defense by both teams.

In overtime, the Bullets scored the first three baskets and held on to win, 102–98.

Now it would come down to a single game—at the Coliseum.

The chants rattling the locker rooms before warm-ups—"We want the Cavs!"—segue smoothly into "Let's go Cavs!" as the team trots out onto the floor. In a seeming aural impossibility, the volume has increased. Tait can't hear himself talk, even with his headphones cranked up.

One game. Forty-eight minutes. A crowd of 21,564 on a heart-pounding Thursday night in April.

Neither team will crack. The lead changes hands 16 times. Eight more times the game is tied. Cleveland is ahead by four after one quarter and by one at the half. After three quarters, Washington has slipped into the lead, 71–69.

Late in the fourth quarter, the Cavs reel off eight straight points and pull ahead, 83–79. But shots by Nick Weatherspoon and James Jones tie it with two minutes to play.

Snyder misses a 12-foot jumper from the left wing, but rebounds his own shot and puts it back in. Snyder, a floppy-haired white guy who played high school ball in North Canton and college ball at Davidson, now has 21 points, and the Cavs lead by two.

Whistle. Foul on Cleamons. With a minute and a half in the game, Hayes goes to the line. Will this be Elvin Hayes, Superstar, or Elvin Hayes, the Game Five Goat?

He bricks his first shot. The crowd roars. He bricks his second, and Thurmond grabs the rebound as the crowd explodes.

Russell passes to Snyder, but the ball is knocked loose and picked up by Unseld. Jones dribbles across midcourt, then moves toward the foul line. Suddenly, the Bullets are whistled for a three-second violation.

With one minute to go, Cleveland still leads, 85–83.

Snyder inbounds in the backcourt to Cleamons, who passes back to Snyder on the left wing. Snyder passes back to Cleamons at the top, who swings it around to Brewer. Brewer hands to Russell, who passes to Snyder. Snyder drives against Chenier, but his layup is blocked. Two Cleveland tips miss, and Jones grabs the rebound.

At the other end, Unseld feeds Chenier on the right wing, and the six-three guard drills a 15-foot jumper. Tie game. Twenty-four seconds to go. Chenier has been Dick Snyder's worst nightmare, having scored 31 points.

Now Cleamons inbounds to Thurmond, who gives it back to Cleamons. Cleamons dribbles down the clock, and Fitch orders a time-out with nine seconds left.

All 21,564 fans are delirious. (The real "miracle" of Richfield: that fans were still able to make this much noise after two hours of relentless wailing.)

Tait is broadcasting to a massive audience. Here's what his listeners hear:

"Nine seconds left in the game and it's tied at 85. Cleamons will inbound on the left side. Cleamons looks and waits. Flips to Snyder. Snyder sideline left. Snyder on the dribble-drive, to the hoop, put it up . . . GOOD! It's GOOD! Snyder scores with four seconds to go!

And the Bullets take time! Cleveland 87 and the Bullets 85 with four seconds to go!"

It was a high-arching shot that hit high on the glass before coming down through the net, a right-handed runner from the left side of the backboard. And it was the biggest shot in Cavaliers history.

Still is.

But four seconds is a lifetime in the NBA. (See "The Shot.") So nobody is taking anything for granted as Washington comes out of the huddle.

"Unseld gets the ball from [referee] Jake O'Donnell at center floor," says Tait. "Here comes the play. Unseld lobs it underneath . . . Snyder knocks it free! Ball picked up by Chenier. Shoots it . . . NO GOOD! NO GOOD! CAVALIERS WIN! THE CAVALIERS WIN! 87–85! The Cavaliers have defeated the Washington Bullets, 87 to 85, and the crowd is going berserk at the Coliseum!"

Instantly, the floor is flooded by fans sprinting toward the players from all points on the compass. Some of the players grow uneasy in the sea of humanity, but they have nothing to fear. These fans aren't trying to tear off jerseys for souvenirs or tear down the baskets or smash the windows of the loges. This is a love fest. The fans are indulging in pure celebration, trying to commune with the players they have come to view as their own personal representatives, players who have pulled the home team from the dregs of pro basketball to an honored pedestal. Although most of the folks on the floor are young white males, this team has brought together white folks and black folks, young fans and old.

At the scorer's table between the two benches, a security guard who is trying to shield Tait from the commotion long enough for him to conduct a postgame wrap-up is knocked to the ground but is not hurt. Nobody else is seriously hurt, either.

The next morning, the newspapers were brimming with Cavs stories, and the same television stations that had expressed no interest in carrying the games were splashing the Cavaliers onscreen as their top news story.

The madness was fueled in part by the futility of the town's other pro teams. The spring of 1976 was not a good time to be a Cleveland sports fan. The Browns were coming off a 3–11 season, preceded by a 4–10 season. The Indians were coming off their seventh straight losing season, and their 21st without a pennant. But now, suddenly, the lowly Cavaliers, the team branded as the "Cadavers" by a Cincinnati reporter during their first year in business, had parted the clouds.

Fortunately, the players had six days to catch their breath and nurse their wounds. And Northeast Ohio had six days to revel in sports ecstasy.

And then, without warning, the Curse of Moses Cleaveland struck again.

That is the real reason Cleveland never wins. The city's founder was honked off that his descendants spelled his name wrong, dropping the "a," and he put a curse on the city that has remained unbroken for centuries. How else to explain the injury to Jim Chones?

Here are the Cavs, on a roll, primed for the Boston Celtics, fine-tuning their game on the eve of the second round of the playoffs, and Chones goes up to block a Campy Russell shot in practice, comes down on somebody's foot, and breaks his own foot. In *practice.* The team's leading scorer in the regular season and the playoffs. The leading shot-blocker. The second-leading rebounder (behind Brewer). The monster in the middle for 33 minutes a game. Suddenly, out of the blue, he is gone.

And now 34-year-old Nate Thurmond is the one and only center. An old man who averaged only 17.4 minutes per game during the regular season.

Lurking right around the corner was not only a solid basketball team but a storied franchise with an ongoing mystique, a team with 12 NBA titles. The ceiling of Boston Garden flew more flags than the United Nations.

The Celts had a nice blend of experience and young stars. There were big names like John Havlicek and Dave Cowens, steady hands like Paul Silas and Don Nelson, and flashy guards like Charlie Scott and Jo Jo White. It was an imposing lineup for any team, much less a team missing its best player.

But Big Nate marched onto the revered parquet floor of Boston Garden for Game One of the Eastern Division Finals and more than held his own. He played 39 minutes, yanking down 16 boards and contributing nine points. It wasn't nearly enough, though. Although the game was tied after three quarters, Boston sprinted away in the fourth, cruising home with an easy 111–99 decision.

Game Two was also in Boston, three days later. The well-rested

Cavs looked strong early, surging to a pair of nine-point leads. But Boston again was stronger in the fourth quarter, immediately pushing out to an eight-point lead and waltzing home with a 15-point win.

Finally, for the first time in 12 days, the action returned to the Coliseum. Game Three, on a Tuesday evening, was a defensive battled in front of another 21,564 rowdy fans. If possible, the noise level was even higher. Boston's Cowens, a veteran of six seasons and nine playoff rounds, said he had never heard as much noise in his entire life.

The fans were rewarded. With 10 minutes left in the game, the score was tied. But this time, the Cavs were the ones who put on a fourth-quarter surge to pull away and win, 83–78. Thurmond played 40 minutes and collected nine rebounds, six points, six assists, four blocks, and three steals. The old fossil certainly had Boston's attention. And the Cavs seemed to be back in business.

That notion was confirmed three nights later during Game Four at the Coliseum. Another sellout, another riotous atmosphere. And in the fourth quarter, the Cavs offense exploded, led by Bingo Smith, who wound up with 27 points. With 2:20 left, the Celtics threw in the towel, clearing their bench, saving their starters for what now would clearly be a tough, lengthy series. Cleveland had blown out the proud Celtics, 106–87, and tied the series at two games apiece.

Thurmond played another 37 minutes and held Cowens to 5 of 20 from the field. Big Nate also registered 12 points, eight boards, and—best of all—six blocked shots.

Now Boston was the team that seemed to be showing its age. The 36-year-old Havlicek had to leave the game in the first quarter with a bad foot. His status for Game Five was very much in doubt.

Two days later, back at the Garden, the people of Greater Boston for the first time began to challenge the decibel level of the people of Greater Cleveland.

But not right away. As late as the third quarter, the Cavs were rolling. They were up 12 points, and coach Tom Heinsohn had gotten so frustrated that he screamed at the officials and got thrown out of the game.

Retired coaching legend Red Auerbach was sitting up in the stands. He stood up, walked down the aisle to the floor, and slowly circled the floor, heading toward the Boston bench. All eyes were on him by the time he reached the team. League rules prohibited him from sitting on the bench, but he sat right next to it, at the press table, in a seat normally occupied by Boston's PR man. As Auerbach sat down, he dramatically pulled out one of his trademark cigars— the ones he lit only when victory was assured—and laid it on the table. The Garden went absolutely ballistic. The Celtics, fueled by the noise, went from 12 points down to 10 up.

It didn't help matters that Thurmond picked up his fifth foul early in the third quarter and got his sixth—on a questionable call—with five minutes left in the game. At that point, the game was tied. And that's when the Celtics pulled off another psychological blockbuster. Havlicek checked into the game, bad foot and all. When the Boston fans saw the six-foot-five legend, wearing his low-cut black shoes and his white uniform with the dark green "17" on the back, they exploded again. Although Havlicek didn't score at all, his teammates ripped off 19 points in the final five minutes. Boston won, 99–94.

Game Six came two days later, on a Thursday night in Boston. It was yet another war, tied several times down the stretch. With four minutes left and Boston ahead by one, Carr hit a jumper for his 23rd and 24th points, giving Cleveland the edge. Then Cowens pump-faked twice, hoping to fool Thurmond, but Big Nate batted away the shot.

Boston edged ahead on a long bomb by White, then Russell retaliated with a 25-foot jumper from the wing for a one-point lead.

Brewer stole the ball but Russell missed a jumper. Another jumper by White gave him 25 for the game and gave the Celtics a one-point lead with about a minute left. Cleveland then fell apart. Russell had the ball stolen, Scott drove the length of the floor for the layup, and the miracle was over.

Bingo Smith fouled out with 17 seconds left. He sat down next to Fitch and started to cry. Thurmond waited to cry until he got into the locker room. Then, the balding giant of a man, sitting on a stool in front of his cubicle, put his head in his huge hands and wept.

Fitch was voted Coach of the Year. Mileti's accountants were smiling, because the Coliseum had hosted 148,603 fanatical fans for the seven games playoff games, an incredible average of 21,229 per game.

Hometown fans were disappointed, but hardly suicidal. They treasured the moment. The six-year-old basketball team had generated so much interest that a full-length record album was cut featuring Tait's play-by-play descriptions from throughout the season. It

was produced at WWWE by longtime Cleveland broadcast personality Larry Morrow. Ten thousand copies were made, and 10,000
copies were sold.

The album was titled *The Miracle in Richfield*, a phrase first uttered
by flaming sports-talk host Pete Franklin. Somehow, over the years,
the event has come to be known as the Miracle *of* Richfield. But regardless of the precise terminology, April 1976 continues to stand as
the most glorious moment in the history of the franchise.

Thurmond's performance was miraculous in itself, the very per-
sonification of willpower. Within nine months, he would be finished.
He played only 49 games in 1976–77 before tearing cartilage in his
left knee in Houston and hobbling off into the sunset.

Despite appearing in fewer than 1,000 pro contests, Thurmond
scored more than 14,000 points and grabbed more than 14,000 rebounds. It wasn't too far into that career when his mom stopped
being angry with him for quitting piano lessons.

She told him when he quit that he could do what he wanted as
long as he did it as well as he could.

Mission accomplished.

Outsiders look at Thurmond's retired jersey hanging from the
rafters and ask how a team can retire a jersey that was worn for less
than two seasons.

You just had to be there.

Rank: #6

RED RIGHT 88

SUNDAY, JANUARY 4, 1981

All season long, the 1980 Cleveland Browns won games in thrilling, come-front-behind fashion. They seemed poised to do it again as the clock wound down on a frigid playoff game against Oakland. But the season came to a shocking end when revered quarterback Brian Sipe threw an interception on a play called "Red Right 88."

BRIAN SIPE was not one of us.

Unlike Bernie Kosar, he didn't grow up here, and he had no particular reason to want to move here. Unlike the people who paid to watch him play, he didn't spend his childhood tuning in Ghoulardi or shoveling snow or rooting for the Browns.

Sipe's formative years were set in the absurdly temperate climate of San Diego, where he lived in year-round comfort, frequently on a surfboard, learning about the complex interworkings of reefs and currents and swells in the magical zone where the Pacific Ocean breaks over the continent.

Sipe loved sports and played them all. But he was fascinated with a lot of other things, too. His mother was a painter who used a Chinese brush technique. His father, an executive in the accounting department of the TraveLodge motel chain, was design oriented too. When Brian was a kid, Dad would load the family into the car and cruise to various parts of San Diego to look at neighborhoods and buildings.

Brian took a mechanical-drawing class in high school and something clicked. When the high school yearbook came out his senior year, the line under Sipe's picture for "Career Goal" read "architect."

In French class, he sat in front of a perky cheerleader named Jeri. She didn't think he was particularly handsome—in stark contrast to an opinion millions of Northeast Ohio women would voice a decade later—but she liked the way his hair curled over the back of his collar. She thought that was cool.

They dated others in college, but kept coming back to each other because it felt right. They would marry in 1973, and eventually have three kids. But before Sipe was ready to find a wife, he wanted to find himself.

The young Californian was not only fascinated with wood and masonry, but with things beyond the physical world. One of his early intellectual sparks was *Siddhartha*, the novel about Buddha and the search for life's ultimate answers.

Sipe read the book while he was living in a lean-to on the island of Maui, back in the days before regular airline flights serviced Hawaii. He considered *Siddhartha* the most important thing he had ever read. The book stuck with him and influenced the way he lived.

When Sipe was drafted by the Browns, both parties suffered a bit of culture shock. That would only intensify as Sipe's career unfolded. Playing quarterback for the Cleveland Browns is the single most prominent position in all of Northeast Ohio sports—not exactly the optimum job for someone who is not drawn to the spotlight.

Sipe's father had grown up on an Indian reservation—Sipe's grandfather was an Indian agent—and young Brian had adopted some of the thinking of the American Indian, particularly in regard to photographs. Many tribes believed that a photograph invades your privacy and steals some of your spirit.

When Sipe discovered the kind of attention that is lavished upon a Browns quarterback, he began to feel stifled, as if the life were being sucked right out of him.

Cleveland fans had a bit of adjusting to do too. They'd had a mathematician as a quarterback in Frank Ryan, but never a quarterback who could quote existential literature, who spoke less about his football stats and more about the satisfaction he derived from mastering the nuances of the game, the same type of satisfaction one might derive from learning the play the violin.

Yet it didn't take long for the city to embrace this outsider. Ironically, the reluctant hero was an awesome interview, charming and accommodating with reporters—which only added wattage to the spotlight that made him so edgy.

Male fans could relate to Sipe because he looked more like an architect than a quarterback, and his arm wasn't much stronger than theirs. Women thought he was gorgeous. The fact that their new hero was reluctant to assume that role made him all the more intriguing to Cleveland fans.

What they didn't know, not right off, neither the women nor the men, was that Brian Sipe was tough—tougher than a riptide off the coast of Swami's Beach in Encinitas. Tougher than any 300-pound offensive tackle from Texas. Tougher than any inner-city cornerback with forearms of steel. The Browns' longtime physician, Dr. John Bergfeld, would eventually proclaim Sipe to be the toughest player he had ever seen, period.

But in the early days, Sipe wasn't known for much of anything. Sure, he had led the nation in passing during his senior year at San Diego State, but his future appeared to be far brighter at a drafting table.

No coincidence he wasn't chosen until the 13th round—the 330th player taken. The Browns called his name one round after picking the immortal Bernard Chapman of Texas-El Paso, and one round before tabbing the legendary Ed Stewart of East Central Oklahoma. Today, the NFL draft doesn't even last 13 rounds.

No coincidence that Sipe was cut in 1972, and again 1973.

Actually, in those days, pro teams had something known as the "taxi squad," which was the sports equivalent of a human slush fund. The name stemmed from the Paul Brown era, when the first owner of the Browns was Mickey McBride, president of the Cleveland Yellow Cab Company. Brown and McBride stashed extra players by putting them on the cab company's payroll. Supposedly, the players drove taxis. But they seemed to spend an awful lot of time on the practice field. And if one of the regulars got hurt, the so-called taxi drivers didn't need much time to, ahem, change professions.

By Sipe's era, the players were no longer paid by a cab company, but the spirit was the same. The Browns paid Sipe $1,000 a week to practice with the team. On game days, he'd take a seat.

During his first year, he sat behind Bill Nelsen, a gritty man of limited skills but several years of NFL experience, and Mike Phipps, a hot young prospect from Purdue.

The second year, Nelsen was gone and Phipps was the starter. But the Browns had so little confidence in Sipe that they brought in a Green Bay also-ran, Don Horn, to back up Phipps.

Sipe finally was handed his No. 17 game jersey in 1974. Even then he was just another guy standing in the shadow of the bonus baby, Phipps. Phipps was the designated savior. Unlike Sipe, he looked like a quarterback, standing six-foot-three and weighing 220 pounds. Phipps threw darts. His passes had a tight spiral that made some of Sipe's efforts look amateurish.

Sipe was listed on the roster as six-foot-one, 195 pounds, but he was actually only six feet and maxed out at 185. When the pro scouts came to measure him his senior year in college, he wore three pairs of gym socks so his heels would appear to be touching the ground when he stood on his toes.

If Sipe didn't have a cannon attached to his right shoulder, his arm was certainly accurate. He was also nimble, and very savvy. And in the fall of 1980, he became absolutely magical.

But it had been a long climb. Playing sporadically his first two years, he threw for two touchdowns and 10 interceptions. Not until 1976—when Phipps ripped up his shoulder during the third quarter of the season opener—did Sipe get a real chance to show what he could do. And it wasn't much.

His first start, in Pittsburgh, resulted in a 17-point loss. His second start, in Denver, became a 31-point blowout. The offense was so horrid in Denver that, after the game, team official Peter Hadhazy told the media that Sipe simply wasn't good enough to play in the NFL.

The Browns had nobody else to take Sipe's place, though, so he remained the starter and eventually showed flashes of the good things to come. When new coach Sam Rutigliano showed up in 1978 with a fetish for the passing game, Sipe was in heaven. Still, it was not until 1979 that Browns fans got a true foreshadowing of the 1980 magic.

During the fall of 1979, Sipe led the league with 28 touchdown passes and threw for nearly 3,800 yards. The team finished 9–7 and almost made the playoffs for the first time in seven years. During the off-season, the team sold an astounding 47,000 season tickets.

The nation remained skeptical. In its preseason football issue, *Sports Illustrated* noted that "seven of the nine Cleveland wins last year came in the fourth quarter or overtime. In 12 of the Browns' games the issue was in doubt in the final two minutes. Their highlight film is called *Kardiac Kids*." The magazine figured much of that success was luck, and predicted a third-place finish and an 8–8 record.

"Their biggest problem is the division they're playing in," *SI* opined. "In the NFC, Cleveland would be a Super Bowl contender, but in the AFC Central, it's just trying to survive against Pittsburgh and Houston."

This was the start of a new decade, though, and things were changing everywhere. The year had opened with a vivid reminder of the incredible possibilities of sport: In the Winter Olympics at Lake Placid, New York, a theoretically overmatched U.S. hockey team upset the powerful Soviet Union team in the "Miracle on Ice."

The new decade brought a new start in national politics as well. Ronald Reagan took office in January, and the American hostages held in Iran were soon released. (Other conflicts were not resolved as quickly. An unknown tyrant named Saddam Hussein led Iraq into a war with Iran that would last a decade.)

Ted Turner launched the world's first all-news network, CNN, which would transform the media but was initially ridiculed by critics as "Chicken Noodle News."

Box-office biggies included *Coal Miner's Daughter, The Elephant Man, The Empire Strikes Back, Raging Bull, Ordinary People*, and *The Shining*.

Among the musical hits that year were *Another One Bites the Dust*, by Queen, *Hit Me with Your Best Shot*, by Pat Benatar, and songs by two groups with roots in Akron: the Pretenders' *Brass in Pocket* and Devo's *Whip It*.

In the fall of 1980, the Cleveland Browns could have used any of those songs as their theme. After losing their first two games, they rolled over 11 of their next 14 opponents—often in the most dramatic fashion imaginable.

The Kardiac Kids played 16 regular-season games, and 13 of them were decided after the two-minute warning. Of their 11 wins, nine were by less than a touchdown.

Part of what was going on was the advent of the "prevent defense." Every coach in the NFL thought the best way to hang on to a lead was to not contest short passes, play conservatively, and force the offense to chew up the clock. With Cleveland trailing so often in the fourth quarter, Sipe was able to cash in on the loose coverage.

Still, some of the comebacks were absolutely absurd. Exhibit A: a home game against the Green Bay Packers in Week 7. The Browns trailed by two touchdowns with a little more than seven minutes left. They were still behind by two points with a mere 16 seconds left and the ball sitting out near midfield.

As Sipe faded to pass, flanker Dave Logan sprinted straight down the right side of the field, toward the open end of the stadium. Sipe lofted the ball in his direction. Logan cut sharply inside his defender, leaped to grab the ball, then sprinted the rest of the 46 yards into the end zone. Browns fans of that era can still see, in their mind's eye, Logan holding the ball aloft with one hand as he passes the goal line.

Logan was an amazing athlete. He grew up in Colorado and became a three-sport star at the University of Colorado. He was so good in football, basketball, and baseball that he was drafted in all three. In Cleveland, if things had gone as planned, Logan would have been the primary receiver on the biggest single play in Browns history, which was to take place 11 weeks after the Green Bay game.

But first, there were a lot more thrill rides to ride.

A week after the miracle against the Packers, the Browns were getting thumped by the dreaded Steelers, trailing 26–14 in the fourth quarter and showing few signs of life. But suddenly Sipe cranked it up again, hitting shifty running back Greg Pruitt for a short TD and then nailing tight end Ozzie Newsome for another. The Browns won, 27–26.

On and on it went. Eight days later, on *Monday Night Football*, with the Browns trailing the Bears with only 4½ minutes left, a well-juiced Cleveland crowd erupted as running back Mike Pruitt ripped off a game-winning, 56-yard run.

As of that moment, Brian Sipe owned Northeast Ohio, lock, stock, and kicking tee. Every Browns fan in the land was convinced that this was the magic man, that this charismatic Southern Californian had arrived to lead Cleveland to the elusive joys of the Super Bowl. It was destiny.

Fans loved the fact that Sipe had been widely disrespected, much like the city itself. They loved the Browns' high-powered, fancy offense, especially in the wake of the plodding offenses of former coach Forrest Gregg.

Sipe's style was a bit unusual, but nothing spectacular. Unlike many quarterbacks, he didn't backpedal. He turned the bottom half of his body and ran backward, scanning the field as he dropped, and set up quickly. He threw the ball directly overhand, which, given his lack of height, was fortunate, because it helped his passes escape the big claws of onrushing linemen.

Sipe was having as much fun as the fans. Professional football fit perfectly with the philosophy he had learned about in *Siddhartha*—living in the "here and now." Life on the field was total immediacy—no telephones, no children, no world events. It was wall-to-wall football, packed with constant decision-making and gamesmanship.

Sipe liked the fact that he was in physical danger. Win or lose, he felt good, like a warrior who has survived a battle—except, that is, when he suffered one of his many concussions.

If God had given Sipe a body that was too small for his job, God also gave him something that was essential in both architecture and quarterbacking—an excellent spatial awareness. Sipe had good depth perception and a knack for quickly analyzing the relationships of various objects. His passes weren't the straight-line bullets of rivals like Terry Bradshaw, but stealthy grenades dropped into various zones at precisely the right instant.

As you might expect, Sipe did not settle his family on Cleveland's beaten path. He and Jeri took a glorified shack in the southern Medina County village of Seville, far from the lights of the city. Although they were initially content there, they realized they needed something more substantial after the arrival of their first child; daughter Lani's bedroom was a bathroom. After four years in Seville, they moved north to Granger Township, then up to Hinckley, getting closer to Brian's workplace but never leaving Medina County.

After each season, the Sipes would immediately return to San Diego, where they would drive up a winding, dusty road, past a glorious field of poinsettias, toward their new house. The field was part of the largest poinsettia farm in the world, operated by the family of the man who first domesticated the Christmastime flower. The combination of sunshine and sea breezes wafting over the little valley north of Del Mar created the perfect microclimate for the flower.

Farther up the road, they'd pass a bizarre structure belonging to an eccentric-artist neighbor named Klimo. His "house" consisted of a doughnut-shaped swimming pool with a dome over it.

Finally, at end of the road, the Sipes could retreat to their comfortable house, which had an in-ground swimming pool and fine views all around. It did not have the Spanish flavor typical in San Diego. In fact, it would have looked right at home in suburban

Cleveland. But it offered that rarest of Southern California commodities: isolation.

Isolation was becoming nearly impossible in Northeast Ohio. As the 1980 season progressed, even the offensive linemen had become household names, and Sipe had turned into an icon on the magnitude of Elvis.

The Browns' eight home games drew 601,496 people—a record that may never be broken.

Houston songwriter Clark Walker fed the frenzy—and was fed by the frenzy—when he set new lyrics to "The Twelve Days of Christmas" and put out a 45-rpm single through Paid Records in Nashville. His little production, "The Twelve Days of a Cleveland Brown Christmas," sold a quarter million copies during the 1980 holidays.

> *On the first day of Christmas Art Modell gave to me,*
> *A Rutigliano Super Bowl team.*
> *On the second day of Christmas Art Modell gave to me,*
> *Don Cockroft kickin'.*
> *On the third day of Christmas Art Modell gave to me,*
> *Brian Sipe a-passin'.*
> *On the fourth day of Christmas Art Modell gave to me,*
> *Alzado attackin'.*
> *On the fifth day of Christmas Art Modell gave to me,*
> *Both the Pruitts' moves.*
> *On the sixth day of Christmas Art Modell gave to me,*
> *Newsome a-catchin'.*
> *On the seventh day of Christmas Art Modell gave to me,*
> *Darden interceptin'.*
> *On the eighth day of Christmas Art Modell gave to me,*
> *The Kardiac Kids a-winnin'.*
> *On the ninth day of Christmas Art Modell gave to me,*
> *DeLeone a-hikin'.*
> *On the tenth day of Christmas Art Modell gave to me,*
> *Doug Dieken blockin'.*
> *On the eleventh day of Christmas Art Modell gave to me,*
> *Dave Logan leapin'.*
> *On the twelfth day of Christmas Art Modell gave to me,*
> *The Browns in the playoffs.*

The songwriter had no particular affinity for Cleveland sports. He released similar records in eight other NFL cities, crafting words of love for those players. But nowhere did the song take off like it did in Cleveland.

As the season wound down, the Browns were given a taste of their own medicine. Up at the Metrodome in Minneapolis, they led the Vikings by two touchdowns but coughed up the lead when the home team scored three TDs in the final five minutes—including a tipped-around, 46-yard Hail Mary that Ahmad Rashad grabbed as the clock struck zero.

That heartbreaker meant the Browns had to go into Cincinnati in the final week of the season and beat the Bengals to clinch the AFC Central Division Championship. Although the Bengals were only 6–9, the rivalry was intense, and anything could happen.

On the cold artificial turf at Riverfront Stadium, Sipe came through again, putting together his sixth 300-yard passing game of the season. Two passes were touchdowns to unsung wide receiver Ricky Feacher. Don Cockroft kicked a short field goal with less than two minutes to go to seal the deal, 27–24.

When the team got back to town that night, 25,000 people were waiting at Hopkins Airport. They were holding signs and cheering and fawning. Among the Browns working their way through that gantlet, grins on their faces, was the quarterback, a guy who would soon be voted the Most Valuable Player in the entire 32-team National Football League. In a contest in which the winner normally edges out the runners-up by only a handful of votes, Sipe was named on 47 of the 84 ballots—a landslide.

Sipe's final regular-season statistics were enough to overwhelm even a certified public accountant: 4,132 yards and 30 touchdowns, against a mere 14 interceptions. He completed 61 percent of his throws and racked up a quarterback rating of 91.4.

Browns fans, though, were focused on another number: two. That's how many victories their team needed to get to the Super Bowl, because the win in Cincinnati bought a first-round bye.

When playoff tickets went on sale December 23, they were gobbled up in two hours. Now the Browns and their fans could sit by the fireplace and wait for an opponent to emerge. And the frenzy had a chance to build over a two-week period.

Halfway through, Browns fans gathered around their televisions to see who would be the Browns' next victim. If Oakland beat Houston, the boys in black would be coming to town. If Houston won, the

Browns would face Buffalo. That was because Cleveland and Houston were in the same division, and playoff rules dictated that teams from the same division couldn't run into each other before the league championship game.

Houston featured running back Earl Campbell and colorful coach Bum Phillips. The Raiders were known for their bull of a fullback, Mark Van Eeghan; a sticky-fingered cornerback, Lester Hayes, who led the league with 13 interceptions; and the surprising play of quarterback Jim Plunkett. The only reason Plunkett was starting was a midseason injury to the regular signal-caller, Dan Pastorini. Until the 1980 season, Plunkett, a former Heisman Trophy winner, had been another Mike Phipps—a college sensation who tanked in the pros. But Plunkett was on a roll, and the Raiders thumped the Oilers, 27–7.

The weather during the week leading up to the playoff game was exactly what you'd expect during the first week of January in Cleveland—bitterly cold. The field was covered with a tarp, but heavy snows covered the tarp, and the playing surface was frozen solid. A couple of days before the game, tractors with rubber blades were dispatched to shove the snow off the tarp without tearing the material apart. Hot air was pumped under the edges to try to thaw the field.

The Raiders didn't fly into Cleveland until they absolutely had to—36 hours before the game, by NFL rules. So much for getting acclimated. Not that being here early would have helped; the Browns were scheduled to work out the day before the game but had to cancel practice because the field was still saddled with ice and snow.

With the game sold out well ahead of the 72-hour deadline, the local television blackout was lifted. Still, few of the ticket-holders would have dreamed of watching this contest from the warmth of their living room, not after everything they'd witnessed in 1980. An amazing 77,655 people walked like Michelin Men into the stadium, squeaking along in their heavy down coats and ski pants to watch a bunch of frozen players slip-sliding away on the concrete turf below. The fans hung banners designed to encourage their team and get themselves on TV—not necessarily in that order. The NBC broadcast crew was, of course, quite taken with signs reading, "Nobody Beats Cleveland."

The Ice Bowl began as scheduled at 1 p.m. Snow covered every square foot of the ground except for the perfect rectangle of the playing field. On the sidelines, behind the benches, on top of the snow, sat the big, green, jumbled-up tarps, looking like abandoned sleeping bags.

The Raiders wore their white jerseys and silver pants, while the Browns went with their dark-brown tops and orange pants.

The players looked like little steam locomotives—every breath they took was visible, emerging from their noses and mouths in narrow jets before spreading out and dissipating.

The footing was terrible, and so were the offenses. The Raiders would average 3 yards per play, the Browns 3.7. Sipe would complete a dismal 13 of 40, Plunkett a very ordinary 14 of 30. Given the weather—1 degree, with a wind-chill factor of 35 below—it's a wonder anybody could move at all.

Oakland took the opening kickoff, ran three plays, and punted.

Cleveland also went three and out.

Oakland threw an interception, but after one first down, the Browns had to punt again.

Oakland went three and out.

Sipe threw an interception, but Oakland had to punt.

Cleveland had to punt.

Oakland had to punt.

Sipe threw a perfect pass to Reggie Rucker in the end zone—and Rucker dropped it. After one quarter, nobody had done anything.

In the second quarter, heading toward the open end of the field and into the teeth of a 16-mile-per-hour wind, the Browns began to move a bit. But Don Cockroft came up short on a 47-yard field-goal attempt. A few minutes later, he missed a 27-yard boot.

The first score of the game came by the defense. The Browns' left cornerback, Ron Bolton, picked off a Plunkett pass and skated 42 yards—after which, of course, the extra point was blocked. Cockroft was now zip-for-January.

With six minutes left in the half, the Raiders passed midfield for the first time in the game, and eventually scored on a one-yard run. They made their kick, and took a 7–6 lead into the locker room.

In the third quarter, Cockroft finally connected, nailing a 30-yarder with the wind behind him. Oakland sputtered again, and Cockroft lined up to try to extend the 9–7 lead. But this time the holder, backup quarterback Paul McDonald, couldn't catch the snap. The kicking game was now 1-for-5.

An interference call later put Cleveland on the Oakland 9-yard line, but that drive stalled, too, and Cockroft kicked a 29-yarder, again with the wind at his back. The quarter ended with Cleveland ahead, 12–7.

The Raiders came out strong in the fourth quarter, mounting a drive that ate up six minutes. Van Eeghan took it in from the one to give the visitors a 14–12 edge.

After some unproductive efforts by both offenses, the Browns got the ball at their own 28 with 4:39 left. The crowd started to buzz in anticipation of yet another fourth-quarter drive. But Sipe promptly fumbled, and the Raiders recovered on the Browns' 25. The crowd fell silent.

Just when the magic appeared to be gone, the defense pulled its own miracle. Van Eeghan was sent into the line three straight times, gaining a total of nine yards. Oakland decided not to try for a 32-yard field goal, and, on fourth down sent their bull, Van Eeghan, back up the middle. He was slammed by linebackers Dick Ambrose and Robert Jackson, and the Browns had the ball back at their own 16.

Now, the fans thought, the real fun starts. Two minutes and 22 seconds. Eighty-four yards to go. Showtime!

Sipe throws incomplete.

Sipe hits Newsome for 29 yards, and the two-minute warning is called with the ball on Cleveland's 45.

Sipe throws another incompletion. Then he's sacked. On third down, he spots Rucker. Rucker can't catch the ball, but the Raiders are flagged for interference. First down on Oakland's 49.

Sipe hits Greg Pruitt, and Pruitt steps out of bounds at the Oakland 28. The clock reads 1:12.

Sipe misses on a pass, but then Mike Pruitt roars up the middle for 14 yards, giving the Browns a first down at the Oakland 14. Cleveland calls time.

Mike Pruitt runs again, and picks up only a yard. Another time-out.

The game clock now shows only two digits: 49.

The Browns have a decision to make. Do they run a couple more plays up the middle and try a field goal, or do they go for the touchdown?

Rutigliano is skeptical about the kicking game. Cockroft has had a miserable day, which is in keeping with a rather miserable year. He went 16 of 26 on field goals during the regular season, far below par, and missed five extra points. After 13 years in the game, his best days are behind him. Part of the problem is torn cartilage in his left knee. Although he kicks with his right leg, he has to plant with the left one, which produces plenty of stress as well.

The regular clock reads 3:30 p.m. Everyone has been out in the cold for two and a half hours. And everything has all come down to this.

On the sideline, Sipe, Logan, Rutigliano, running back Cleo Miller, and quarterback coach Jim Shofner gather around to plot the next step. Sipe argues in favor of a field-goal attempt. But given the circumstances—the weather, Cockroft's injury, and the previous ineptitude—Rutigliano orders a pass.

The head coach looks at Sipe and says, "Red slot right . . . "

Sipe interrupts. "Slot right or regular?"

"No, no," responds Rutigliano. "Red slot right, halfback stay, 88."

"Red" is the formation. "Slot right" means that the "Y" receiver, Rucker, will line up on the right side. "Halfback stay" means both running backs, Miller and Mike Pruitt, will stay in and block, rather than run a pass pattern. And "88" is the blocking scheme for the offensive linemen.

Newsome is supposed to line up on the left side as the "X" receiver against Raider cornerback Dwayne O'Steen. Logan and Rucker will line up right. Their job is to attract attention and lure most of the defenders out of the target area, the right corner of the end zone.

Newsome is the one and only target. "If he's not open," Rutigliano tells Sipe as the meeting adjourns, "throw it into Lake Erie."

But when Sipe runs back onto the field in front of the bleachers, he tells his teammates: "Red right 88, halfback stay."

That changes the primary receiver from Newsome to Logan. Instead of what Rutigliano has envisioned, Rucker and *Newsome* will start on the right side and clear the path for *Logan*.

Although it isn't the same play, the hot receiver is still covered by O'Steen, which is essentially the arrangement Rutigliano was looking for.

Newsome is supposed to sprint to the back of the end zone and then cut across to the left side of the field, taking along the two deepest defenders. Rucker will head to the right side of the end zone, then cut back behind Newsome, drawing his defender, Lester Hayes, to the left side. Then, in theory, Logan will have to beat only one man, O'Steen.

As Sipe approaches the line of scrimmage, he silently tells himself, "Don't get sacked. Don't get sacked."

The ball is snapped. As Sipe begins to drop, he sees two Raider linebackers blitzing. He sees Newsome breaking open. What he doesn't see is that the guy covering Logan, O'Steen, has been knocked off stride by one of his own teammates, and Logan is crossing toward the right corner wide open.

On the sidelines, Browns defensive tackle and full-time lunatic Lyle Alzado swears aloud, then yells to linebacker Dick Ambrose, "I can't believe they're throwing the ball!"

The blitzing linebackers, Ted Hendricks and Rod Martin, begin closing on Sipe, who has set up at the 22-yard line. He unloads a hurried throw to Newsome. The ball wobbles noticeably. As Newsome moves toward the pass, he slips. Mike Davis does not.

Mike Davis, of all people. Davis, a college teammate of Logan's. Davis, who has the worst hands in the Raider secondary. Yes, Davis. Davis grabs the ball as if it and his gloves are made of Velcro.

Logan looks back, sees the interception, and drops to one knee on the frozen turf, devastated. Newsome lies on the ground for a moment. His first instinct is to congratulate Davis on a great play. Sipe is buried under linebackers and doesn't see what happened, but he doesn't have to. He knows by the reaction of the crowd.

Cleveland Stadium is silent—completely, astoundingly, awe-inspiringly silent. It is the sonic equivalent of suddenly flipping off the main circuit-breaker in the middle of a Rolling Stones concert.

As Sipe walks off the field and pulls off his helmet, he looks shocked and horrified. Rutigliano walks up to him, throws his arms around him, and says, "I love you, Brian." A moment later Sipe bends over at the waist and stares at the turf in emotional agony.

Already, both men have absorbed the enormity of the moment. But they do not yet realize that this moment will brand both of them for life.

In the years before and after, Brian Sipe threw 3,439 passes for the Cleveland Browns and completed 1,944 of them. But this one pass, this last heave of the 1980 season, would be the one pass people would talk about until the end of time.

Rutigliano would suffer too. Nearly a decade later, as he took the field as the head coach of the tiny religious school Liberty University for a big game at Eastern Michigan, he saw concrete evidence of his lifetime sentence. At one end of the stadium, EMU fans unfurled a big banner that read, in orange-and-brown letters, "Red Right 88."

How many play calls in the history of football have been nationally known by their technical names?

As the gray daylight faded that Sunday at Cleveland Stadium, the second-guessers were having a field day. *Akron Beacon Journal* columnist Tom Melody sat up in the crowded press box and categorized Rutigliano's decision to pass as "a wholly remarkable example of malpractice in the business of football coaching."

Melody said the pass proved that Rutigliano "is not yet [and] might never be a technically sound coach. Instead, he is a coach mesmerized by the oft-miraculous powers of his quarterback, Brian Sipe. A coach whose idea of logic would be to jump out of his 24th-floor hotel room in order to get a breath of fresh air."

In the Browns locker room, the players initially sat in stunned silence. When they began talking to reporters, their comments ran the gamut. Alzado, one of the most distraught, could have been speaking for hundreds of thousands of Browns fans.

"When you have a dream, it's with you night and day," said Alzado. "It becomes part of your life. It's like losing somebody you love. You want something so bad, you would do anything to get it and when it goes away, you feel something's missing. And that's how I feel."

Sipe slowly pulled on his best postgame face. Standing in front of his locker, wearing a heavy jacket over a turtleneck sweater, a cap from a heli-skiing resort pushed back on his dark, thick hair, he told reporters: "I'm disappointed, but I'm going home and [will] be damned happy with what we accomplished. We had a dream and we almost made it come true."

But he was feeling a deep ache, one that would never fully leave.

That wintry afternoon, at 3:30 p.m. Eastern Standard Time, 12:30 p.m. Pacific Time, Brian Sipe, the California surfer, officially became one of us.

PERFECT

FRIDAY, MAY 15, 1981

On a cold, drizzly night at Cleveland Stadium, Len Barker pitched the first perfect game in all of baseball in 13 years. No runs, no hits, no errors, no forgetting.

INSIDE LEN BARKER'S small condominium in Parma, every workday began the same way. No alarm clock jerking this guy out of dreamland. He would simply sleep until his body didn't need any more. Then he'd slide out, usually about 11 a.m., get something to eat, and hack around for six hours before heading down to the ballpark.

Barker was only 25 years old, and his neighborhood—just off Broadview Road in the center of town—was full of young families. He and his wife fit right in, all the way down to his new, blue, four-wheel-drive Chevy Blazer. With a salary of $125,000, he was in a better financial position than most of his neighbors, and he could have driven something sexier, but that just wasn't his style.

On this particular day, Barker had to make a side trip before reporting to the office. His brother, Charles, was flying in from New York to watch him pitch, and Lenny had promised to pick him up at Hopkins.

The plane was late. The pitcher waited and waited. Finally, he could wait no more, and he hopped back into the Blazer and drove to Cleveland Stadium.

Barker wasn't particularly stressed out by missing the rendezvous. He knew his brother was capable of finding his way to the ballpark. As usual, Lenny wasn't about to let the little stuff get to him. What good would that do? Besides, the weather was so bad he wasn't even sure the game would be played.

The starting pitcher for the Cleveland Indians pulled into the players' parking lot at 6 p.m.—about 45 minutes later than usual. Still, he had time to get his usual rubdown from trainer Jimmy Warfield. Before every start, Warfield would rub Barker's arm and rub his legs and rub up his spirit with jokes and encouragement.

Barker then pulled on his white game uniform and stuck his feet into his black Spalding cleats. A few minutes after seven o'clock, he grabbed his Wilson XLC2000 glove, the one he had begun to break in several months earlier, and began the long walk through the dank tunnel onto the soggy field, where he began to stretch.

Unlike many ballplayers, Barker paid no attention to which shoe he put on first or how many people touched him in the locker room or where the second hand was when he made his first warm-up toss. He wasn't the least bit superstitious. He was a pitcher, and pitchers pitched. They didn't mess with voodoo.

The secret to success, he believed, was simple: hard work. During his early years as a pro, he played winter ball. Once he became established with the Indians, he bought a condo in Tucson, Arizona, and headed out there every year immediately after Christmas to beginning working out. That way, he was already in the groove when the rest of the players showed up for training camp in mid-February.

At six-foot-five, 220 pounds, Leonard Harold Barker III was a big Kentucky-born boy with a big, distinctive delivery. He would rock back slowly, lifting his hands over his head, then turn his right foot almost 90 degrees, planting it parallel to the rubber. Rocking forward, he would raise his left knee way up—all the way above his eyes—before pushing off with his right leg and firing the ball with a three-quarter delivery.

The knee action certainly wasn't textbook, and it required a lot of extra effort. But no coach was going to mess with that delivery: by the age of 16, Barker could throw a baseball 96 miles per hour.

In the pros, he occasionally hit 97. But on this drizzly night, his fastball ranged from 91 to 95 miles per hour. That was still plenty fast. Even better, on this night his curveball was incredible. It came in as fast as a slider but was breaking almost as big as a curve. It was the best of both worlds—a "slurve." And after a couple of innings, he discovered he could throw that slurve exactly where he wanted. Mix that in with the fastball and you have a hitter's nightmare.

Barker had a changeup, too. But on this night, he only threw it once. Why bother with slow stuff when you have two pitches that are lethal?

The weather didn't make the opposing hitters any happier. Although the skies were not so much raining as misting, the 49-degree temperature made the thin precipitation seem far more intense. A drying agent was spread on the mound and around home plate, giving the field a sloppy look. In the stands, umbrellas were popping up and down throughout the ballgame.

At least partly because of those conditions, all but 7,290 residents of Northeast Ohio decided they could find something better to do on a Friday evening. (Odd that now 72,900 people claim to have been there.)

Herb Score and Nev Chandler were calling the game in the WWWE (1100 AM) radio booth. They were baseball traditionalists and made a point of adhering to baseball's just-barely-unofficial protocol, carefully noting the number of batters Barker had dispatched but never *ever* uttering the phrase "no-hitter," much less "perfect game." Same with Joe Tait and Bruce Drennan, who were manning the mikes in the WUAB (Channel 43) TV booth.

Tait was in a particularly good mood. The previous evening, his pal, former long-suffering Cavs coach Bill Fitch, had won an NBA Championship with the Houston Rockets. Having virtually lived with Fitch during the Cavaliers' death marches of the early '70s, Tait was relishing the title almost as much as Fitch.

And now Tait was about to get a little taste of athletic perfection.

"Perfection" is almost an understatement. Barker threw 103 pitches, and only 19 of them were balls. In other words, 82 percent of his pitches nailed the strike zone. That's all the more remarkable given his reputation for wildness. In one game he missed so badly with a pitch that it ended up in the press box behind home plate.

Barker's wildness had delayed his ascent to the majors, but not by much. Drafted by Texas in 1972, he made his first big-league start in 1976, stopping the White Sox on a three-hit complete game. From there things went straight downhill. The Rangers eventually tried him as a closer, but in 1978 he blew more than half his save opportunities and was shipped to the Indians with Bobby Bonds in exchange for Jim Kern and Larvelle Blanks.

Halfway through the following season, Tribe pitching coach Dave Duncan decided Barker was better suited to a starting role, and switched him back. Finally, Barker began to settle down. Although his ERA was an atrocious 4.92, he finished the season 6–6 and earned a spot in the rotation.

The next year, 1980, he rang up 19 wins against 12 losses and cut nearly a full run off his ERA.

By the spring of 1981, Barker seemed to be putting it all together. He still had the good heater, but now he had learned how to pitch. When he took the mound on May 15, he owned the third-best ERA in the American League, 1.67.

The Indians were on a surprising roll as well. They were all alone in first place with a 15–8 record, one game ahead of Baltimore and New York. That simply didn't happen, even early in the year. During the previous 12 seasons, the Indians had never once finished higher than fourth.

Despite the crummy weather, the Tribe looked sharp, wearing their simple home whites with INDIANS across the front, the letter "C" on their blue caps, Chief Wahoo on the left sleeve, and their names and numbers on the back. One red and one blue stripe ran down the outside of each leg. The same combination ran around the waist and collar and around the sleeves. The uniforms were classic and classy.

This was the era when players knew how to wear their socks. The uniform pants came down to the middle of the shin, and the colored outer socks, or "stirrups," were worn high, with plenty of white sock showing underneath. The bottom of the pants touched just above or below the arc of the stirrups.

The Blue Jays, by contrast, looked odd, wearing powder-blue jerseys and pants. The logo on the front of their shirts was so complicated that from more than a foot away you couldn't tell exactly what it was.

Barker was an intimidating sight standing up on the soggy mound. Wearing Number 39 on his broad back, he would stare out at the hitters through a forest of hair. He sported a big, thick, Sundance Kid mustache, and his hair covered his ears and hung well over his collar.

Umpire Rich Garcia was behind home plate. He brought a liberal strike zone to the game that night, but not an unreasonable one. Most of the players who barked about calls—and there were plenty of them—were just killing the messenger. Barker was simply unhittable.

And he got better as he went along. His first strikeout didn't come until the second batter of the fourth inning. After that, 11 of the next 17 Jays ended up with a "K" after their name. And every K was swinging. As Tait noted in the eighth inning: "The Blue Jays appear to be opting for the theory that if he's throwing like that, you might as well go up there and wave at it. Maybe you'll get lucky."

The Tribe scored two runs in the first inning, but otherwise the early stages of the game were nothing special.

Barker's fourth inning was relatively rocky. He almost hit the first batter, Alfredo Griffin, with an inside fastball. And when Griffin later lifted a fly ball to left-center field, outfielders Rick Manning and Joe Charboneau nearly collided. Then, the second batter of the inning, Lloyd Moseby, ripped a shoulder-high fastball down the right-field line. It went foul by only four feet.

Then, suddenly, as if someone had flipped a switch, Barker locked into a groove. He struck out Moseby, then struck out George Bell, prompting Drennan to proclaim, "Lenny brought a little heat to the ballpark tonight!"

When the smoke cleared, Barker had 12 consecutive outs, the last two by strikeout, and a bit of a buzz began to spread through the stands.

Barker started the fifth by punching out yet another batter, cleanup hitter John Mayberry. Then he got a defensive gem from his third baseman, Toby Harrah. When Willie Upshaw hit a foul popup toward the seats just past the Jays' dugout on the third-base side, Harrah sprinted over, flipping his eyes back and forth between the ball and the wall. At the last instant, he lunged into the seats, the metal railing striking him just above the knees, and stabbed the ball as it was about to hit the concrete floor.

Harrah got a standing ovation. "That was worth the price of admission," said Tait. It was also worth one twenty-seventh of a perfect game.

The next batter, Damasco Garcia, foul-tipped a pitch off the left leg of catcher Ron Hassey, who was starting to build up quite a collection of bruises. It was at least the third time he had been nailed since the game started. But Hassey walked off the pain and got back into position.

Garcia fanned to end the inning—the fourth strikeout in five batters—and the crowd really began to sense that something special was brewing. So did the players. Barker became a nonentity in the dugout. He would sit at one end of the bench and all 24 players and the coaches would sit at the other. Nobody wanted to jinx him, so most people said nothing at all. Only Manning and Harrah talked to him, and their remarks consisted almost entirely of, "Come on, Big Guy, we know you can do this."

The first batter in the sixth, centerfielder Rick Bosetti, hits a ball off the handle, but he hits it sharply enough to present a challenge to second baseman Duane Kuiper. Kuiper short-hops it and flips to first baseman Mike Hargrove for the out.

Up steps Danny Ainge, the two-sport pro who will soon put away his baseball glove and devote himself full time to the NBA. Ainge has an odd stance. The right-hand batter moves as far back as possible in the box, brings his left foot well toward the plate, and bends over. It doesn't work. He strikes out swinging.

Barker's fastball is not only fast, but dancing. Each strike is bringing cheers now, as catcher Buck Martinez discovers after taking a called strike. Soon Martinez is a strikeout victim—Barker's sixth—and Drennan announces: "He's retired 18 in a row!"

At the top of the seventh, Barker is looking at the top of Toronto's order.

Griffin smacks a grounder to Kuiper's left. He makes a nice stop on the grass, but the fleet-footed Griffin is flying down the line and Kuiper must shift his feet and get rid of the ball in a hurry. He does. One out.

Now the fans are cheering on every delivery. When Moseby strikes out on a breaking pitch, they erupt.

The third batter, Bell, is so befuddled that he asks the ump to check the ball. The ball is fine. There's no hanky panky going on; all the tricks are coming from Barker's right arm.

Something happens during Bell's at-bat that could knock Barker right out of his rhythm: while delivering a pitch, his left foot slips on the moist ground, he nearly falls, and the pitch misses by a mile. But Barker doesn't even blink. He comes right back and strikes out Bell on a low slurve.

Now it's the eighth. Cleveland 2, Toronto 0. Cleanup hitter John Mayberry steps up to the left side of the plate, as so many Blue Jays have done on this night, and soon fans on a breaking ball.

The next hitter, Willie Upshaw, manages to make contact, but he hits an easy grounder toward Kuiper for the second out.

Now Garcia stands in from the right side, and, prepared for

Barker's heat, is paralyzed by a changeup—Barker's only changeup of the game. Says Tait: "It is almost criminal to throw as hard as Lenny Barker does and then give you something off-speed."

Garcia swings and misses for strikeout No. 10.

In the bottom of the eighth, the Tribe's right-fielder Jorge Orta, hits a solo home run to give Barker a 3–0 lead. As if he needs it.

Ninth inning. Fans on their feet. Toronto catcher Rick Bosetti in the batter's box. First pitch: a curveball that Bosetti fouls out of play. After missing with a high fastball, Barker throws a curve that Bosetti pops into foul territory near third base. An easy play for Harrah.

Two outs left.

Al Woods strides to the plate, pinch-hitting for Ainge. He fouls off a breaking ball, which hits Hassey near the left knee. Once again Hassey has to walk around in circles until the pain subsides.

A swing and a miss on a curve.

A swing and a miss on another curve. Woods sits down.

Everybody else is standing. Even the cold, stiff pitchers in the Tribe bullpen, huddled up in red jackets and, in some cases, wearing full-length red parkas, are on their toes, bouncing up and down and cheering.

Up steps another pinch-hitter, Ernie Whitt, hitting all of .188.

Barker walks behind the mound, facing home, and rubs up the baseball. His lips aren't moving, but he is talking to himself. "I know you can do this. I know you can do this. *Concentrate.*"

First pitch: curve. Called strike.

Second pitch: a curve in the dirt.

Third pitch: a swing and a miss on a high fastball.

One ball, two strikes.

At 9:43 p.m., two hours and eight minutes after his first pitch, Barker stands on the back of the mound, staring in at the plate. He adjusts his cap with his right hand, wipes his fingers over his forehead, wipes them on his pants, shrugs his shoulders, gives his right arm a little shake, steps onto the rubber, and takes such a big breath that you can see his shoulders heave.

He leans over for the sign. Hassey puts down two fingers for a curve. As Barker rocks back, Hassey is motioning with both hands to keep the ball low. Barker does, delivering a knee-high curve.

Whitt swings, and as radio announcer Score puts it: "Fly ball, shallow centerfield, Manning racing in . . . he catches it! A perfect game for Lenny Barker! The first perfect game in 13 years!"

Next door, in the TV booth, Tait's description is even more sparse: "Fly ball! Centerfield! Manning is there! GOT IT! A perfect game for Lenny Barker!"

After grabbing the 27th out, Manning immediately leaps into the air, shooting both hands toward the night sky. When he lands, he starts running toward the infield, then leaps again. The left-fielder, Charboneau, a few yards to Manning's right, pulls off his cap and joins the rush to the mound.

Meanwhile, the three players closest to Barker—Hassey, Hargrove, and Harrah—have already arrived and are pummeling him with congratulatory backslaps. The pitchers from the bullpen are closing in fast, along with a remarkable number of civilians. Some are news photographers, but many are overly excited fans who have jumped the barricades in an attempt to get a hand on history. The cops lead some of them away without incident. During his trip back to the dugout, Barker has a cop on each side. He puts his left arm around one cop as the other cop stoops to retrieve the pitcher's cap.

It is only the 10th official perfect game in more than a century of baseball, and only the 8th of the modern era.

Compared to a perfect game, a no-hitter is almost pedestrian. By May 15, 1981, big leaguers had already thrown 183 no-nos.

Even some games that appear to be perfect don't qualify. The oddest perfect game, one that isn't officially recognized, was thrown by Ernie Shore of the Boston Red Sox in 1917. The starting pitcher was Babe Ruth, who in his previous appearance had thrown a complete-game victory without walking a single batter. This time, the first batter he faced, Ray Morgan, took four straight pitches, and home plate umpire Brick Owens called four straight balls.

Ruth started wolfing at Owens, and Owens threatened to run him out of the game if he didn't calm down. Ruth responded by telling the umpire he'd punch him if he was thrown out. Owens did throw him out, and Ruth did punch him—whacked the ump right on the side of the head, earning a 10-game suspension.

After Ruth was escorted off the field by a cop, Shore was summoned from the bullpen, despite having pitched only three days earlier. He was given as many pitches as he needed to warm up, and eventually was ready to face the game's second batter.

On the first pitch, Morgan tried to steal second but was thrown out. Shore then mowed down the next 26 consecutive batters. Not a bad job of relief pitching. But not good enough for a perfect game. You need 27 batters and 27 outs. Period.

As Barker approached the Tribe's crowded little locker room that night, his teammates and the clubhouse personnel weren't about to let his achievement go unheralded. Towels were laid out on the floor from the clubhouse door to his locker, serving as a red carpet. A bottle of cold champagne was waiting on ice. On Barker's chair, clubhouse manager Cy Buynak had arranged six cans of Heineken in the shape of a zero. Barker popped the champagne top and took at big swig as the news photographers fired away.

Heineken was Barker's normal postgame weapon of choice, though, and one of his favorite ways to wind down after a game was to quaff a couple at Captain Frank's seafood restaurant on the pier at the end of East Ninth Street. But the postgame commotion dragged on and on. There were lengthy interviews to give, and the clubhouse was packed with people who normally didn't set foot in the place, such as general manager Phil Seghi and team president Gabe Paul.

Because the hour was late and the team had a day game on Saturday that would be televised nationally, Barker skipped Captain Frank's and invited a handful of pals back to his condo. Manning and Harrah were there, along with Charboneau and pitcher Dan Spillner. They sat around and pounded Heineken into the wee hours. In fact, Barker didn't sleep a wink. He was too excited.

Fortunately, he didn't have much to do the following day, other than signing autographs and giving a few more interviews. A healthy crowd turned out—24,964—to watch the Tribe lose to the Blue Jays, 4–1. Manning, Harrah, and Charboneau went a combined 1-for-11. Charboneau made two errors. Clearly, Heineken was not the Breakfast of Champions.

The payoff for Barker was considerably better. The GM called him into the office and gave him a $5,000 bonus. In an era when the better players like Barker were making $125,000, that was a marvelous chunk of change. Barker passed along $1,000 of his bonus to his catcher, Hassey.

Hassey was a solid defender, but he was overshadowed in 1981 by Bo Diaz, who played well enough to make the All-Star team. Barker felt more in synch with Hassey, so manager Dave Garcia usually wrote down Hassey's name on the days Barker pitched. During his night of perfection, Barker shook off Hassey's signal only once or twice.

What a summer. A perfect game. The Tribe in first place. And a few months later, Barker would throw two innings in the All-Star Game—held in Cleveland—and face the minimum of six hitters.

Like so many other chapters in Indians history, though, this one turned sour. Right before that All-Star Game, baseball shut down for 50 games because of a players' strike. The game was pushed back to August and became the first competition after the strike. Because of the long work stoppage, the All-Star Game, to many fans, suddenly seemed meaningless at best and insulting at worst. By the time the truncated season ended, both Barker and the Tribe were off their games. Barker finished a pedestrian 8–7; the Tribe was only one game over .500, too, at 52–51, and finished fifth.

The following year, Barker rallied to 15–11, but that would be the last time he would break .500. During the 1983 season, he was sent packing to Atlanta for Brett Butler, Brook Jacoby, pitcher Rick Behenna, and $150,000. He floundered in Atlanta, needed arm surgery in 1984, and was cut in 1987—washed up at the age of 31.

But on that one precious spring night in 1981, "Large Lenny" Barker pitched as well as any pitcher in the history of the game.

Barker knew right away that he had done something special. As a kid, he had watched Catfish Hunter's perfect game on TV as it happened. He also had seen replays of perfect pitching by Sandy Koufax and Jim Bunning. What he didn't realize was that nobody had done it since the night he watched Catfish 13 years earlier.

Barker was inundated with requests for interviews from the national media and invitations to TV shows. He agreed to field questions at the ballpark, but he wasn't about to fly anywhere to go on TV. Not with the Indians in a pennant race. He didn't want the distraction.

As it turned out, Lenny's brother did make it to the ballpark that night. But he didn't immediately tap into the drama. In the sixth inning, Charles Barker initially couldn't figure out why the fans were so riled up.

At least Charles had a better handle on his brother's achievement than their 96-year-old grandmother. When a reporter tracked her down for a comment on Len's perfect game, she said, "Well, I hope he does better next time."

THE DRIVE

SUNDAY, JANUARY 11, 1987

The Browns were five minutes away from their first Super Bowl appearance, and the hometown fans were blowing the roof off the stadium. Then Denver's John Elway engineered an unbelievable 98-yard march that became one of the most talked-about in NFL history.

HE LIKES US! He really, really likes us!

That was the reaction of Browns fans upon discovering that somebody—somebody good—actually *wanted* to play in Cleveland.

Were we a tad insecure? You bet. Even worse than actress Sally Field accepting her Oscar. But not without reason.

During the first half of the 20th century, Cleveland was viewed as one of the most powerful, most sophisticated cities in America. Nobody was the least bit embarrassed to live here. In 1944, when the Cleveland Electric Illuminating Company launched its advertising campaign calling Cleveland "the Best Location in the Nation," nobody smirked.

Cleveland's self-image began to take its first heavy hits in the 1960s. The true slide began in the summer of 1966, when the Hough neighborhood erupted in race riots. Two years later, Glenville, which was in far better shape than Hough, spawned even worse riots. Those outbreaks spurred on massive urban flight by whites and exacerbated all of the other growing problems that were beginning to weigh down the nation's "rust belt" cities.

Cleveland's reputation hit rock bottom on June 22, 1969. At

around noon on that sorry summer day, the Cuyahoga River caught fire. The blaze may have started with sparks from a passing train. Nobody was ever certain, and it didn't much matter. The only thing that really counted was that the whole world was reading stories about a burning river.

The fire was fueled by a 50-foot-wide oil slick. Flames from the oil shot nearly five stories into the sky and burned two wooden railroad bridges at the foot of Campbell Road. Fortunately, the blaze broke out on a Sunday, so there wasn't much activity in the area. The city's lone fireboat finally snuffed it, with help from a fire truck on shore, after 20 minutes. But those 20 minutes would haunt the city for decades.

The incident prompted singer/songwriter Randy Newman to record what would become Cleveland's unfortunate, unofficial theme song, *Burn On*. Even by Newman's standards, the level of sarcasm and scorn was impressive, and his trashing of the city unleashed a nationwide torrent of Cleveland jokes.

And that was just the beginning of the Cleveland abuse. In 1977, the city elected a confrontational, 31-year-old mayor who became known as "Dennis the Menace" and "the Boy Mayor" and plenty of other names that were far less flattering. Within 10 months of taking office, Kucinich had outraged so many people with his in-your-face style that a recall election was authorized. He survived the vote, but just barely.

Kucinich not only antagonized every element of the traditional Cleveland power structure but seemed to flip-flop at a moment's notice. He fired the city's police chief one month after calling him the best police chief in the nation.

The mayor must have set a record for drawing death threats. The Cleveland Indians' 1978 home opener was typical. Kucinich, on hand to throw out the first pitch, was wearing a flak jacket, and sharpshooters from the Cleveland Police Department were standing on the roof, ready to take out anyone who looked to be launching an assassination attempt. Nobody in the stands took aim, but when Kucinich was introduced, thunderous boos rained down from 70,000 people.

Later that year, Kucinich made international news by presiding over the first American city to default on its bank loans since the Great Depression. Analyses of what happened vary, but the bottom line was that Kucinich so alienated the city's business community that six Cleveland banks refused to roll over short-term loans.

At that point, Cleveland-bashing became a national art form. Cleveland was the "Mistake on the Lake," replacing Philadelphia as the comedic whipping boy.

What's the difference between the Titanic and the city of Cleveland? Cleveland has a better orchestra.

But even the comedians couldn't top reality. The funniest joke of all was supplied by the president of the Cleveland school board, who was arrested for "mooning" his brother through a car window while driving down the highway. Now that's the kind of image any city would love to project, eh?

Laid over the top of this civic nightmare was the ongoing ineptitude of the city's professional sports franchises. The Browns hadn't won anything since 1964. During the Cavaliers' best season, the so-called "Miracle of Richfield," the team didn't make it past the conference finals. The Indians were even more hideous. During the 25 seasons from 1960 to 1985, the Tribe finished in fifth place or worse 21 times. Their *best* finish was third place. Most years, they were essentially eliminated by Groundhog Day.

Yet now, in the mid-1980s, a college football star named Bernie Kosar was actually scheming to find a way to end up living and playing in Cleveland. What kind of knucklehead was this guy?

Actually, he was brilliant, one of the most intelligent people ever to don an orange helmet, an academic All-American who finished college in three years and, after his NFL career, went on to become a multimillionaire as a business entrepreneur.

The key to fulfilling Kosar's hometown dream was something called the "supplemental draft." Designed to help the NFL raid the juiciest prospects from the rival USFL, the supplemental draft was held for only two years, 1984 and 1985.

For the Browns, the first supplemental draft yielded a powerful running back named Kevin Mack. Before the second draft, the Browns, eager to comply with Kosar's wishes, launched trade talks with the Buffalo Bills, who held the first supplemental choice. Finally, a deal was struck: Cleveland would get Buffalo's supplemental pick in exchange for Cleveland's regular first-round picks in 1985 and 1986, plus a third-round pick in 1985 and a sixth-round pick in 1986.

Despite his incredible success at the University of Miami, Kosar initially was not obvious on the professional radar screens because, in terms of college eligibility, he was only a sophomore, having been red-shirted his freshman year. He didn't declare himself eligible for the regular draft, so when most of the other names were called in April of 1985, Kosar wasn't on the board. But he was set to graduate that spring with a degree in finance and economics, and therefore became eligible for the special draft in May. And what a coincidence: Cleveland owned the top choice.

Kosar also was a proven winner. In the Orange Bowl, on national television, under massive psychological pressure, he passed for 300 yards and two touchdowns against number-one-ranked Nebraska, leading the Hurricanes to their first national football championship. He set 22 school passing records and left with a 19–6 win/loss mark.

During college, while others were sitting around the locker room studying the sports section, Kosar was reading the *Wall Street Journal*. He actually negotiated his own pro contract. His business acumen was such that, less than five years after he retired from football, he sold his stake in Precision Response Corporation, a company he had formed, for $49.4 million.

Good thing Kosar was bright, because, physically, he was not exactly the second coming of Jim Brown. When No. 19 first took the field in training camp at Lakeland Community College in the summer of 1985, *Akron Beacon Journal* reporter Ed Meyer took one look at him and wrote, "Everything about Kosar's official unveiling was unspectacular, which is surprising considering the 21-year-old phenom from Boardman is expected to bring back the hordes to Cleveland Stadium and make the Browns an instant playoff contender . . . Kosar's first pass was anything but a missile. It was a short flip over the middle . . . "

The story quoted coach Marty Schottenheimer offering the faintest of praise: "I think he threw the ball adequately." Meyer also forced quarterback coach Greg Landry to defend the "somewhat awkward" appearance Kosar displayed while running footwork drills around orange cones. "He looks slower because of his size," Landry offered.

But the expectations of Browns fans were gargantuan. Despite his Big Bird style, Kosar had led the Hurricanes to the summit. Now he was joining a team with a weak starter, Paul McDonald, and an aging backup, Gary Danielson, imported from Detroit. The year before—

their third losing season in the last four—the Browns were a dismal 5–11.

Kosar was a glamour boy, arriving at that first practice in a new brown Datsun 300ZX with his omnipresent sunglasses atop his head, projecting a quiet but steely confidence.

He played in 12 games the first year, splitting the duties with his tutor, Danielson, and completed half his passes, quite impressive for a rookie. He was helped immensely by a powerful running attack: both Mack and Earnest Byner racked up 1,000 yards on the ground. The Browns improved to 8–8, and the expectations grew even higher.

During this era, the Browns were putting together some great drafts. Their first-round picks in 1981 and 1982, cornerback Hanford Dixon and linebacker Chip Banks, became Pro Bowl players. With their first two picks in 1984, the Browns took two stellar defensive backs, Don Rogers and Chris Rockins. The team uncovered Brian Brennan in the fourth round of '84 and—even better—found Byner in the 10th round. Their second pick in '85 was a lightning bolt from San Diego State named Webster Slaughter. The pieces were coming together for Kosar.

So was the theme.

In the summer of 1985, on a hot July day in training camp at Lakeland, the star cornerbacks, Dixon and Frank Minnifield, were trying to find a way to fire up their defensive comrades. The guys on the defensive line simply weren't putting enough pressure on the quarterback. So Dixon started talking about cats chasing a dog. To emphasize his point, he started barking. Minnifield began to bark too.

At Lakeland, the spectators were right on top of the players. The fans heard the barking and began to join in. Training camp soon became a kennel, and the dogs—quickly dubbed The Dawgs—went forth and multiplied. Their main home became the end zone at the east end of Cleveland Stadium.

The "Dawg Pound" was the bleacher section, which had long been considered among the *least* desirable locations in the entire horseshoe. The seats had no backs, and no roof above them. Because they were situated at the open end of the stadium, the autumn winds would sweep unimpeded off the lake and cut to the bone. And when the football was positioned at the other end of the playing field, the players looked microscopic. This was the back alley of Cleveland Stadium, an entirely fitting locale for a Dawg Pound.

The back line of that end zone was literally within reaching distance of the front row of the bleachers. When the ball was near that end of the field, the players could hear what the fans were yelling. And the players were well within throwing distance.

The bleachers began to fill with people wearing dog masks and full dog costumes. People wore hats with bones on them. They painted their faces to look like dogs. They wore dog collars. They barked from the introduction of the starting lineups until the final whistle. They brought dog biscuits, threw them at the players, and, sometimes, ate them. Fans in the pound displayed all the subtlety of a convention of pit bulls.

Not that these behaviors were entirely new. The bleachers had always been rowdy, home to the drinkin'est, fightin'est fans in the stands. Well before the advent of the bones, the bleachers were a war zone every time the Browns hosted their archrivals, the Steelers.

In 1976, when the Steelers' Terry Bradshaw was lifted off his feet and smashed head first into the turf near the bleachers by Joe "Turkey" Jones, his prostrate body became the target of people throwing batteries and whiskey bottles. Never mind that doctors feared he had a broken neck, and strapped him to a board before carrying him off the field.

The bleacher behavior wasn't always so boorish, though. In general, the Dawg Pound was looked upon fondly. Starting in the mid-1980s, it became one of the most recognizable fan subgroups in all of sports.

The relationship between the players and the Pound was unlike anything seen before on the North Coast. The interaction was more in keeping with a college setting, with well-lubed fraternity brothers avidly rooting on people they actually knew.

The players went to extraordinary lengths to buck up the relationship. Many of them sincerely believed that the Pound was a competitive advantage. Backup quarterback Mike Pagel said he thought the Pound gave the home team an extra one- or two-touchdown advantage every game, primarily on defense.

But with a couple of exceptions—notably, the colorful Bob Golic, a graduate of St. Joe's—almost all of the 1986 Browns were, as usual, football mercenaries, imported from foreign lands to do battle wearing the orange and brown. Never had the most important guy on the team grown up in Northeast Ohio.

Kosar's hometown of Boardman, a small berg in Mahoning

County, was only 60 miles from the stadium as the football flies. As a youth, Bernie made the trip often.

Boardman didn't have any burning rivers, but, like the rest of the kids growing up in Northeast Ohio at the time, Kosar learned to function under that same psychological impediment. That's why few Browns fans cared that he didn't have a picture-perfect release, or that he wasn't the most mobile guy around, or that his hair looked like it was styled with a Cuisinart, or that he had a weird, side-saddle stance under center that always made him look like he was tipping off the play, even though he wasn't. We simply shrugged off shots taken by outsiders such as *Los Angeles Times* columnist Jim Murray, who once wrote that Kosar passed "like a guy losing a bar of soap in the shower."

Okay, maybe he did throw that way. But he was homegrown, he was six-foot-five, he was a winner, and he was ours.

Quite a contrast to the evil John Elway, the "spoiled" Stanford product with the straight blond hair and blue eyes who was drafted by Baltimore but said he'd rather play in hell. He forced a trade within a month. The Broncos got a steal, receiving Elway in exchange for their top draft pick, Chris Hinton; backup quarterback Mark Herrmann; and the rights to their top pick the following year.

Elway had been the biggest hotshot in the best crop of quarterbacks in eons, the Class of 1983. He was everything Kosar was not: fast, quick, muscular, a constant threat to run, a man with a Howitzer attached to his right shoulder, a QB with a classic delivery. Elway was so athletic that he probably could have played professionally as a running back.

Laboring under heavy expectations and the usual acclimation process, Elway's debut in the Mile High City was rocky. After starting five games as a rookie, he was benched in favor of Steve DeBerg. When DeBerg was hurt at midseason, Elway became the starter again, and didn't do much better. He finished the year ranked 17th in the conference. Still, the Broncos made the playoffs as a wild-card team before losing to Seattle.

The next year, Denver fans fell in love. Elway started 14 games and won 12 of them, completing 56 percent of his passes. The team finished 13–3, the best in franchise history. However, Denver lost again in the first playoff game, to Pittsburgh.

In his third year, 1985, Elway became The Man. He set team

records for passing and led the NFL in total offense. He was the clear leader of a team that finished with a sparkling 11–5 mark. But, remarkably, that was not good enough to make the playoffs.

The following year was a different story. That year, Denver's 11–5 tally won the AFC West.

Meanwhile, the Browns were even better.

Danielson was expected to be the starting quarterback when the season opened in Chicago, but he broke his ankle in the final exhibition game. Suddenly, the team was Kosar's.

Although he was only 23 years old, he moved in like he owned the place. He beat Don Shula's Dolphins on *Monday Night Football*, throwing for 401 yards. He led the Browns into Three Rivers Stadium, where they had failed to win a game in *17 years*—and came away with a victory. In the rematch at home, he threw for 414 yards, including a late, dramatic touchdown strike to the rookie Slaughter. In one season, the Browns had changed from a running team to a passing team.

They won their last five regular-season games and finished at 12–4—the best winning percentage since 1965.

The team's performance was all the more remarkable considering the way the season began. Right before training camp, standout safety Don Rogers, a key to the defense, dropped dead on the night of his bachelor party from an overdose of cocaine.

Some ugly injuries cropped up too. The week after Danielson broke his ankle, the man who was replacing Rogers at free safety, Al Gross, was lost for 10 weeks with a knee injury. Then the team's kicker, Matt Bahr, was knocked out for the season, requiring the team to go out and sign the elderly Mark Moseley.

But as the season marched on, nothing, and no one, could stop the Browns.

The previous year, the young Brownies had managed to sneak into the playoffs with their .500 record and give Miami a good game in the first round. But this was different. This team had been dominant. This team could go all the way.

The 12–4 mark earned the Browns a bye during the first week of the playoffs, then a home game against the wild-card winner, the New York Jets.

The Jets game was Bernie's official coming-out party. On a sunny Saturday afternoon at the stadium, he set NFL records for passing yards in a playoff game (489) and passing attempts (64), and tied the mark for completions (33). Even more remarkable was the way he pulled his team out of a nearly impossible hole.

With 4:14 left to play and the Browns losing by 10 points, things looked so bad that many of the 78,106 cold spectators got up and left. They left muttering about Kosar, who had just thrown his second consecutive interception after 133 passes without one. Those cranky people missed one of the most amazing rallies in Cleveland history.

When the Browns got the ball back, they immediately lost 14 yards. And on their second play, Kosar threw an incompletion. But as Kosar followed through, the Jets' hotshot defensive end, Mark Gastineau, blasted Kosar in the back with his helmet and drew a flag. First down.

Kosar threw for four first downs in a row, and the Browns scored on a short run by Kevin Mack to close the gap to 20–17 with just under two minutes left.

The home team tried an onside kick, but the Jets recovered at Cleveland's 45. Once again, the end looked near. But the defense held, and Cleveland got the ball back at its 33.

After an interference penalty, Kosar flung a 37-yard pass to Webster Slaughter, who caught it over his shoulder and took it to the Jets' 5. With 18 seconds to go, the Browns went for the win. But Kosar threw a terrible pass, forcing it to Slaughter, and it looked like yet another interception. Brian Brennan was trailing Slaughter, though, and stripped the ball from the defender, giving the Browns another chance. Moseley hit a field goal to send the game to OT.

Then Moseley, 38, nearly turned into the goat. With 8:53 left in the first overtime, he blew an absurdly easy 22-yarder, missing to the right. The Browns defense was relentless, though, and Moseley atoned with two minutes gone in the second overtime, nailing a 27-yarder at the open end of the field.

The game was the third longest in NFL history and put the Browns one victory from the Super Bowl.

Tickets for the AFC final sold out in two hours. People camped in tents in freezing temperatures to buy them.

The dramatic win put the whole town way over the top. During the eight days between the Jets win and the invasion of the Broncos, local newscasters wore Browns jerseys and tossed around dog bones on the set. (So much for journalistic objectivity.)

No fewer than two dozen Browns songs were aired on area radio stations. The most popular was a low-rent, garage-band effort called

Bernie, Bernie, sung, badly, to the low-rent, garage-band tune *Louie, Louie.* Sample lyric: "Bernie, Bernie, oh, yeah, how you can throw." The, um, artists were known as the Bleacher Bums—never heard from before or since.

Some efforts were more professional. Longtime local music stars Alex Bevan and Pat Daley recorded and released an original number called *Browns Town.* Another tune available in stores was *Bad, Bad Cleveland Browns,* set to the relentless wedding reception favorite, *Bad, Bad Leroy Brown,* by the Cleveland Beat.

An Akron band, Nite Shift, contributed a rap song called *Super Bowl Bound.* It was only one of two songs with the same name. The other *Super Bowl Bound* came from singer Tim Perry.

Almost every musical style was dumped into the mix. Among the others: *Super Bowl Brownies,* by Brownsville 11; *Browns Town Rap,* by Hit Man & Buzz; and *Dawg City,* by the Cosmic Generation.

Music by Randy Newman was nowhere to be found.

In Denver, after the Broncos dispatched New England despite an injury to Elway's ankle, Bronco fans turned their attention to the North Coast. They printed posters showing broken dog bones. Their radio and TV commentators let fly with comments like this, from Greg Moody of TV station KUSA: "Ohio is bordered on the west by Indiana and on the east by Pennsylvania—all things considered, it's a pretty miserable place to be. And it is bordered on the north by Lake Erie—the only body of water that people can actually walk across."

A man on the street, collared by another TV crew and asked why he thought the Browns were so named, replied: "I think it's because they're always being pushed into the dirt."

By most accounts, Broncomania had not reached the fervor it attained in 1977, when the team made it to the Super Bowl and people were painting their houses Bronco orange. But there was still enough of a frenzy that at least three Denver ministers changed the times of their Sunday services to avoid a conflict with the 12:30 p.m. kickoff, which was 10:30 a.m. Mountain Standard Time.

Meanwhile, the Browns were down in Florida for the week because the weather was so rotten on the North Coast (a move that certainly did not go unnoticed in Denver). Coach Marty Schottenheimer wanted to avoid pulled muscles and get in some quality practice time.

Game day wasn't pretty. At kickoff the temperature was 30 degrees, and a 17-mile-per-hour wind was blowing in from the northwest, making it feel like 6 degrees. Snow was piled all around the sideline, but the field itself was in decent shape.

The sky was overcast, with a steady downpour of Dawg bones. Even Bob Costas and Don Shula, sitting in chairs on the sidelines for NBC's pregame show, were pelted. By the end of the pregame, NBC's Ahmad Rashad was barking and Paul Maguire was stuffing a dog biscuit in his mouth.

Costas was loving every minute of it. "Who needs domes? Who needs AstroTurf? It's cold. It's dark. It feels like a football game. And it's for the championship of the AFC."

Browns fans agreed. Only 58 ticket-holders failed to show up.

Banners flooded the stands. "Next year is today," read one. Another featured a drawing of a can of dog food named "Elpo." The contents were "Bronco chunks," a suitable "dinner for Dawgs." Countless signs made reference to Pasadena, the site of the Super Bowl that was two weeks—and one game—away.

Vegas had Cleveland as a three-point favorite, at least partly because Denver was 8–1 at home and only 4–4 on the road. Advised Maguire: "Take the Browns, give the points."

Outside the Browns locker room, Rashad couldn't resist taking a 19-year-old cheap shot at "a town more known for its river having caught on fire."

NBC's top team was in the booth: Dick Enberg on play-by-play and Merlin Olsen teaming with Bob Griese for the analysis.

The Browns, dressed in white with brown numbers and orange trim, introduced their starting defense:

LDE: Reggie Camp, 96
NT: Bob Golic, 79
RDE: Carl Hairston, 78
LOLB: Chip Banks, 56
LILB: Eddie Johnson, 51
RILB: Anthony Griggs, 53
ROLB: Clay Matthews, 57
LCB: Frank Minnifield, 31
RCB: Hanford Dixon, 29
SS: Ray Ellis, 24
FS: Chris Rockins, 37

Two non-starters also were honored with personal introductions: defensive end Sam Clancy, 91, and "defensive end and running back Dave Puzzuoli," 72. Puzzuoli had become the Browns' version of Chicago's Refrigerator Perry, a massive defensive lineman used in the offensive backfield in short-yardage situations.

The Browns won the toss and took the ball, fielding their usual lineup:

WR: Webster Slaughter, 84
LT: Rickey Bolden, 77
LG: Paul Farren, 74
C: Mike Baab, 61
RG: Dan Fike, 69
RT: Cody Risien, 63
WR: Reggie Langhorne
TE: Ozzie Newsome, 82
QB: Bernie Kosar, 19
HB: Earnest Byner, 44
FB: Kevin Mack, 34

Most of the Browns used hand-warming pockets sewn into their jerseys. Kosar had two. His left hand was thrust into a pocket in front of his stomach. His right hand went into a pocket behind his number. Between plays, he looked like a mummy.

Many of the Browns had Don Rogers's old number, 20, written on their wristbands or the back of their helmets.

Cleveland won the toss and, despite the wind and increasing snow, elected to receive.

They did nothing. Two runs, a near interception, and a punt.

Denver went out quickly too.

On its second possession, Cleveland started to roll. Mixing runs and passes, the Browns rang up five first downs and were first-and-goal at Denver's 4-yard line. Then they almost fell apart. Backup tight end Harry Holt was wide open in the end zone but dropped it. Mack fumbled. The Browns recovered, but lost two yards.

Now, on third and six, probably the last chance before a field goal attempt, Kosar threw a swing pass to the right side to backup halfback Herman Fontenot. Fontenot caught it at the 10, put a great fake on the only defender near him, and literally jogged across the goal line. After 14 plays and nearly 7½ minutes, Cleveland had a 7–0 lead.

Denver could manage only one first down, and Cleveland got the ball back at its own 36. But on the second play, Kosar threw an interception that was returned to the Browns' 35.

As the second quarter began, Denver stalled. Elway stood in shotgun formation on fourth-and-10, but, failing to draw the Browns offside, punted it out of bounds on the Cleveland 17.

Kosar looked highly fallible again. On the third play of the drive, he threw a hideous, looping pass that was picked off by linebacker Jim Ryan. The QB with the lowest interception rate in the entire league had thrown two in the last four plays.

Somehow, the Cleveland defense held Denver to a field goal and kept the lead.

Cleveland's offense immediately self-destructed again. Mack fumbled—the Browns' third turnover in 10 minutes—and Denver had the ball 37 yards from the end zone. Elway scrambled for all but four of those yards and would have gotten them all except for a stumble caused by his bad ankle, which was heavily wrapped both inside and over his shoe.

On fourth-and-one, with the Browns so confused that they had only 10 men on the field, running back Gerald Willhite rammed into the end zone and gave Denver a 10–7 lead.

By now the uniforms were plenty muddy, but the footing was still reasonably good. Little bits of paper were blowing around the field. By the end of the game, the field would look like the floor of the stock exchange at the close of trading.

After an exchange of punts, the Browns staged a long drive that featured a 43-yard bomb to backup receiver Carl Weathers. But they stalled, and Moseley tied the game with a 29-yard field goal.

At halftime, a frigid Ohio State Marching Band took the field and capped its act with Script Ohio and the time-honored tradition of dotting the "i."

The halftime rest did little for the offensive units. Neither one moved much until the middle of the third quarter, when Denver picked up a 26-yard field goal to take a 13–10 lead.

As the quarter ran down, Cleveland began an impressive drive from its own 17 that included a 20-yard pass to Slaughter, a 22-yard pass to Langhorne, and two great power runs by Mack—who at one point was handed the ball six consecutive times. The drive slowed deep in Denver territory, though, and Moseley hit a short field goal to tie things up with 12½ minutes left in the game.

Early in the fourth quarter, with a fourth-and-one at midfield, the Browns tried a trick play. Offensive tackle Cody Risien reported in as a tight end. In the middle of the count, he rose up, took a step backward, and set up again. The Broncos came flying across the line, thinking that an offensive lineman had moved illegally. The result was exactly what Schottenheimer had hoped for. But the officials flagged Risien, claiming he had purposely drawn the Broncos offside. Schottenheimer was so incensed that he called a time-out to rail at the officials. That conversation had the usual effect—none.

After a punt, Denver went nowhere, and punted the ball back with only 6½ minutes left in the game—and in somebody's season.

Kosar started at his own 48. He threw a screen that Mack dropped, then handed the ball to Fontenot on a draw play. Fontenot picked up only four, and the Browns were looking at third-and-six at the Denver 48.

The fans are roaring as Cleveland comes to the line with four wide receivers. Weathers is split wide to the left, and Brennan is in the left slot. McNeil and Langhorne are split on the right side. Fontenot is the lone running back.

Kosar fades. He sees that Brennan is in single coverage and, at his own 43-yard line, lofts a long, high pass. Brennan looks over his left shoulder, sees the ball is coming on his other side, and swivels his head around to the right. The defender, Dennis Smith, slips. Brennan stops, stays on his feet, and grabs the ball at the 17-yard line. The only person between him and the goal line is Smith—and he's on the ground.

Brennan cuts to the outside and hits the end zone untouched. He winds up with his right hand and spikes the ball into the turf with gusto.

Cleveland Stadium erupts. The roar from the throng of 79,915 can be heard by all the ships at sea. It's so loud that NBC's Enberg doesn't bother to say anything for one minute and four seconds.

Cleveland 20, Denver 14.

In the owner's box, Art Modell kisses his wife.

The Browns are 5:43 away from their first Super Bowl. They are 5:43 away from a chance to recapture the glory of 1964—when Bernie Kosar was one year old.

The cheer on the ensuing kickoff nearly matches the one that followed Brennan's catch: Moseley hits a knuckleball that is botched by

Bronco rookie Ken Bell, who falls on it at his own 2 yard line.

Now, Denver must go 98 yards in 5½ minutes, heading directly into the wind blowing in from the open end of the stadium.

If Elway is uncomfortable, he certainly doesn't show it. As he walks into the Bronco huddle in the west end zone, he is smiling. "If we work hard," he says, "good things will happen."

A couple of plays into the drive, something odd happens—the wind almost completely dies down.

Facing a third-and-2 at its own 9-yard line, Denver calls time. Coach Dan Reeves decides to hand the ball to Winder. Winder barely picks up the first down, then gets another four yards on another run.

On the fifth play, Elway's receivers are covered and he scrambles for 11 yards. Next, he rifles a high pass to Steve Sewell, who jumps and makes a great catch over the middle for 22 more yards. Suddenly, the Broncos are at midfield.

They cross into Cleveland territory on the next play, a short pass to Steve Watson on the right side. Elway then heaves a long pass down the sideline to Vance Johnson . . . incomplete.

The action is furious. Linemen on both sides are beating each other to a pulp, and backs from both sides are flying all over the place. There is enough adrenaline coursing through the bodies on the field and in the stands to fuel the *Queen Mary*.

Elway fades again, and is sacked by Puzzuoli. The Broncos call time with 1:47 left. The ball is at the Cleveland 48, and it's third-and-18.

On the first play after the time-out, another very odd thing happens: with Denver in a shotgun formation, Watson goes in motion from the left to the right. Just as he is passing between the center and the quarterback, the ball is snapped. It actually hits him in the butt and changes direction. But not enough for the Browns. Elway reaches down by his ankles and grabs it. The timing of the play doesn't suffer one iota—Elway hits Mark Jackson for 25 yards. Egads.

Elway throws the next pass out of bounds, stopping the clock at 1:19.

A screen pass to Sewell on the left side takes Denver to the Cleveland 14-yard line—and the sinking feeling in the stands has grown to monumental proportions.

On the 13th play of the drive, Elway shoots for Watson on the right side, but misses. Forty-nine seconds left.

Elway looks for a receiver, doesn't see one, and rumbles out of bounds at the Cleveland 5-yard line. With 42 seconds left, it's third-and-1.

Everyone is standing and roaring for a defensive stop. With the ball on the right hash mark, Jackson goes in motion. Elway drops straight back, Jackson comes open on a post pattern, and Elway fires a low pass into the end zone. Jackson goes down on both knees and hauls it in—in almost the identical spot where the Browns lost the 1981 playoff game on Red Right 88.

Elway shoots both fists in the air in celebration.

The extra point is good, the score is tied, and only 37 seconds remain.

After the kickoff, Cleveland makes a token effort to move the ball with a screen to Fontenot. Then Kosar kneels down, hoping for better things in overtime.

Denver's star linebacker, Cleveland native Tom Jackson, is asked to call the coin flip. "Heads," he says. It's tails. Marty wants the ball. Denver wants to go toward the closed end of the field.

Diminutive Gerald "Ice Cube" McNeil returns the kick to the Cleveland 30, and the offense goes to work. Sort of.

Kosar is sacked because of tight defensive coverage. Brennan catches a pass in the right flat, but is short of the first down. On third and two, Kosar hands the ball to Fontenot. Fontenot? A guy who doesn't weigh a whole lot more than the 137-pound McNeil? Yep. And right guard Dan Fike misses a block on linebacker Karl Mecklenburg, who tugs Fontenot to the ground. The Browns have to punt.

It is the last time they will see the football.

Winder gains five up the middle.

Tight end Orson Mobley makes a nice catch on a 22-yard throw that moves the ball a yard into Cleveland territory.

Winder loses one on a sweep, and a screen falls incomplete. It's third and 12.

Yet again, Elway comes to Denver's rescue. He scrambles left, chased by Clancy and Hairston, and unloads a bullet to Watson on the left sideline. Watson leaps and snatches it at the Cleveland 22.

Now it's just a matter of when.

Winder gains five up the middle. He runs again and is stopped for no gain. On his third run, his goal is simply to get the ball to the middle of the field for the kicker. He does, and Rich Karlis comes on to try a 33-yard boot.

Karlis is from Salem High School, a mere 13 miles from Kosar's Boardman. Odder still, he wears no shoe on his kicking foot. He's just more comfortable that way—even with a six-degree wind-chill factor.

The snap is good . . . the ball is down . . . the kick starts off to the left . . . and stays there. It is so close to the left upright that, even after it passes the post, Karlis and his holder, backup QB Gary Kubiak, stand watching, waiting for a signal from the officials. The men in stripes put their hands straight up, sending Denver to Pasadena and Greater Cleveland to the brink of clinical depression.

Denver 23, Cleveland 20.

The Broncos pile onto each other in a riotous celebration as Browns fans grind their teeth. Then, no more than 20 seconds after the field goal, a funny thing happens. The crowd erupts in a spontaneous, thunderous ovation. The fans are thanking the Browns for the great, entertaining season. In a city so hungry for a championship, a city so tired of fighting the good fight without the ultimate payoff, the reaction is remarkable.

In the locker room, Elway declared it "a game that brought out the greatness in both sides."

Schottenheimer kept a stiff upper lip. "This football team is not finished," he said in the postgame interviews. "This football team is coming back."

Ozzie Newsome, who was heading to the Pro Bowl but was shut out on this day, was even more specific. "You can start the Cleveland jokes or whatever you want to," he said, "but I guarantee you we'll be right back here in this same position next year, and go one step further."

When the game was over, the field was littered with dog biscuits. But not all of the visitors were appalled. At least three Broncos—Karlis, Vance Johnson, and general manager John Beake—picked up a few biscuits for souvenirs. Beake's secretary had his doggie treat lacquered and mounted on a plaque that he hung in his office. Beneath it was a brass label reading: "AFC Championship. Denver 23, Cleveland 20. January 11, 1987."

Which gave him the last laugh. At least for one year.

Rank: #11

THE FUMBLE

SUNDAY, JANUARY 17, 1988

One year after John Elway led "The Drive" to deny the Browns their first appearance in a Super Bowl, the tables seemed to be turning. This time, it was the Browns who were staging a dramatic drive late in the AFC Championship Game. Then, suddenly and sickeningly, Cleveland running back Earnest Byner coughed up the football.

EXACTLY 371 DAYS after The Drive, two classic forces were dueling for control of the football universe: poetic justice vs. déjà vu.

The Browns vs. the Broncos for the Super Bowl.

Again.

Kosar vs. Elway.

Again.

Good vs. evil.

Again.

This time, the setting was dramatically different. Instead of the frigid shores of Lake Erie, the action would take place at Mile High Stadium, just across the South Platte River from downtown Denver, where the dry, sandy surface was 4,600 feet higher than the floor of Cleveland Stadium. And it would take place not across a flat tableau of gray, but on a sunny, comfortable winter's day with a high blue sky and bright white snow visible on distant mountain peaks.

Denver, sad to report, averages 300 days of sunshine per year. Yet another reason to hate the Broncos.

Denver probably doesn't look like you think it does if you've never been to the place. Yes, the city is a mile above sea level. Walk up to the 15th step of the state capitol in the center of downtown—it's the building with the round dome topped with 200 ounces of pure gold—and you're exactly 5,280 feet above the oceans. But downtown Denver is literally flatter than Manhattan.

As you move west through the Great Plains, through the endless, numbing sameness of Kansas and on through eastern Colorado, the ground rises so slowly that you don't even notice. By air or by car, Denver skyscrapers pop up unexpectedly out on a flat expanse, like tree branches jammed upright in a wide, sandy beach.

In other words, Toto, when you're in downtown Denver, you *are* in Kansas some more. The big-time geology doesn't begin to assert itself until you get 15 miles west of the city. But when that finally happens, it happens in a big way. The things they refer to as "foothills" look like Mount Everest to people from the Midwest. Not far past the city, the elevations soar to as much as 11,000 feet.

Why, compared to that, Mile High Stadium is almost subterranean. But never say that to a visiting athlete. Most pros are convinced that Denver teams have a home-field advantage because Denver's players are accustomed to the thin air.

That belief led Browns coach Marty Schottenheimer to take his boys on another pregame field trip a week before the game. Instead of Florida, where they had practiced a year earlier to escape Cleveland's cold, the coach rounded up his troops and hauled them to Albuquerque, New Mexico—elevation 4,945 feet—so they could get accustomed to the physiological demands of strenuous activity at higher elevations.

Schottenheimer ran the place like Area 51. Fearing spies, he hired a dozen guards to patrol the outskirts of the practice facility, rented from the University of New Mexico.

How much effect Denver's elevation actually has on the performance of a football team was the subject of considerable debate. Some experts said the difference in available oxygen was insignificant. Others, citing the term "Mountain Sickness," said the problems were very real, that people moving into high altitudes frequently have headaches and difficulty sleeping. Most NFL doctors seemed to subscribe to the theory that teams should go one of two ways: either move into the high altitude well before game day so the players can adjust, or arrive at the very last minute so the effects don't kick in before the game is played.

If nothing else, the issue was always in the back of the minds of the visiting players, giving them yet another small away-from-home-field disadvantage. No coincidence that Denver always went to great lengths to let visiting teams know that oxygen tanks would be available on their benches.

Mountain Sickness or not, one scene at Mile High Stadium was enough to trigger a wave of nausea in any Browns fan. Down by the Denver locker room, in a special lounge created for the players' wives, 10 large photographs hung on the wall—every one of them taken a year earlier during The Drive. Behind those 10 shots, from floor to ceiling, pasted directly onto the wall, was a 30-foot-long mural of Elway throwing the winning pass.

Pass the Tums.

Other than the setting, this 1988 AFC Championship Game looked like an instant replay of the 1987 AFC Championship Game.

For starters, the network TV announcers were exactly the same. NBC again put Dick Enberg and Merlin Olsen in the booth, used Bob Costas and Don Shula for commentary, and sent Ahmad Rashad and Paul Maguire on the prowl. And once again, Maguire would play the buffoon, at one point donning a blue motorcycle helmet with a big, broken Dawg bone attached to the top and a big Bronco horseshoe on top of that.

And, yet again, Maguire would assure the nation's armchair gamblers that Cleveland was a lock. "A major turnover is going to lead to a score," he proclaimed. "The Denver Broncos are going to have the turnover, the Cleveland Browns are going to pick it up and score, and Cleveland is going to win the game by three points."

Even the uniforms were unchanged. Like most teams, Denver wore its colored jerseys at home. Unlike most teams, Cleveland, for much of the 1980s, wore its white jerseys at home. As a result, for the second consecutive title game, it was Denver in bright orange jerseys with blue-and-white trim, white pants, and blue helmets, and Cleveland in its sleek white jerseys and pants, topped by the famous orange, logoless helmets.

Mile High Stadium and Cleveland Municipal Stadium were strikingly similar—well, except for that gigantic statue atop the Mile High scoreboard, a white horse rearing up on its hind legs. Both facilities were big, multi-tiered, multi-sport horseshoes seating more than 76,000 for football, with a big section of bleachers at the open end. When the home team made a key play, the noise in both places could get loud enough to crack your contact lenses.

The main sonic difference was that, at Mile High, the noisy end was the *closed* end of the stadium, rather than the open end. That's because the seats were so close to the field all the way around. Although you could nearly reach out and touch the players from Cleveland Stadium's Dawg Pound, seats on the 50-yard line were a healthy seven-iron from the players' benches. By contrast, the front row of nearly all the lower sections at Mile High was just a few yards from the playing surface. And the distance between the visitors' bench and the first row of seats was a mere 25 feet—five feet less than the distance needed for a first down.

No matter where you sat, Mile High was the noisiest outdoor stadium in football. That was not merely a function of architecture; the Broncos had sold out for 17 straight seasons—*seasons*, mind you, not *games*—and Denver fans were every bit as fanatical as Cleveland's. When the 76,000 Broncomaniacs cranked things up, the windows of the loges would literally rattle, and the TV cameras would shake so much that viewers wondered whether the camera people were suffering from severe hangovers.

Colorado's capital was settled in the mid-1800s by gold prospectors, and although the city is a scant 350 miles west of the exact geographic center of the continental United States, it thinks of itself as part of the old Wild West. The most visible fan was a guy who dressed in a cowboy hat, cowboy boots, a metal barrel held up by suspenders, and not much else, regardless of the weather.

Tim McKernan was his name. He was 47, and worked at Denver's Stapleton Airport as a mechanic for United Airlines, which had a hub there. But everybody knew him as The Barrel Man.

The Barrel Man had missed only nine games—home and away—in 10 years. Naturally, his life was significantly easier at home games. The previous year, in Cleveland, he had drawn a perpetual barrage of Dawg bones and beer.

In fact, a major moral issue was facing the Denver faithful in the days leading up to the rematch: to bone or not to bone. That was the Mile High question because of all the abuse the Broncos had taken the year before in Cleveland, where they were pelted with dog biscuits from the moment they stepped off the plane until they departed. Even the departure was ugly, accompanied by death threats phoned to Hopkins airport, threats that were taken quite seriously by authorities.

Denver residents prided themselves on being good sports. They considered Mile High Stadium an oasis of sanity in the often-nasty world of pro football fandom. But their self-control was being sorely tested by this particular rivalry.

Bronco coach Dan Reeves pleaded with viewers of his regular weekly television show to refrain from limbering up their throwing arms. Broncos owner Pat Bowlen was even more direct: toss anything, he vowed, and you lose your season tickets. Bowlen's threat had the teeth of a Doberman; the waiting list for season tickets contained 18,000 names.

The Browns brought four extra security officials to guard against dirty tricks at their Denver hotel, the 26-story Hyatt Regency in the heart of downtown. Nothing particularly untoward took place, and the Browns were able to rest in peace.

Bronco fans were more intent on just getting into the game than disrupting it. When radio station KOAQ promised to give two tickets to the listener who staged the most outrageous stunt, a woman pulled a Lady Godiva act, riding a horse through the city's bustling 16th Street Mall at high noon. She was not only completely nude but painted Bronco blue.

And she finished fifth.

Just kidding.

A bit of promotional crossover action was taking place as well. In Friday's *Denver Post*, the Browns Backers of Denver, about 120 strong, bought a quarter-page ad that read: "Go Dawgs. Our address might be in Denver, but our hearts are with the Cleveland Browns."

Elsewhere in the *Post*, the content was downright ugly. Wrote columnist Buddy Martin: "The BrownDogs are coming to the Mile High City, barking every step of the way. You'd bark, too, if you lived in Cleveland and they let you out for the weekend."

In the crosstown *Rocky Mountain News*, columnist Mark Wolff was only slightly more subtle: "To quote an obscure passage from Philistines 1:17: 'The bones of the dog shall be scattered amidst the lair of the wild horses.'"

Things were over the top back in Cleveland as well. President Ronald Reagan, in town to help raise $250,000 for Mayor George Voinovich's race for the U.S. Senate, was photographed holding a

Browns sweatshirt and, later, carrying a football autographed by Bernie Kosar onto Air Force One.

Cleveland radio's playlist had been loaded up with even more Browns songs than the year before. Added to the mix were "The Dawgs from Browns Town," "Browns Dawg," "Super Bowl Road," "The Super Bowl Brownies," "Come On Brownies," "Born and Raised on the Cleveland Browns" (to the melody of "Born in the U.S.A."), and a rewrite of "Mack the Knife" ("When the Dawg bites . . .").

Denver's radio playlist was not as lengthy, but one song had jumped to the top of the list and was played obsessively. It was a reasonably professional effort sung to the tune of Kenny Rogers's "The Gambler" and was, of course, focused on Elway:

> *You got move from the pocket*
> *And launch another rocket*
> *As you execute your spin move*
> *And chuck it on the run;*
> *With great blocks from all the Broncos*
> *And great moves from the Three Amigos*
> *We'll walk on as winners*
> *When we hear the final gun.*

As the song noted, the Broncos had ratcheted up their PR game from the previous year by carving out their own special persona. Denver now had the Three Amigos to line up across from the Dawgs.

Wide receivers Mark Jackson and Vance Johnson were joined during the '87 season by a talented rookie, Ricky Nattiel, drafted out of Florida. All of them were small, quick, black, and young, with great hands. Their numbers were 80, 82, and 84. They hung out with each other away from the field. Amigos, indeed.

The tag sprung from an offhand locker-room comment made by Elway. It was a reference to the not-so-funny 1986 comedy starring Chevy Chase and Steve Martin.

Elway's Amigos had certainly asserted themselves the previous week, when Denver took care of the wild-card Houston Oilers, 34–10, at a rollicking Mile High Stadium. The place was louder than a squadron of F-18s. The crowd was egged on with a then-obscure rock song by Gary Glitter called "Rock and Roll, Part 2." It was primarily an instrumental, punctuated occasionally by the word "Hey!" About 76,000 people made "hey" whenever the cut was played.

Even after a trip to the Super Bowl, Bronco fans were taking nothing for granted, and for good reason. Until 1987, Denver had not won a postseason game for nine years.

Elway was good against the Oilers, as usual, throwing for two TDs and running for a third. And, as usual, so was the Denver defense, coming up with two key interceptions. All year, the Bronco D had shown a knack for forcing key turnovers.

Kosar's offense, by contrast, had been almost devoid of turnovers. The Browns had the fewest turnovers in the AFC for the second year in a row, coughing up the football only 29 times.

Cleveland wasn't going to sneak up on anyone in the fall of 1987, though, having won 12 games the previous season and coming within an eyelash of the Super Bowl. Their opponents were pumped. And the team's record slipped to 10–5 (a labor dispute erased one game). It could have been far worse: the Browns rallied to win their last three games.

Denver finished 10–4–1.

Unfortunately, the Browns' drafts had begun to turn a bit sour. The year's top choice, Duke linebacker Mike Junkin, famously billed by a Browns scout as "a mad dog in a meat market," turned out to be a lame duck with a big contract. He played badly for half a season, then blew out his wrist. This from a guy taken fifth overall in the draft, a choice Cleveland acquired by trading linebacker Chip Banks and some draft picks.

The team's third-round selection was kicker Jeff Jaeger, obtained at the hefty price of three subsequent picks. In the end, he couldn't beat out senior citizen Matt Bahr.

And a few months after this game, the Browns would waste a first-round pick on another dog-eared linebacker, Clifford Charlton.

But that damage had not yet settled in. The core of the 1987 Browns was still young and aggressive and hungry. Kosar told reporters that, rather than being discouraged by Elway's crushing drive the season before, the Browns had been given even more incentive to work hard. More players than ever before stayed in Cleveland during the off-season, spending many of their days in the weight room.

After losing the season opener in New Orleans, the Browns came home and handled Pittsburgh, 34–10, in front of 79,543 crazies.

They settled into a pattern of playing .500 ball on the road and winning absolutely everything at home. The first loss on the lakefront didn't occur until December, when they dropped a 9–7 decision to the Indianapolis Colts.

The Browns turned things around against those same Colts in the first round of the playoffs. With the score tied at 14 halfway through the third quarter, linebacker Eddie Johnson blew through on a blitz and drilled Colts quarterback Jack Trudeau as he was throwing. The pass was intercepted by Felix Wright, and the Browns set off on an 86-yard TD march that demoralized the Colts. The final score was 38–21.

Cleveland's defense had a breakout season in 1987, partly because of a new, more aggressive philosophy that called for attacking the run by putting more men near the line of scrimmage. The secondary, anchored by all-pros Hanford Dixon and Frank Minnifield, was its usual stellar self. The D held opponents to 285 yards a game, compared to 329 the previous season.

But this was the Broncos, this was Mile High, and good things usually didn't happen here to visiting teams. In the previous two years, Mile High visitors had won only one game.

Besides, the Browns were a battered bunch. All-pro nose tackle Bob Golic would watch the game wearing not his number 79 jersey but a cast on his right hand and a colorful sweatshirt containing big splashes of the Olympic colors, a drawing of an equestrian, and the words "Melbourne, Australia, 1956." (Don't ask.)

Starting left guard Larry Williams would dress, but he planned to spend his time on the bench, recovering from an ankle injury. He might be used as a last resort. In his place at left guard would be rookie Greg Rakoczy.

On offense, the Browns began like this:

WR: Reggie Langhorne, 88
LT: Paul Farren, 74
LG: Greg Rakoczy, 73
C: Mike Baab, 61
RG: Dan Fike, 69
RT: Cody Risen, 63
TE: Ozzie Newsome, 82
WR: Webster Slaughter, 84

QB: Bernie Kosar, 19
HB: Earnest Byner, 44
FB: Kevin Mack, 34

Cleveland's defense came out this way:

LDE: Sam Clancy, 91
NT: Dave Puzzuoli, 72
RDE: Carl Hairston, 78
LOLB: David Grayson, 56
LILB: Eddie Johnson, 51
RILB: Mike Johnson, 59
ROLB: Clay Matthews, 57
LCB: Frank Minnifield, 31
RCB: Hanford Dixon, 29
SS: Ray Ellis, 24
FS: Felix Wright, 22

Injuries had been killing Denver as well. Their strong safety, Dennis Smith, was playing with a broken right forearm and was wearing enough adhesive tape to hike the share price of Johnson & Johnson. His broken arm was the least of it. Earlier in the year he had messed up a finger so badly that the surgeon had to repair it with two metal pins. And at halftime of this game the finger would act up again, and Smith would reach down and yank out one of the pins. He was in the starting lineup only because somebody had to replace Mike Harden, who—you guessed it—broke his arm the previous week. Harden had replaced Randy Robbins, who blew out a knee.

One of the Three Amigos was in even worse shape. Vance Johnson was in the hospital. He had been drilled the week before on a late, cheap hit by Houston linebacker John Grimsley and sustained a severely hemorrhaged artery in his groin. At first it was thought to be a bad bruise, but he nearly passed out after Thursday's practice and was rushed to the hospital.

Elway rode into battle with this lineup:

WR: Ricky Nattiel, 84
LT: Dave Studdard, 70
LG: Keith Bishop, 54
C: Mike Freeman, 62

RG: Stefan Humphries, 79
RT: Ken Lanier, 76
TE: Clarence Kay, 88
WR: Mark Jackson, 80
QB: John Elway, 7
RB: Sammy Winder, 23
FB: Gene Lang, 33

Defensively, the Broncos had been completely retooled. Because of injuries and retirements, only one of the 11 starters from the previous year, Ricky Hunley, was in his same spot. As usual, though, the Bronco D was undersized but quick.

LE: Andre Townsend, 61
NT: Greg Kragen, 71
RE: Rulon Jones, 75
OLB: Simon Fletcher, 73
ILB: Karl Mecklenburg, 77
ILB: Ricky Hunley, 98
OLB: Jim Ryan, 50
LCB: Mark Haynes, 36
RCB: Steve Wilson, 45
FS: Tony Lilly, 22
SS: Dennis Smith, 49

The TV announcers were locked in on just two of the 44 starters. Enberg talked at length about the "two brilliant young quarterbacks." Rashad compared Kosar to Johnny Unitas, and said Elway "is as strong as a linebacker and runs like a running back, not to mention his arm."

Several banners hanging from the stands made reference to the previous year's heroics, including an end-zone sign reading, "Just another Sunday drive."

Kickoff was set for 2 p.m. Denver time, which was 4 p.m. for most of the key television markets. Fans would be able to catch it right after the Redskins and Vikings elected the NFC's Super Bowl representative at Washington's RFK Stadium.

That NFC game ended in dramatic fashion, with the Redskins stopping a late Minnesota drive to win 17–10. Expectations for the AFC final were even higher. Said Costas: "Perhaps it's too much to ask these two teams to repeat the drama of a year ago. We'll settle for half the drama."

Not to worry, Bob.

At kickoff, the conditions were comfortable. Although most spectators wore winter coats, some showed up in sweaters. Unfortunately, the Browns began the game as if they were wearing concrete spikes.

Their first quarter was a disaster from the opening kickoff. Gerald "Ice Cube" McNeil fielded the ball at the noisy end of the field and only got to the 12-yard line.

On the first play from scrimmage, Kosar faded, looked around, couldn't find anyone, and was sacked. A handoff to Earnest Byner gained seven, unleashing a torrent of praise from Enberg. "The heart of that Cleveland offense," Enberg said of Byner. Enberg then quoted Schottenheimer as saying, "After Kosar, he is the last man I'd trade."

Facing a third-and-12, Kosar tried another pass. This time, he hit Webster Slaughter right in the hands. Bad spot. The ball bounced out, caromed around, and was picked off by defensive lineman Freddy Gilbert, who had hustled downfield in pursuit.

In a scant three plays, the AFC offense with the fewest turnovers had fallen victim to the AFC defense with the most turnovers.

The Broncos had the ball at Cleveland's 18. The first three plays were handoffs to Sammy Winder, who gained six on the first carry and six more on the second before losing two yards. At that point, Elway dropped for his first pass. He looked right, looked left, and followed with a laser shot over the middle to Nattiel, who caught it, all alone, right on the letter "N" in the word BRONCOS painted on the grass in the end zone.

Confetti flew out of the stands, orange pom-poms were shaken into a frenzy, and the window-rattling roar made another appearance.

Denver 7, Cleveland zip.

The Browns began to move on their second drive. Byner and Mack gained steady yardage and poked their way into Denver territory. But after a great power run, Mack coughed up the ball and Denver recovered at its own 40. Elway went right back to work. He gained seven on a scramble, then called a quick pitch to Gene Lang, who roared around left end for 42 yards, all the way to the Browns' 11.

Cleveland's defense stiffened and forced an incompletion on third down. But Minnifield was flagged for holding, giving Denver a first down at the two. The Broncos made an odd play call, given their field position, running a slow-to-develop reverse to Steve Sewell. It obviously fooled the Browns, because as he rambled into the end zone, no orange helmet was in the same ZIP code.

Denver had a two-touchdown lead after barely more than 11 minutes of play.

Cleveland responded with a sustained drive that lasted into the second quarter and resulted in a field goal, but the price was heavy. On the second play of the quarter, center Mike Baab was helped off the field with a knee injury and would not return.

The Browns had already lost their best offensive lineman, Ricky Bolden, early in the year and were starting a rookie at guard because of Williams's bad ankle. After Baab went down, Williams was the only viable player left. He hobbled in to left guard, and the rookie, Rakoczy, had to switch to a new position, center.

With Cleveland deep in Denver territory, Kosar walked away from center, complaining about the noise. (In those days, the NFL had a ridiculous rule that enabled the referees to halt play until the home crowd quieted down enough to permit the visitors to hear the signals.) Immediately after the pause, on third-and-3, Kosar threw to Byner in the right flat, but Byner, looking back into the sun, dropped it.

The consolation prize was Bahr's 29-yard field goal.

On their third position, the Broncos were cruising again. And on the fifth play of that drive, Cleveland's nose tackle, Puzzuoli (who was, of course, playing for the injured Golic), went down with a bad knee. The Browns temporarily went to a four-man line, then eventually sent in their third-string nose tackle, Darryl Sims.

The first play after the Puzzuoli's injury, Elway ran a quarterback draw. He got the first down and was drilled in the head on a late hit by Chris Rockins. That triggered a short fight and moved the ball all the way to Cleveland's 39.

Nattiel picked up 14 on a crossing pattern through Cleveland's porous zone, and two plays later picked up 20 more on the same pattern. The final yard came on a plunge by Lang.

In three possessions, Denver had three touchdowns and an 18-point lead. Elway had thrown only five passes. And Cleveland fans had the Mother of All Migraines.

Most Browns fans found themselves thinking, *Well, at least our hearts won't be broken this time. It's a blowout. We won't invest any more emotion into this game. We'll pull back. Starting today, it's basketball season.*

The Browns continued to look comatose. Three plays and a punt.

On Denver's next drive, which started at their own 32, they really began to pick on Sims. Winder gained five yards straight up the middle. Next play, same call. This time Winder gained nine. Four plays later, Lang got five more, again right over Sims. Finally, the drive died on two incomplete passes, and a 50-yard field goal attempt was pulled to the left. This was Denver's first unsuccessful drive in the first half—and only 3½ minutes remained.

Which was plenty of time for Cleveland's offense to screw up again. After a nice power run by Mack to start the drive and a nine-yard completion to Slaughter, Kosar threw a horrible pass to Newsome, leaving a third and one. Byner went up the gut and was stopped. On fourth and one, Schottenheimer gambled, and Cleveland picked up the first down on a handoff to Mack.

Then things got ugly again. After an incomplete pass to Slaughter, Slaughter took a punch at the defender, Lilly, and was counterpunched with a 15-yard penalty.

Kosar then hit Brennan in the left flat. Brennan was hit by a little-used defensive back named Jeremiah Castille, and fumbled. Denver ball.

Three Cleveland turnovers, and the game wasn't even half over.

As Denver started moving again, Sims suffered a stinger and had to leave. Now the Browns' *third-string* nose guard was temporarily out, forcing another shift to a 4-3 alignment.

Up in the broadcast booth, Olsen was amazed at the devastation. "I don't know when I've seen a game with more critical injuries," he said. The words were barely out of his mouth when Denver's Rulon Jones had to leave temporarily after taking a finger to the eye.

The field resembled a battlefield, sandy, dry, and dusty, and littered with papers. The players' spikes continually kicked up chalk from the yard lines and logos.

The fresh face in Cleveland's lineup, Al "Bubba" Baker, soon sacked Elway. Sam Clancy sacked him on the next play, pushing Denver out of field-goal range. Even though a punt was in the offing, Cleveland squandered 30 seconds before calling a time-out.

The Browns threatened, but, short on time, missed a 46-yard

field-goal try by Bahr, who had been rehabbing an injured knee and was struggling with any kick longer than 45 yards.

First half summary: All Denver, All the Time.

Not only was the score 21–3, but Denver was in line to get the second-half kickoff.

Two city-side reporters from the *Akron Beacon Journal* had seen enough. Armed with press credentials but without seats in the maxed-out press box, they headed out to the parking lot, climbed into their rental cars, and started typing away on their laptops, certain of the tone their stories would take. They typed throughout halftime and most of the third quarter.

So much for working ahead. They had not only wasted a lot of typing, but missed perhaps the most amazing offensive explosion in the 42-year history of the Cleveland Browns.

Within three plays, it became obvious the second half would be different. The immortal Elway suddenly looked quite mortal. Facing a third-and-11, he rolled to his right, rolled back into the middle, and uncorked a long pass down the center of the field into triple coverage. It was a horrid throw, flying well past the target and into the hands of Felix Wright. Cleveland's ball at the Denver 35.

Three-quarters of the field was now in shadows, but Cleveland's offense was just beginning to see the light. Kosar began to look like he was directing an attack against the local CYO team.

Mack powered for 13 yards, and Byner picked up four more. With the ball on Denver's 18, Kosar came to the line and didn't like what he saw. So he changed the play, spending so much time doing it that the play clock was down to one second when Rakoczy snapped the ball. Langhorne, flanked to the right, ran a post pattern. As he sped downfield, Kosar slung a sidearm, falling-away toss that hit him right in stride. Touchdown. Only four minutes into the second half, Cleveland had closed the gap to 21–10. The momentum seemed to have shifted.

Or maybe not. With the ball at Denver's 20, Elway went into the shotgun. He caught the snap, faded to the 12, moved forward, ran into the back of his right guard, Humphries, rolled to his right, and was nearly clobbered by Hanford Dixon. But at the 8-yard line, he got off a throw to Mark Jackson. Jackson caught it on the 25-yard line, near the right sideline, and spun inside, shaking off a tackle by Mark Harper. At the 30, he broke another tackle, this one by Wright.

The Amigo roared down the right sideline, going 80 yards for a score.

"Hey!" The entire stadium shook. "Hey!"

This broken play, this Elway improv show, became the longest touchdown in postseason history.

Denver 28, Cleveland 10.

When Jackson's feet finally stopped flying, you could see the number 82 written on the back of his left shoe in honor of his fallen Amigo, Vance Johnson. Over the tape on his right shoe he had written "The Vance." The script for this game seemed to have been written as well.

But Kosar didn't even flinch. Two runs by Mack, an 11-yard pass to Byner, and a 29-yard pass to Slaughter put Cleveland on Denver's 32. Kosar then faked a draw to Byner, couldn't find a receiver, began to run, and then lofted a little touch pass to Byner, who rambled 32 yards down the right side into the end zone. The Browns had scored again in only five plays.

Denver did nothing, and after a lousy punt, the Browns began at Denver's 42. A screen to Mack netted nine. A Kosar pass to Slaughter could have been intercepted, but Slaughter came back hard to the ball and grabbed it for a 16-yard gain. A flair to Mack gained eight. With the ball on the 4, Byner ran it up the gut and scored.

"Earnest Byner is a money player," Olsen announced. "Money players know where the goal line is."

Now it was 28–24. Now it was Cleveland that had scored 21 points in barely nine minutes. Now the momentum was running against Denver like an avalanche rolling down one of the nearby foothills.

Denver's next drive featured a collision between cornerback Mark Harper and tight end Orson Mobley that left both men on the ground for an extended period of time. Mobley eventually got up, but Harper was carried off with a leg injury, thinning Cleveland's defensive ranks even further.

Nattiel dropped a pass and Elway overthrew another, and Denver settled for a 38-yard field goal, bumping out their lead to 31–24.

At the start of the fourth quarter, the light was fading, the temperature was dropping, and Kosar stood on the sidelines, making the sign of the cross as an NBC camera watched. The Catholic gesture prompted Enberg to note that, when owner Art Modell first drafted Kosar, "Modell thought he was Jewish."

Wrong. But in the second half, through whatever avenue, Kosar seemed to have a direct line to the Man Upstairs. His first play of the quarter—a screen to the right side to Mack, good for six yards—gave Kosar his eighth completion in eight second-half tries.

He missed Newsome when the pass hit a Bronco in the back of his helmet, but he came right back and found Byner over the middle. Byner caught it at the Cleveland 44, turned on the jets, and reached Denver's 27.

Mack contributed a great run, breaking four tackles and moving the ball to Denver's 5. From there, Kosar threw a pass to Fontenot in the right corner that was not caught but could have been.

The next pass was perfect. Slaughter lined up wide left, with Brennan inside of him. Brennan took a couple of strides and cut to his right. Slaughter put four stutter steps on his defender and slanted toward the goalpost. Kosar nailed him at the goal line, his 11th completion in 13 passes.

Better still, the plodding, mistake-prone Browns of the first half seemed to have been fitted with bionic parts at the intermission.

Denver 31, Cleveland 31. It was a shocking turnaround. And now, with 10:45 left, the winner of the trip to San Diego was anything but clear.

Elway's initial response was a pass to Mark Jackson for 23 yards. Winder got six more up the middle, and Denver had nearly hit midfield. On third down, Elway ran a quarterback draw and was nailed a yard short of the first down by a rejuvenated Sims. It was an apparent punting situation, but Cleveland spotted backup quarterback Gary Kubiak coming into the game and called time to set up for a trick play. Denver came out of the time-out with Elway in the backfield, but he delivered a little pooch punt to the Cleveland 32.

For the first time in a long time, the Browns offense struggled as well. Slaughter got two steps on defender Steve Wilson, but Kosar overthrew him with a pass that traveled 55 yards in the air. Later, on another potential blockbuster, Kosar threw a bomb to Brennan that seemed to have a good chance, but Slaughter ran the wrong route and brought his defender into Brennan's territory, where he broke up the play.

The Browns punted back to Denver, and Elway began at his 25 with exactly 5:14 left on the clock—a figure eerily similar to the one the previous year (5:32) when The Drive began to unfold.

Nattiel beat Dixon, Elway hit him, and in one play Denver was at midfield. On the next play, Elway tried to get it all, overthrowing Nattiel near the Cleveland goal line. Nattiel's number was called yet again. He ran another crossing pattern, this time right to left, and Elway hit him, advancing the ball to the Cleveland 20, where the Broncos called time.

The time-out was a good investment: on the next play, Elway threw a screen over the middle to Winder, who made a great run to the right side and scored. Denver had gone 75 yards in only five plays, taking not much more than a minute.

"Hey!" exclaimed Gary Glitter, with 76,000 backup singers. "Hey!"

Denver 38, Cleveland 31. Four minutes left.

McNeil ran the kickoff out to the 25, and Kosar took the field with 3:53 to play. As he stood there, 75 yards from a tie, he momentarily flashed back to Elway's drive of the previous year. He was thinking about poetic justice.

The once-fresh afternoon has turned to night. The field is awash in scraps of paper from previous celebrations. The national television audience has been carried into prime time now, and few viewers have any desire to tune out. Each play has become mountain sized.

Would this be *Son of The Drive*?

First play: a handoff to Byner, who blasts up the middle on a quick-hitter and reels off 16 yards.

Byner again for two.

Kosar fades, looks to his left and lets fly for Brennan, who is completing a hook pattern. It's good for 14 yards and another first down. The ball is on Denver's 44.

Kosar scrambles left and throws to Brennan, who runs all the way to the Denver 24. The two-minute warning is called with Cleveland needing to cover only a quarter of the football field to tie the game.

On the next play, Rakoczy, who had been sensational filling in for Baab, is bowled over by Denver before the snap. The penalty gives the Browns a second-and-5 at Denver's 19.

Byner gets the handoff and runs left. A trap block by Dan Fike helps get him a first down at the Denver 13. He is brought down with help from cornerback Castille.

Castille is an NFL reject, cut from the Tampa Bay Buccaneers during training camp—cut from a team that would wind up 4–11. He had been given a governor's reprieve by Denver, but has spent much of the day stapled to the bench. Only when right cornerback Steve Wilson goes down do the Broncos call on Castille.

As Castille comes back to the huddle after tackling Byner, he tells some teammates, "I almost got the ball loose."

Byner's number is called again on the next play, this time as a pass receiver. Kosar slings one near the back line of the end zone and . . . too long. Byner nearly crashes into the goalpost going after it.

In the TV booth, Olsen again refers to Byner's wonderful versatility. "We've mentioned Byner's ability as both a runner and blocker and catcher."

Second down. Kosar barks out the count, drops, and fires a pass to Langhorne. Incomplete. But Denver has jumped offside. Coach Dan Reeves is livid at the offender, his star linebacker, Mecklenburg.

The official steps off five more yards, moving the ball to Denver's 8. It's second-and-5, with only 1:12 left on the clock.

Merlin Olsen utters a sentence that goes virtually unnoticed at the time: "These are the toughest yards in football right here."

Indeed.

Kosar walks into the huddle and says, "13 Trap." The Browns line up with four wide receivers—Slaughter wide left, Brennan in the left slot, Langhorne wide right, with Clarence Weathers in the right slot—and one running back. That's Byner, who is slightly to Kosar's right, standing on the 13-yard line.

Byner will get the handoff. It will be the third consecutive play in which he has gotten a handoff or been the target of a pass, and the fourth time in the previous six.

The ball is snapped. Kosar whirls and hands it to Byner with his left hand.

Fike has pulled from his right guard spot and is sealing the left side of Denver's line with a great block. Farren is doing a nice job of holding off his man as well.

Slaughter and Brennan have crossed paths, and Brennan is heading to the corner of the end zone while Slaughter moves toward the goalpost.

Byner takes the ball at the 12 and cuts outside at the 9.

He cuts back to his right at the 7 and seems headed for the tying score.

At the 4, Castille hits him in the left elbow with his left shoulder pad. The ball is tucked to Byner's chest, but not tightly enough. It pops out.

Castille falls on it at the 2.

Byner looks back and sees Castille recover. He looks skyward and drops flat on his back. He knows it's over.

So does the Denver crowd. Mile High Stadium explodes.

"Byner fumbled the ball and Denver has recovered!" yells Enberg. "Oh, MY!"

"HEY!" roars the crowd. "HEY! . . . HEY!"

The Browns walk in slow motion toward their bench. Brennan pats Byner on the helmet. Slaughter comes up and puts an arm around him. Kosar moves methodically back and forth on the bench, offering encouragement to his battered and bloody linemen.

Byner pulls off his helmet and sits on it. He stares straight ahead, chewing on his mouth guard, idly pulling off his wristbands.

Offensive coordinator Lindy Infante walks over and puts an arm around him. Kosar comes by and gives Byner a hug.

But the game isn't over.

Denver is trying to run down the clock, but the clock seems to be in slow motion. Kosar begins to warm up again, and Byner pulls his wristbands back on.

On fourth down, with 13 seconds left, Reeves orders his punter to run out the back of the end zone, taking the safety. That makes the score 38–33, and Denver must kick the ball from its 20.

Only eight seconds remain when McNeal calls a fair catch of a booming punt, giving Kosar one last shot from the Cleveland 27-yard line.

He hurls it deep down the right sideline to Brennan, but a mass of orange jerseys knocks it down. The Broncos are heading to their third Super Bowl. The Browns are headed away from their 22nd straight.

The hard-hitting marathon left football fans everywhere exhausted, and left NBC so mixed in its emotions that it declared both Elway and Kosar the game MVP.

A strong argument could have been made for Byner as well. At five-foot-ten, 218 pounds, he put the Cleveland offense on his back the second half. He scored two of the third-quarter touchdowns and for the game rushed for 67 yards and caught seven passes for 120 more yards. This from a guy chosen 280th in the 1984 draft, reeled in from that legendary football powerhouse, er, Eastern Carolina.

The football was the only thing Byner left on the field. When he fumbled, the two teams had been going at each other for three hours and 22 minutes. They had been playing a mile above sea level. And Byner had been involved in all but two of the previous six plays. If he was exhausted, he never once used it as an excuse.

Enberg: "Two cities, football crazed, and how unkind it is for the fans of Cleveland—again."

This time, it was even worse. At least the previous game had been decided by the opponent's heroics. This game had a goat. Earnest Byner's name was now written next to Bill Buckner's and Jackie Smith's. And Cleveland had suffered another severe case of poetic injustice.

THE SHOT

SUNDAY, MAY 7, 1989

As the clock ticked down on a thrilling final game of a playoff series between the Cleveland Cavaliers and the Chicago Bulls, Michael Jordan hit a 15-foot jumper to send the Cavs home for the summer and propel Jordan toward the realm of international icon.

THEY WERE MORE LIKE a college team. They passed the ball and moved without it. They set screens. They played defense. They boxed out. They trusted each other, cared about each other. They even liked their coach.

They were mainstream guys, guys with names like Mark and Larry, Ron and Brad, Craig and John. They had grown up on farms or in small towns—not, like most professional basketball players, in the nation's biggest cities. And they chose to live not in Greater Cleveland, but in quieter, smaller Akron. Most of them were married. They were, by contemporary NBA standards, total outsiders.

The Mark of the group—Price—looked like a middle school gym teacher, or maybe the guy who does your taxes. Six feet tall, slim, white, with squinty eyes. The eyes were the key. The low-hanging upper lids served as a veil, pulled down to provide distance between the people staring at him and his own corneas, which seemed to be perpetually unfocused but in reality never missed a thing. Price's peripheral vision must have pushed 360 degrees.

Instead of jumping into limos with his posse, Price would jump into his Pontiac and drive his family to the Chapel, a nondenominational Christian church in downtown Akron. In the team's press book, he listed his favorite song as "Praise Ye the Lord," by a group called Petra, and, for the "person you'd most like to meet," cited Billy Graham. Price recorded songs with a Christian singing group and, for a while, hosted a weekly program on a Christian radio station, WHLO, where he talked about his faith, read Bible verses, and played contemporary Christian records.

The Larry of the group—Nance—was even more unassuming, if such a thing is possible for a six-foot-ten black man with a two-mile wingspan and the springing ability of a kangaroo. When the league held its first slam-dunk contest in 1984 in Denver, Nance, then a Phoenix Sun, soared into the rafters with a basketball in each hand and tomahawked each one through the net before floating back to earth with the winner's trophy. Among the eight defeated competitors were legendary high-flyers Dr. J and Dominique Wilkins. In subsequent years, Nance declined to participate in the slam-dunk contest. Why do it again when you've already done it?

He was similarly reticent during games. After swatting away one of his 200 blocked shots per year, he would never glare at the man he was defending. He wouldn't stick a fist in the air, or pound his chest, or look for the replay on the scoreboard, or even high-five a teammate. He would stare straight ahead, almost sheepishly, and simply trot back down the court, reloading for the next play. Nance was one of the most unassuming All-Stars in NBA history.

The most distinctive person in the group had the most common name—John. But he also had a cool nickname: "Hot Rod," given to him by his mother when he was a baby because he would make engine noises while scooting himself backward across the floor of their tiny home in rural Louisiana.

Unlike the others, Hot Rod Williams hadn't emerged from college toting armloads of plaques and universal praise. Upon leaving Louisiana State University, Hot Rod had been branded with a scarlet letter—a big "P," for point-shaver. Other NBA teams wouldn't touch him. But the Cavs knew something the others did not. After the Cavs drafted him, and long after the label was affixed, Williams was cleared of all charges—with the possible exception of being hopelessly naïve in his choice of college companions—and was freed to play professional basketball.

Hot Rod's look was unusual too. At the very top of that six-foot, eleven-inch frame, he wore a big, old-fashioned flattop haircut. He was a big man with a big 'do, and his head looked like an aircraft carrier.

But Hot Rod had the shooting touch of an ace fighter pilot. He also hit the boards, played defense, and hustled every night. He played well in the clutch. He kept his nose clean. People liked him.

Same with Craig Ehlo. If Hot Rod's head looked like it could be moored at the naval base in San Diego, Ehlo looked like a fellow you might see manning a lifeguard tower on a California beach. He had long, blond, wavy hair, a jaunty gate, and a laid-back demeanor.

Ehlo was actually from Lubbock, Texas, and stood six-foot-seven, but nothing about his manner was big. Cut by the Houston Rockets after three ordinary years, Ehlo was signed as a free agent and always gave the impression he was happy just to be around.

Like most of these Cavs, Ehlo lived in Northeast Ohio year round. Fans would frequently see him strolling around Summit Mall, not far from his house. Heck, in the summer, fans could play basketball with him if they showed up at nearby Croghan Park, where he often joined pickup games. Superstar? Never. Great guy, solid player? Absolutely.

In contrast to Ehlo, Brad Daugherty was a household name among basketball fans, the first pick in the 1986 draft and a onetime teammate of Michael Jordan at perennial collegiate powerhouse North Carolina. In a sense, though, Daugherty was the anti-Jordan. Nothing he did was spectacular—unless you count his remarkable passing skills; the evening TV highlights never did.

Brad was a good-ol' country boy in African-American skin. He was so low key and down home that he made truck-drivin', Utah-livin' Karl Malone seem as gaudy as Clyde Frazier. Daugherty wore number 43 because it was the number painted on the hood of the stock cars driven by his hero, NASCAR's Richard Petty.

Brad was soft, they said. Too soft for the NBA. No heart inside that seven-foot-one, 265-pound frame. Then how did they explain those 20 points and 10 rebounds that showed up every night next to his name?

This Cav had weird hair too, but not Hot Rod hair. Brad's was a simple buzz cut. The funkiness involved his hairline: it came down so low on the sides that you thought it was going to grow right into his eyebrows. He was a helmet head.

Ron Harper was the only one of the regulars who reminded you of a normal NBA player. He was a city kid, a kid with moves, a kid with attitude. But the city he was from, Dayton, was smallish, and the college he went to, Miami of Ohio, was smallish, and, hampered by a stutter, his proclivity for speaking in front of a microphone was smallish as well.

The man coaching this group was not exactly a loose cannon, either. Although Lenny Wilkens was the product of a tough New York City ghetto, three decades in the spotlight had long since worn away any rough edges. In fact, Wilkens, a nine-time All-Star point guard during his playing days, had become quite sophisticated—refined, reserved, a sharp dresser.

"Coach Lenny," as Hot Rod always called him, never made the TV highlights for screaming in people's faces or breaking clipboards or throwing chairs. Coach Lenny was the steady hand on a ship that had to navigate 82 regular-season games each year. He was the voice of experience, the guy who consciously smoothed out the peaks and valleys.

As was fitting, this laid-back group reported to work each day at the most laid-back arena in the NBA, the Coliseum in Richfield.

The television networks were fond of showing pregame scenes with the Coliseum in the background and sheep grazing in the foreground, compliments of a nearby farm. But the innocent little Cleveland Cavaliers were not the ones being led to slaughter. Not during the 1988–89 season. This group of Cavs was dismembering the opposition. Home-court advantage? How about 37 wins and four losses? How about a home winning percentage of .902? How about not losing a home game from mid-December through early March?

One night in Richfield, against Golden State, they scored an unheard-of 142 points. At various times, all five starters scored 30 or more points in a game.

Not that the entire season was sweetness and light. During a home game in late February, the Cavs were blowing out the Detroit Pistons when, in the fourth quarter, Detroit's Rick Mahorn delivered a vicious cheap shot that gave Mark Price a concussion. As Price was running down the floor, near the middle of the court, Mahorn threw an elbow that hit Price right in the temple. Mahorn was fined $5,000. Why he was not suspended, too, is an enduring mystery.

Price was still groggy three days later for a rematch in Detroit. On that trip, Wilkens received a death threat, and later the team had to leave its hotel because of a bomb threat.

Getting picked on by bad guys made the team even more lovable.

The franchise not only charmed the fans for what it had become, but from where it had come—namely, the NBA's outhouse. The 1988–89 season was only six years removed from the Ted Stepien Era, which may well have been the nadir of professional sports in Cleveland.

Stepien owned the team for only three years, but it seemed like 30. The founder of Nationwide Advertising became a nationwide joke. Among the six coaches he hired—that's right, six coaches in three years—was a pal of his, Don Delaney, whom Stepien somehow managed to snatch away from that perennial basketball powerhouse, er, Lakeland Community College in Mentor. At least Stepien didn't have to pay to fly him in for an interview. Among the coaches Stepien fired was Chuck Daly, who, of course, moved on to Detroit and won back-to-back NBA titles.

Teddy's idea of a dance team was the Teddi Bears, a nowhere-near-ready-for-prime-time collection of lasses who danced haltingly to the team's fight song—a polka. And, for your additional halftime pleasure, he brought in a fat guy to eat beer cans. Seriously. A porky fellow dubbed "The Amazing Boot" entertained the masses—okay, the dozens—by chomping on beer cans, raw eggs, and firecrackers.

But that was the least of it. The moves made by Stepien's front office were so horrific that the league banned further trades by the Cavs in an effort to protect Stepien from himself—or at least protect the future of the faltering franchise. At one point, Stepien had discarded six years' worth of first-round draft picks to assemble a collection of players who would have had a hard time winning the intramural championship at Kent State.

When Cleveland hosted the All-Star Game in 1981, league officials moved into the Coliseum and took over the operation so Teddy wouldn't screw things up and soil the reputation of the entire NBA.

By Stepien's third year, attendance had plunged to 3,900 per game. When he finally bailed out—lugging away a record of 66 wins and 180 losses—he was replaced by two polished, experienced businessmen with real money, George and Gordon Gund. The Gunds were in the business of buying struggling companies and pumping life back into them, which made the Cavs a perfect takeover target.

The Gunds did what Stepien did not: using a patient, steady hand, they began to slowly, methodically cart away the wreckage. In 1986, they went out and hired somebody who knew talent—veteran general manager and former NBA star Wayne Embry—and let him do his thing. His thing was beautiful, at least in the early years.

Embry's first draft choice was Daugherty. His second was Harper, chosen eighth overall. That pick was part of a deal the Gunds struck with the NBA; because their franchise had been so mismanaged, they were permitted to buy additional first-round picks in both 1985 and 1986.

Embry's third key move was hiring Coach Lenny.

The same year, the team was gaining the services of Hot Rod. He had been drafted the previous year, but had just now been judged innocent, and therefore eligible for the NBA. Mark Price came aboard, too, acquired in a little-noticed trade with Dallas.

That first year under Coach Lenny, the crowds averaged only 10,900. But those fans were slowly falling in love. Sure, Harper ended his first season just 10 turnovers short of an all-time NBA record. But he also averaged 23 points per game and played with as much flair as any Cavalier—ever. He and his teammates were raw, but they were fun. Mixed in with all their rookie mistakes were moments of pure brilliance.

The momentum began to grow. In Coach Lenny's first year, the Cavs won 31 games. The next year, they improved by 11 games and made the playoffs. Then, in 1988–89, they added 13 more wins, giving them a franchise record of 57.

If 1975–76 was the "Miracle of Richfield," the '88–'89 season was nothing of the sort. This was totally expected. These guys were good—young, athletic, coachable, hungry. Three of them—Price, Nance, and Daugherty—were voted to the All-Star team. During the second half of that contest, held in Houston, all three were on the floor at the same time—60 percent of the East's lineup.

The future looked so bright that no less an authority than Magic Johnson dubbed the Cleveland Cavaliers "the Team of the '90s."

They could have been, except for one small thing. Actually, he was a medium-sized thing by NBA standards, six feet, six inches tall and 215 pounds. But by any standards, he was remarkable. The "Team of the '90s" had the misfortune of coming into its own at precisely the same time as the Player of the Century.

Like the reborn Cavs, Michael Jordan had been a bit of a sleeper. Only the third pick in the 1984 draft (behind Hakeem Olajuwon and, yes, Sam Bowie), he came out blazing in his rookie year, averaging 28 points per game. By his third season, he had cranked up that average to an amazing 37 points. But Chicago still had not won a playoff series. Jordan's first year, the Bulls dropped three of four to Milwaukee. Jordan's second season, they were swept by Boston (despite a game in which Jordan exploded for 63 points). Same thing happened the following year. That left the Bulls with exactly one playoff win in Jordan's first three years.

Lots of big scorers had come and gone without winning a championship, and those players were never viewed in the same light as players who owned rings. So the jury was still very much out on Jordan's place in history.

Finally, in Jordan's fourth year, 1987–88, the Bulls won a playoff series—against the Cavs. Even though Chicago had a better overall record, and therefore home-court advantage, the Cavs had held their own that winter, splitting the six regular-season games.

The home court was an advantage, indeed. Chicago won the first two games in Chicago, Cleveland won the second two games in Cleveland, and the Bulls won the deciding game at creaky old Chicago Stadium.

That series helped lift Jordan into the realm of superstar. Not only did he average 45 points during those five games, he showed that, with a little help, he could get his team into the winner's circle. The help had arrived in the form of Scottie Pippen and Horace Grant, two youngsters with grown-up skills.

But the 1988–89 season promised to be different. The Cavs had swept all six regular-season games from the Bulls, including the season finale in Chicago, which Price, Daugherty, and Nance sat out, resting injuries.

And this time, the Cavaliers were playoff-tested. They knew the drill. And, with 57 wins, they also held the home-court advantage.

At least until the first game.

Game One took place on a Friday night at the Coliseum, but the Cavs played as if it were an exhibition game at a neutral site. They were awful, shooting 19-of-29 from the foul line and 1-of-6 on three-pointers. It didn't help that Price missed the game, still nursing his pulled groin, or that Daugherty virtually disappeared, scoring only nine points and grabbing only seven rebounds. Cleveland needed a 31-point fourth quarter just to come within seven.

In Game Two, on a Sunday afternoon in Richfield, Daugherty was MIA again, and was booed by the sell-out crowd. Fortunately, Price was back, acting as if he had never been hurt, and Harper stepped up, scoring 31 points and outplaying Jordan at both ends of the floor. The Cavs won by eight.

For Game Three at Chicago Stadium, Bulls fans put on a cheering clinic. They were roaring a half hour before the game, and never let up. The Bulls charged out to a 15-point first-quarter lead. The Cavs closed the gap to three late in the game, but Chicago hung on. Once again the Cavs were hampered by injuries: Ehlo missed the game because of a sprained ankle suffered in practice. In his place, the Cavs tried three different players on Jordan—Harper, Mike Sanders, and backup point guard Darnell Valentine—with little effect. Jordan poured in 44.

Game Four, on enemy turf, was a true test of Cleveland's character. Lose that game and the season was over. The Cavs won a wild shootout in overtime, 108–105. The only reason the game reached overtime was a gutsy performance by Daugherty, who shook off the "choke" label by sinking two free throws with four seconds left in regulation, not to mention grabbing a playoff-record 17 rebounds. The Big Guy was back, and just in time.

For the second year in a row, the Bulls–Cavs series would come down to a final game. Winner stays, loser goes home for the summer.

On a sunny spring day, the 80 acres of blacktop surrounding the Coliseum filled up early for the 3:30 p.m. start. People normally loathe to surrender a beautiful May afternoon after a harsh Northeast Ohio winter couldn't wait to get inside, into the darkness, to watch the Cavs put the icing on their remarkable season.

The CBS cameras were in place. Dick Stockton and Hubie Brown were behind the microphones at the scorer's table, and James Brown was the rover.

In place of the Teddi Bears, the nation's viewers saw the infinitely more watchable Cavs Dance Team, attired in tight blue bodysuits and drilled to near perfection, and dancing to mainstream rock, rather than polkas.

The nation also was watching a group of Cleveland Cavaliers that was quite likely the best in the 18-year history of the franchise.

Unfortunately, that group was not entirely healthy. Price was still battling a groin injury, Ehlo was still having trouble with a sprained ankle, and Daugherty had a hip-pointer. The Bulls, by contrast, were 100 percent—or at least as close to 100 percent as you can be after eight straight months of basketball.

Shortly before the tip-off, in the visitors' locker room, Jordan was wearing headphones and listening to an Anita Baker song, "Give It Your Best." As if he would give anything less.

The atmosphere was electric. Although the fans had been criticized in the media for sitting on their hands during the first two games and for booing Daugherty, the lack of wild abandon came less from not caring than from caring too much. Fans, like players, can be too tight for big games. Their hearts had been in their throats.

But this time, with the Cavs' backs to the wall, the fans were on a mission. They brought their "A" game, and that was obvious from the beginning. Thunderous boos filled the bowl with the introduction of No. 23 in the visiting red jersey with the black letters and white trim. The rafters rattled with cheers when the Cavs ran out in their simple but tasteful white warm-ups, with blue and orange piping, the players' last names arching gracefully across their backs. First Williams. Then Nance. Then Harper. Then Price. Then Daugherty.

For the first half, the good guys were set to move toward the north end of the floor (right to left as you faced the scorer's table and the team benches). Nance squared off against Cartwright for the opening tip and won it, batting the ball backward to Hot Rod.

The Cavs' first possession was a microcosm of the season. Before a single shot was taken, every Cav touched the ball. After Nance's tip, Hot Rod passed to Harper, who passed back to Hot Rod, who passed to Price, who passed to Daugherty, who passed to Hot Rod, who took a good shot from just left of the foul line. He missed, but Price used his blazing quickness to grab the long rebound. He then dribbled into the heart of the key and, without looking, flipped the ball to his right to Harper, who was wide open on the wing. Harper drilled the 12-foot jumper. The crowd erupted.

On the Bulls' first offensive foray, Pippen drove to the basket and was hacked by Nance—but missed both of his free throws. That set the tone for a sub-par game by one of Chicago's key players.

The performances of Pippen and Nance were crucial to their respective teams. During the first four games, Pippen had averaged 16 points and 8 rebounds while shooting 43 percent; Nance had averaged 20 points, 8 rebounds, and 57 percent. If Nance could outplay him again, the Cavs' chances looked bright.

Back at the other end of the court, Harper found himself open again, in the same spot, and launched another jumper. Same result.

This was a good omen, because Harper was known less for his outside shooting than for his slashing moves to the basket.

Before his trade for Danny Ferry, before he blew out his knee with the Clippers, Ron Harper was a sight to behold. He wasn't the least bit intimidated by Jordan. He was the same size as Jordan, nearly as athletic, nearly as difficult to stop in the open floor, nearly as flashy, and every bit as confident.

Unfortunately, he wasn't Jordan. Subtract Jordan from the equation and the Cleveland Cavaliers may have won a couple of NBA titles.

On this Sunday afternoon, the Cavs tried their best to subtract him. Harper and Ehlo took turns guarding him straight up, and for a while Jordan was quiet.

Someone far less elegant was doing the early damage: Bill Cartwright, the pointy-elbowed center with perhaps the ugliest shot in NBA history. Cartwright would raise the ball way up over his head, fully extending both arms, before dipping his hands and flipping the ball toward the basket with a whole-body jerk. But the seven-footer had been around for a long time, as witnessed by the patch of gray at the bottom of his beard, and he knew what it took to win playoff games. It wasn't aesthetics.

Cartwright, Chicago's biggest starter, would have to excel for his team to hold its own against the Cleveland, which boasted one of the biggest front lines in the league: the seven-foot-one Daugherty, the six-foot-eleven Williams, and the six-foot-ten Nance. That trio enabled Cleveland to finish second in the NBA in blocked shots. One January night against the Knicks, Nance blocked 11 all by himself, a team record, and the other guys combined for 10 more.

The Big Three had loomed large during the first four games of this series, averaging an amazing seven blocks per game. They had loomed so large, in fact, that Coach Lenny changed the starting lineup, inserting Hot Rod—normally the league's best Sixth Man—in place of the steady but unspectacular Mike Sanders, who had started almost every game all year.

Two quick buckets by Cartwright kept Chicago close in the early going.

Jordan, playing point guard, seemed content to let his teammates get involved. He didn't even take a shot until well into the first quarter, sinking a left-hand layup to give his team a 15–14 lead.

From a purely athletic standpoint, the game was a gem from the outset. Both teams were executing well, shooting well, diving for loose balls, playing tough defense, and rebounding like their seasons depended on it. For the vast majority of the game, officials Jake O'-Donnell, Jack Madden, and Hugh Evans were invisible—which is the highest compliment an official can receive. The overall level of play was worthy of Game Seven of the NBA Championship.

At the end of the first quarter, Cleveland led, 28–24. Fouls had become an issue. Jordan picked up his second foul near the end of the quarter, and Nance and Daugherty each had two.

Early in the second, Price began to zone in. The kid from Oklahoma, a coach's son, had the prettiest jump shot east or west of the Mississippi. He shot like the drawings in the basketball textbooks: shoulders square to the basket, elbow in, good extension, same motion every time.

Because he was an NBA midget, he had to work hard. And because of both factors, he was a fan favorite, a normal-looking guy beating up on genetic mutants with his guile and long-range jump shot.

One of those jumpers found the mark early in the second quarter and gave the Cavs a seven-point lead. The crowd exploded—goaded, as usual, by public address announcer Howie Chizek: "Mark Price [long pause] for thaa-*REEEEEE!*"

According to the fine print in the NBA rulebook, the P.A. announcers were not supposed to show favoritism. But the enforcement of that rule was even less stringent than the enforcement of traveling violations by superstars.

Speaking of which, Cleveland fans were already complaining that the league's newest superstar, Jordan, was getting more than the benefit of a doubt, on both offense and defense. But some of it, at least, was sour grapes. Some of it simply looked illegal because nobody had ever done those kinds of things.

Jordan's hair was very, very short, but he was not yet shaving his head on a regular basis. He and some teammates had done it in a show of solidarity on the eve of the playoffs, and it was starting to grow back. But it was certainly not yet his trademark. His red shorts were a bit longer than the other players', but still well above his knees. He looked confident, but he did not look invincible. In fact, in Game Four, he had looked extremely human, missing a foul shot with eight seconds left and missing a short jump shot at the buzzer that could have won the game.

Television viewers were not yet seeing a steady stream of MJ commercials. During this game, the most frequent advertisement on CBS was a Miller Lite commercial with a professional wrestling theme. It featured an over-the-top, heavily costumed wrestler named Jesse "The Body" Ventura.

Once again, it appeared to be a case of Jordan against the world. Pippen was pulling his own vanishing act. (He would shoot 4-for-13 from the floor, and he was struggling so badly from the foul line that in the second half he began to line up a foot or more behind the line.) Jordan began to look for his own shot first. And he was heating up.

The P.A. system supplied the recorded bass-drum soundtrack, and the fans provided the chorus: "[THUMP, THUMP] DEEE-fence. [THUMP, THUMP] DEEE-fence . . ."

The pleas were headed. The Cavs' defensive rotation was as good as at any time all year.

On offense, in place of one superstar, the Cavs had rolled out five starters who were all playing up to their capabilities. Halfway through the second quarter, they combined for a vintage offensive assault.

Standing in front of Coach Lenny, who was wearing a tasteful, charcoal-gray suit, Harper inbounded the ball to Ehlo . . . who threw it back to Harper . . . who threw it inside to Hot Rod . . . who threw it back out to Harper . . . who threw it back in to Hot Rod . . . who threw it out to Ehlo at the top of the three-point arc. Before the ball was even out of his hand, thousands of fans simultaneously exclaimed, "THREE!" And it was. After six quick, sharp passes and one wide-open shot, the Cavs had extended their lead.

This group of players had absorbed something that every basketball coach tries to teach: human beings can pass the ball faster than other human beings can move their feet. Pass it often enough, from side to side and, especially, inside and out, and someone will be open. The philosophy makes perfect sense. But even in the 1980s, this kind of ball movement was uncommon in the NBA.

The fans adored this team not only for its winning percentage, but because of that selflessness. Nobody on the floor was thinking about his individual stats or his contract status or his press clippings. They were thinking only about finding a seam in the defense, finding a spot where the opposition was vulnerable. And on defense, they were constantly helping out, constantly rotating toward the ball.

"[THUMP, THUMP] DEEE-fence. [THUMP, THUMP] DEEE-fence . . ."

Jordan still wasn't fully untracked. On one fast break, he rose into

the air to dunk, but jammed it down against the back of the rim and
the ball flew all the way over the scorer's table. The fans roared.

With 15 seconds left in the half, though, Ehlo missed a three, Jordan came down with the ball, zoomed around Price to the basket, and was fouled by backup center Tree Rollins. With three seconds left, he canned both free-throws to draw Chicago to within two points, 48–46.

At the half, Grant, Cartwright, and Daugherty had three fouls apiece.

The Cavs hit their first shot of the second half, and Grant quickly picked up his fourth foul.

"LET'S GO CAVS . . . LETS GO CAVS . . . "

A short time later, Cartwright was whistled for his fourth foul. Although the score was still tight, two key Bulls had gotten themselves in foul trouble. Again, Jordan started to pick up the slack. After going 5-for-13 in the first half, he began to light up the house, hitting long jumpers and driving seemingly at will.

Both teams were playing awesome basketball. As CBS's Stockton told the nation, "This is a game to admire." And there was plenty of game left.

Little Craig Hodges stepped up for Chicago, too, scoring eight points in the third to keep the Bulls within striking distance. At the end of three, the Cavs led 75–69.

They would build that lead to eight points in the fourth quarter, but the Bulls would go on a 16–3 run to take a five-point lead with six minutes left.

But the Cavs battled back. They took a one-point lead on a breakaway layup by Harper and his tough jumpshot over MJ. Both teams then unleashed a flurry of offensive assaults—Jordan, Harper, Jordan, Ehlo, Cartwright, Nance.

Crunch time.

With a minute and a half left, Grant fouls out and is replaced by Warrensville native Brad Sellers. The Cavs lead by one.

During the final 1:13, the two teams will score 12 points. The first comes from an unlikely source, given the events of the day.

Jordan drives, but is double-teamed and has to back out of the lane. With the shot clock winding down, he throws the ball across the court to Pippen, who is right in front of the Cavs' bench, a mile from the basket. With one second left on the shot clock, Pippen launches a three. Nothing but net.

Chicago 97, Cleveland 95. The Cavs take time with 1:13 left.

After five Cav passes, Ehlo pops open behind the three-point arc and drills it.

Cleveland 98, Chicago 97. The clock reads 51 seconds.

Jordan misses a layup. Price grabs the rebound and pushes the ball up the court. The Cavs work the ball around until, with 12 seconds left on the shot clock, Nance hoists a 20-foot jumper. It's a shade short, and during the war for the rebound the ball goes out of bounds off Ehlo.

Now 19 seconds remain. The Bulls call time. Chicago has the choice of taking the ball out at the far end of the floor or at midcourt. They elect to traverse the entire floor, hoping to keep their offense in a more normal flow.

"[THUMP, THUMP] DEEE-fence. [THUMP, THUMP] DEEE-fence . . . "

Jordan gets the ball with nine seconds left. He drives around Ehlo—smacking him in the face with his left elbow—and pulls up for a jumper to the right of the key. Bingo.

In terms of pure execution, this was an even more remarkable shot than the one that would live in infamy. This shot was taken not over a stumbling, half-lame defender, but over one of the league's premier shot-blockers, a guy who was perfectly healthy, had his feet firmly planted, and jumped at precisely the right time. Jordan arched this jumper directly over a sky-high Larry Nance.

During the 1980s and early '90s, watching Nance jump was one of Northeast Ohio's most enjoyable pastimes. He didn't remind you of a Jordan or a Dominique Wilkens, a rocket bursting up through the atmosphere; he was more like a glider. Once aloft, he would hang on the currents, his long arms extended, his long legs, half-covered with knee-high white socks, drifting high above the landscape, seemingly forever, before finally touching back down, softly and gracefully. Nance blocked shots with either hand. He'd turn away shots from point guards driving the lane, or stop hook shots from the biggest men in the game. But he couldn't get to Jordan's jumper.

Chicago 99, Cleveland 98. Six seconds left.

In the huddle, Coach Lenny draws up the play. Six seconds should be plenty. Ehlo will take the ball out near midcourt, just down from the Bulls' bench. Price will start low on the right side of the basket, with Daugherty alongside him. Harper will act as a decoy, standing far away from the action on the right wing. Nance will line up on the left side of the lane, the side closer to Ehlo, and start on the low block. When the play starts, Nance will slide up the lane and receive the pass. Ehlo will streak inbounds, take a return pass from Nance, and, in theory, make a layup.

When the action begins, that's exactly what happens. Nance is able to shield Sellers from the ball. The other three Cavs have kept their distance, clearing the way for Nance and Ehlo. Ehlo throws a perfect pass to Nance. Nance leaps, grabs it, and, as he's coming down, scoops it underhand back to Ehlo. Ehlo takes one right-handed dribble and lays the ball off the glass with his right hand. Good!

He then lands awkwardly on his right ankle, and goes down as if he has been shot.

The crowd goes ballistic. Cleveland 100, Chicago 99. Jordan signals for a time-out a millisecond after the basket.

Three seconds left.

As the teams move toward their benches, Ehlo is grimacing in pain and limping noticeably. But nothing short of an amputation would get him out of the game now.

Now it's time for Chicago coach Doug Collins to draw up his most important play of the season. The "who" is no mystery. Everybody in North America knows *who* will get the ball. The question is *where*.

The local guy, Sellers, will inbound. Cartwright will be at the elbow on the near side. Jordan will start on the far elbow. Pippen will set up on the left block.

Just as Sellers prepares to inbound, the Cavs take their last time-out. Having seen Collins' formation, Coach Lenny can now refine his defensive strategy.

In the huddle, Coach Lenny assigns two men to Jordan. Ehlo will do his best to stay between Jordan and the basket. Nance will face away from the inbounds pass, watch Jordan, and try to deny him the ball.

Sellers resumes his position and takes the ball from the ref. Cartwright runs away from the ball, heading toward Jordan, apparently on his way to set a pick. But he loops outside of Jordan and swings down toward the basket, dragging Daugherty along with him.

Pippen begins to move from the low block to Sellers' side of the court. But all eyes are on No. 23.

Jordan feints slightly toward the basket, then heads directly toward Sellers. He soon encounters Nance. Nance doesn't fall for the first couple of fakes, but another fake catches him leaning. When Jordan takes a step toward midcourt, Nance moves that way, trying to cut him off. Instead, Jordan cuts sharply to his left, losing Nance, and pops into the open about 10 feet from the sideline, roughly in line with the foul line. Sellers flips him the ball, and the race against time is on.

Jordan pivots, dribbles once with his left hand . . . twice with his left hand . . . and arrives at the middle of the floor. Ehlo is playing him perfectly, keeping himself between Jordan and the basket. Right at the foul line, Jordan leaps into the air, kicking his feet back behind him. Ehlo leaps too. But when Ehlo comes back down, Jordan is still up there. After reaching the peak of his jump, Jordan finally releases a flatter-than-usual shot.

It appears to be on line.

The buzzer sounds.

The ball goes in.

Chicago 101, Cleveland 100.

Ehlo falls to the floor in emotional agony. Price grabs the bottom of his shorts and bends over at the waist, staring at the floor in shock and disgust. Nance, Daugherty, and Harper just stand there, numb, trying to convince themselves they haven't really seen what they think they've seen. The crowd falls silent.

Jordan leaps in the air, pumping his fist, and is mobbed by teammates. His coach jumps up, too, perhaps as high as he ever did during his playing days. Collins spins around, punches the air with his fist, and sprints onto the floor.

Across the nation, this will soon become known as "The Shot." It will be replayed on television screens until the end of time.

In retrospect, any of the final three shots could have become legendary had the subsequent shots not gone in. Jordan's jumper over Nance with nine seconds left would have fit the bill. So, too, would Ehlo's gritty drive with only three ticks left. But because of The Shot, those shots are mere footnotes.

Almost immediately, Jordan is collared by CBS's James Brown. Bending over, out of breath, bursting with emotion, Jordan can barely talk. He is beneath the basket where he has just made history, the proud owner of 44 points, nine rebounds, and six assists. Huge beads of sweat are pooled on his forehead. Some of them begin to slide down the sides of his cheeks and over his eyebrows.

The nation is looking at a spent warrior. It is also looking at a man who is so good and—as of now—so timely that he has begun to transcend his sport.

"We came in and we stuck tough," Jordan says, gasping for air. "We hung right in there and gave ourselves a chance to win, and we won the ballgame . . . We're going to New York, baby."

Cleveland fans don't want to hear about it. Twenty thousand, two hundred, seventy-three crushed souls file out into the May afternoon, squinting against the brightness.

Did you ever notice how the sun always seems to be shining in the aftermath of a tornado?

LAST DANCE WITH A GREAT LADY

SUNDAY, OCTOBER 3, 1993

The last baseball game ever played at Cleveland Stadium drew an emotional, sell-out crowd that celebrated its shared history with a tearful farewell.

CLEVELAND STADIUM was not about Jim Brown and Rocky Colavito. Not really. It was about Tom Muscenti.

Tom happened to be from Mentor, but he could have been any one of us, any one of literally tens of millions of Northeast Ohioans whose lives were touched by the gigantic concrete-and-steel structure that hugged the shores of Lake Erie for 65 years.

Muscenti was among 72,390 people at the final Indians game on October 3, 1993. As usual, the Indians lost. They were shut out in the stadium's first game in 1932 . . . they were shut out in the stadium's last game in 1993 . . . and in between they lost a lot more often than they won.

But on that final day, nobody cared about the score. When the game ended and the postgame ceremony began, not a soul got up to leave.

Ninety-year-old Bob Hope, unsteady and hard of hearing, shuffled onto his hometown field to sing "Thanks for the Memories." Members of the grounds crew, wearing black tuxedos, dug up home plate with a pickax and put it in the trunk of a white limousine. The limo slowly drove around the warning track and out through the outfield gate, its eventual destination a new ballpark known as Gateway, where it would serve for one game before being retired.

Finally, after an hour of festivities, the affair was over, and the fans began to trickle out slowly, almost grudgingly. It was 5:30 in the afternoon. The sun had dipped most of the way behind the 115-foot-high roof on the third-base side of the diamond and now lit only the right-field stands. This was the transitional sun of early October, a sun that is bright yet not fully here, a sun in the midst of changing from a throbbing, constant companion to a distant acquaintance.

Muscenti was still sitting out there in that sun. And tears were streaming down his face. Here was a guy in the initial stages of middle age, a guy who each birthday would look in the bathroom mirror and notice that his hairline was farther back than it had been the year before. He was a successful financial planner, the career he had chosen only after realizing he would be unable to make his living on a baseball field.

He was not exactly sobbing, but a steady trickle was visible, including a long streak down his left cheek. Muscenti made no effort to hide the flow. He just sat there, looking straight ahead, blinking against the sun and the drops coming from his eyes.

Muscenti was thinking about his life. About how things used to be. A long time ago—20 years—he had sat in that precise location with his mother. She had taken him by the hand and led him through the massive concrete concourse to the 1963 All-Star Game, the childhood equivalent of nirvana.

Although Muscenti now owned season tickets in a far better location, he wanted to sit out in right field for the last game because that's where he had sat with his mom.

Muscenti's mom was no longer around. She had passed on. He could no longer thank her for taking him to the game. He could no longer thank her for his magical childhood.

At one time, many Octobers ago, this man was certain he would grow up to be a pro ballplayer. Every little boy thinks he's going to grow up to be a pro ballplayer. Or at least every little boy who grew up in the '50s, '60s, and '70s.

Whadya mean it's a lousy field? Any Northeast Ohio kid knew Cleveland Stadium was the perfect field. The only field. We loved Cleveland Stadium. We didn't have any other big-league field to compare it to. The only thing we could match it against was the weed-infested diamond with the rusty wire backstop at our local school or park.

We were awed by the gigantic oval made of steel and yellow brick.

When the Stadium came into view, with the big Chief Wahoo spin-ning around on the right-field roof and Lake Erie in the background, we felt as if we had arrived at a magical oasis.

The best part came after you pushed through the turnstile, walked up one of those concrete aisles, and emerged from the darkness into the bright light of day. You felt like Dorothy entering Oz. Suddenly, unfolding in front of you, were four acres of lush grass. Sliced metic-ulously into that expanse of green, like a gem in a setting, was the big brown diamond, which was not only the focal point of the action but also loaded with geometric intrigue—an oval pitcher's mound, rec-tangular coaches' boxes, and square bases placed within the gentle arc of the infield dirt. The white chalk foul lines—arrow straight—and the pristine batters' boxes were the finishing touches, the glitter radiating off the precious stone.

When football season kicked off near the end of the baseball sea-son, the expanse of green would be marred by yard lines, and the grass would get rough. But compared to the weed-infested fields most fans played on, the Cleveland Stadium turf still looked like a fairway.

The players who trotted around down on that turf were gods. Even when they were in sixth place. We loved the way they dressed, the way they moved, the way they pounded their gloves, the way they pawed the dirt with their cleats. We wanted to be them. We knew the name of the 25th player on the roster. Knew his hometown, too.

Their uniforms were perfect. Even the red-on-red ones of the mid-1970s—the ones that, as some wag once noted, made hefty Boog Powell look like "the world's biggest Bloody Mary."

You couldn't order a Bloody Mary at the ballpark, but the beer and pop flowed, and the odor of hot dogs, Stadium Mustard, and distant cigar smoke seemed to trigger some sort of Pavlovian response that made you never want to leave.

Even the scorecards were magical. The little black-and-white grids provided entree to an exciting world of secret codes, like BB and K and LOB and 6-4-3. Keeping score was a way to bundle up the game and take it home.

During most of the 20th century, there wasn't much separating Indians players and Indians fans. The only real difference was phys-ical: Sam McDowell could throw the ball 103 miles per hour; we couldn't. Rocky Colavito could hit a curveball 425 feet; we couldn't. But the players lived among us in middle-class neighborhoods and, in the off-season, worked other jobs.

Most of the time, if you were reasonably polite, they'd sign an autograph. Heck, at Cleveland Stadium, you could walk right along with them when they came out the clubhouse door and strolled to their cars in an unguarded parking lot. We'd take those autographs home and pin them up on the bulletin board.

Today, players are paid to sign autographs at card shows, where dealers buy them and turn around and sell them to people who haven't been within 50 feet of the player. This is progress?

For every negative at Cleveland Stadium, there was a positive. Sure, 70,000 of the seats often remained empty. But that meant you could roam around and sit almost anywhere you pleased. An inning in right field, another in left. Watch the pitchers in the bullpen.

You could even sneak down to the expensive seats if you knew how to do it: namely, wait a couple of innings to make sure the seats you had in mind were truly empty, then parade down there with an armload of food, acting like you were coming back from the concession stand. On the rare occasions when you were nailed, you could usually succeed if you simply tried again a couple of sections away.

Yes, the seating bowl was littered with 44 steel I-beams. When the crowds were large and you couldn't move to another seat, you'd be in for a long afternoon. On the other hand, if rain came, you didn't have to move to stay dry.

Even at the end of the Stadium's 65 years, most of the seats still had not been converted to molded plastic; they were the same unyielding wooden seats built for 1930s-size bodies. But when you wanted to encourage the Indians to rally, you could grab the front of those seats, bang them up and down, and make such an ungodly racket that the crowd seemed to multiply exponentially.

To get a sense of how the average fan felt about the old lady by the lake, you need only hear about the magical mystery tour taken by home plate after it was dug from the hallowed ground on that final day.

According to the party line, home plate was being taken directly to Gateway, where it would be used for one game before being shipped off to the Baseball Hall of Fame in Cooperstown, New York. Well, one out of three ain't bad. Home plate was indeed used for the first regular-season game at Jacobs Field on April 4, 1994. But the rest of the story doesn't hold Gatorade.

Tribe officials decided they didn't want to surrender such an important artifact to the Hall of Fame. The old plate instead went on display inside the Team Shop on the main concourse at Jacobs Field.

That's no secret to Tribe fans. But the route it took to get there might come as a surprise.

The two limos at the closing ceremony belonged to Paul Zehner of Uniontown, near Akron. He was the co-owner of now-defunct Pegasus Motorcoach. Nobody told him specifically what to do with home plate after it was laid in his trunk, so he decided to give it a ride.

First stop: a parking space near the Crazy Horse strip club on St. Clair Avenue in Cleveland. That's where the two limo drivers had arranged to rendezvous after one limo dropped off Bob Hope and his wife at the former Stouffer Tower City Plaza Hotel. The drivers and their helpers got out, popped the trunk, and stared in amazement. Then they showed some passersby, who were suitably awed.

From the Crazy Horse, home plate went to Akron's North Hill neighborhood, where Zehner, then 41, showed it to his cousin and half the neighborhood. Next stop was Springfield Township, where buddy Chris Madrin lived. Two additional stops were made in Green, to show the plate to another cousin and another buddy.

At each stop, the homeowner called neighbors and friends, who flocked to the slab of rubber as if it were a holy relic. They stared at it, touched it, posed for photos with it, laid it down in the yard and slid into it.

For the next several days, the plate was stashed at Zehner's house in Uniontown. The first night, as he was watching the late sports report on TV, the anchor talked about home plate being dug up and "taken to a safe place." Zehner thought, "Yeah. It's under my bed."

He seriously considered carving his initials on the bottom, but chickened out. He settled for breaking off a little chunk of clay and putting it in a baggy for display in his sports room.

Three days later, the precious platter was driven back to Cleveland and handed over to the team. (When informed later of its sojourn, team officials said, "No harm, no foul.") Zehner later declared the final game at Cleveland Stadium to be one of the highlights of his life.

Tribe fans knew exactly what he meant. So did many of the former players. Even the precious few of us who didn't have to fantasize about being down on the field were awed by the gigantic structure and its history.

Duane Kuiper's most memorable moment with the Indians did not come when he helped Len Barker achieve a perfect game. It did not come when he hit his only home run. The high point of Kuiper's

10-year career came when he merely duplicated an act performed by millions of ordinary fans: strolling into Cleveland Stadium for the first time.

He can still remember walking down West Third Street from his hotel on Public Square. He thought the stadium looked big from three-quarters of a mile away. With each step he took, he was thinking, "Man, I'm not only getting closer to the big leagues, but take a look at this stadium! This thing is huge!"

Kuiper was called up with several other rookies late in the 1974 season. As usual, the Tribe was out of contention and the games were virtually meaningless. But as far as Kuiper was concerned, Cleveland Municipal Stadium was the center of the universe.

"One thing about the people of Cleveland," Kuiper said. "When they came out, they made a ton of noise. We would have 15,000 people in there, and a lot of times it sounded like 40,000. When you jammed in 75,000, it sounded like 150,000."

Even during lean years, the Indians could usually count on a couple of crowds in the 70,000 range. Opening Day. The Fourth of July. A Sunday doubleheader against the Yankees. At times like those, the joint would rock. The surges of crowd noise would raise goose bumps.

What most fans didn't realize was that some of the stadium's worst seats were in the dugout. When you'd sit on the Indians' bench—the home team was along the first-base line in those days, not the third-base line as it is at Jacobs Field—you couldn't see below the knees of the outfielders because of the crown of the field. It was set up that way for water runoff.

Toward the end, players despised the field. As far back as the 1980s, it was voted worst infield in the league. But for its first half-century, the field was one of the best. That changed only after the legendary Bossard groundskeeping family was phased out and the field was dropped 18 inches to accommodate new box seats. Shaving down the field level reminded anyone who had forgotten that the Stadium was originally constructed on a landfill. The playing surface was never the same after it was lowered.

Things got progressively worse for spectators, too. By the end, swarms of summertime bugs and perpetually backed-up restrooms could make Cleveland Stadium a miserable place to be.

And so the last day came. The stadium's work was done. But the mood was bittersweet.

Yes, the place was built on a garbage dump, and the sightlines were atrocious, and, during its golden years, the playing field was a disaster and the plumbing was a joke. But the yellow-brick monster was ours—rotting fangs and all. A person simply couldn't live in Northeast Ohio for any length of time and not be touched by it. This was not just another building that had outlived its usefulness; this place had been a symbol—both personal and communal—of our hopes and dreams.

But the trouble with dreams is this: even if they come true, they don't last. Mel Harder was testimony to that.

Harder, like the tearful Muscenti, was at the final Indians game in '93. The former pitcher was among the ex-players who ran onto the field during the closing ceremony in period costume—Rick Manning in the bright-red top of the '70s . . . Max Alvis in the sleeveless jersey of the '60s . . . and onward back to Harder's baggy wool uniform with the big "C" on the front.

Many of the players had turned potbellied and gray. Some, like the 80-year-old Harder, had a difficult time even trotting onto the field.

In 1932, Harder had thrown the first pitch at the new stadium. Now, in a wonderful piece of symmetry, he was throwing the last pitch, a ceremonial final toss to a youngster who was waiting behind home plate.

Harder peered through his bifocals, wound up, and threw. But the ball landed short and bounced to the young catcher.

"I wanted to throw it 60 feet so bad," Harder said later. "But something happens to my arm about halfway through. It loses its power."

Age happened to your arm, Mel. Age happens to all of us. It happens to the Mel Harders, and it happens to the Tom Muscenties.

It even happened to Cleveland Stadium.

THE DASH IN THE DOME

TUESDAY, OCTOBER 17, 1995

The 1995 Cleveland Indians delivered one of the most impressive seasons in Cleveland sports history. The biggest moment in a season full of them was Kenny Lofton's dash home from second base on a passed ball in the final game of the ALCS in Seattle. His scamper put the Tribe into the World Series for the first time in four decades.

IT WAS A LIGHTNING BOLT, dazzling in its audacity, shocking in its element of surprise. And for Indians fans, it was the ultimate high in a seven-month festival of highs.

Oddly, the biggest single moment of the 1995 baseball season took place at a ballpark located as far away from Cleveland as you can possible get and still be in the major leagues.

The Seattle Kingdome stood 2,028 miles from Jacobs Field, on the banks of Puget Sound in the Great Northwest. But as the Tribe's renaissance approached a climax, the Kingdome may as well have been in Parma. Vicariously speaking, every Indians fan was right there.

More than 58 percent of the television sets in Northeast Ohio were tuned to Game Six of the American League Championship Series. That translated into 815,000 households. And those Nielsen numbers didn't take into account any of the people watching at a bar or a friend's house.

In many ways, Seattle was an odd place for the crowning moment of a beautiful Indian summer. The Kingdome was among the worst ballparks in the league, a 19-year-old hulk of concrete that seemed

three times older. When the facility was on the drawing board, building a dome sounded like a great idea, given Seattle's penchant for
rain. But by 1995, even Seattle's most loyal fans considered the place
an outmoded dump. A year earlier, four big ceiling tiles had fallen
into the stands just hours before a game.

Inside the dome, the dominant theme was concrete—plain, stark,
gray concrete. The most prominent color was the artificial green of
fake grass. The description of the playing surface in the Mariners'
media guide sounded like a newspaper ad for Carpet Barn: "120,000
square feet of Monsanto Astro Turf, half-inch thick above five-
eighths-inch foam pad." The players had a different description: rock
hard.

Imagine that. Clevelanders ripping another city for a bad ballpark.
How the world had changed.

But the atmosphere inside the dome was hotter than blazes, because the villagers viewed their M's as a team of destiny. In the summer of '95, the Mariners had picked up a rallying cry and gained an
identity when a fan stood up in the centerfield seats holding a big
sign that read, "REFUSE TO LOSE." During the intervening
months, seemingly every store and car window in Greater Seattle
had acquired a "Refuse to Lose" poster. It was also on T-shirts,
bumper stickers, and pennants. The phrase was even plastered on the
top of the Space Needle.

Seattle fans had come to believe they could simply will their team
to victory. The belief started when the M's beat the Angels in a one-
game playoff to gain admittance to the postseason. It was reinforced
in the opening series, when Seattle came roaring back from a two-
games-to-none deficit to beat the mighty Yankees in one of the most
dramatic series in playoff history. No true baseball fan will ever forget
Ken Griffey, Jr., scoring the game- and series-winning run from first
base on Edgar Martinez's double and being mobbed by teammates.

So, even though their heroes were trailing by one game in the
best-of-seven league championship series, Mariner fans had no intention of throwing in their scorecards.

The Indians were every bit as excited as the Seattle fans. After a
thrilling victory in Game Five Sunday night in Cleveland, they
needed only one win in two games to make it to the World Series.

But that wouldn't be easy. In Game Six, Seattle's nasty six-foot-ten
fireballer, Randy Johnson, in the prime of his career, would be on the
mound against the Indians' aging, sore-armed Dennis Martinez. And

if the series went to a seventh game, the Tribe's Charles Nagy—who had a horrible record in domes—would be the starter.

If ever there was a good day for baseball in a dome, it was October 17, 1995. Seattle lived down to its meteorological reputation all day long. But the relentless drizzle seemed to have no impact on the crowd of 58,489. The Indians got a preliminary indication of the kind of aural assault they could expect when several hundred fans cheered lustily as the Mariners concluded batting practice a full 90 minutes before the game.

NBC was airing the series with Bob Costas and Bob Uecker, and the network honchos were certainly getting their rights fees' worth. As Johnson—aka The Big Unit—prepared to throw his first pitch, the noise was deafening, so loud that the red plastic seats actually vibrated. The noise got even louder when Johnson struck out the first batter, Kenny Lofton. At that point, the din was measured at 109 decibels—the equivalent of standing next to a chain saw.

Soon, however, Lofton would be personally responsible for cutting the decibel level nearly to zero. In the fifth inning, he singled home Cleveland's first run. Three innings later, the score was still 1–0—and Lofton was about to sprint right into the hearts of all those long-suffering people back in Cleveland.

Top of the eighth. Tribe catcher Tony Pena leads off and launches a double. Every runner is critical now, so manager Mike Hargrove sends in Ruben Amaro to pinch-run for the slow-footed Pena.

Lofton lays down a bunt to try to sacrifice Amaro to third. But Johnson is so slow in fielding the ball that Lofton beats it out.

Runners on first and third. Omar Vizquel comes to the plate.

On the first pitch, a ball, Lofton steals second so easily that he doesn't even draw a throw.

Johnson's next pitch misses the mark too.

His third delivery, a high fastball, ticks off catcher Dan Wilson's glove and rolls to the wall near the Indians' dugout on the first-base line. Amaro scores easily from third to give Cleveland a 2–0 lead. But the play isn't over.

Lofton hits third base at full tilt. He is planning to bluff toward home to try to draw a bad throw. But when he sees Wilson casually jogging after the ball, he turns on his afterburners. The red No. 7 on the back of his blue jersey is nothing but a blur.

When Wilson turns around, he is shocked to see Lofton streaking toward the plate. So is everybody else in the ballpark—including Johnson, who is covering home only by rote. Wilson hurriedly fires to the plate . . . Lofton slides . . . safe!

Tribe 3, Mariners 0. For all practical purposes, the game is over.

That play typified the athleticism and nerve of the 1995 Cleveland Indians. More importantly, it bought the Indians a ticket to their first World Series in 41 years.

But 1995 didn't begin in Seattle, and it didn't end there.

You could say the 1995 season actually began in 1984, when Cuyahoga County voters nixed a plan for a publicly funded domed stadium to replace the aging horseshoe on the lake. Later that year, community leaders sat down to sketch out Plan B, which consisted of a non-domed, baseball-only stadium and a big, all-purpose arena.

Officials started buying land in December 1985 and four months later reached an agreement with the Cavaliers and Indians on the basic designs. In May 1990, voters gave their seal of approval, agreeing to a tax on alcohol and cigarettes to fund the complex, which in those days was known as Gateway.

Although emotions ran high about the impending demise of the Cavs' home at the Richfield Coliseum, almost no one questioned the need for a new baseball stadium. And as the ballpark began to take shape in early 1992, Tribe fans felt as if the franchise were emerging from the ultimate hibernation.

During every Northeast Ohio winter, there comes a numbing stretch during which you begin to believe the solar system has inexplicably become stuck in one alignment and that winter simply will never end. Ever. Then, finally, one day in late February or early March, you detect a small sign that things are changing. Maybe you're sitting in your living room one afternoon and notice that the angle of the sun has increased in relation to your neighbor's house. Or maybe you're driving home from work at the usual time and notice the sky is a tad lighter. That's what time it was for the Cleveland Indians. After 40 years of winter, the team was poised for a spring reawakening like no other. And the whole region sensed it.

The home team's Ice Age had lasted—quite literally—a lifetime. When Jacobs Field opened, 63 percent of the people living in Northeast Ohio were not even alive the last time the Indians reached postseason play, in 1954.

Now baseball was getting a fresh start, with a 42,000-seat facility that was big enough to be exciting, yet small enough to be intimate; a park that was old-fashioned, but brand new; a park that was just a little bit quirky, with a 19-foot wall in left field, 8-foot walls in center and right, and vertical light standards that looked like big toothbrushes.

Opening Day at Jacobs Field—April 4, 1994—was as beautiful as the new ballpark, which by now had been named Jacobs Field by team owner Dick Jacobs to honor his family. He paid $13.9 million over 20 years for the right. The weather was sunny and felt far warmer than the 48-degree game-time temperature.

The gates swung in at 10:45 a.m. to the strains of Emerson, Lake & Palmer tinkling from the spunky new P.A. system: "Welcome back my friends/to the show that never ends/we're so glad you could attend/come inside, come inside."

Management pulled out all the stops. The pregame festivities began with an exhibition of baseball as it was played in the 1860s— with the umpires in top hats and tails, the players wearing frilly shirts and dress pants, and no gloves.

As game time approached, four framed uniforms were handed to the four players whose numbers had been retired (or their representatives)—Earl Averill (3), Lou Boudreau (5), Mel Harder (18), and Bob Feller (19).

Members of the Cleveland Orchestra and Chorus presented a gorgeous rendition of the national anthem. Ten huge baseball-shaped balloons floated on tethers 60 to 80 feet in the air. Higher still was the Goodyear blimp, circling above everything with its television camera.

Before the game, a woman with breasts the size of North Olmsted dashed onto the field and kissed Albert Belle. She received a cheer. By contrast, President Bill Clinton received a decidedly mixed reception as he took the field to throw out the first pitch.

Clinton's visit marked the first time a sitting president had ever attended an Indians game. As the Beatles' tune "Twist and Shout" blared from the sound system, he jogged from the Tribe's dugout to the mound. The big lefty stretched his arms above his head and lobbed a strike to catcher Sandy Alomar, who caught it without moving an inch.

Providing equal time for the Republicans, Governor George

Voinovich, having made his entrance in the rumble seat of a restored 1936 Chevy, tossed a second ceremonial pitch. He, too, was on target.

Ironically, the third tosser, Hall of Fame pitcher Feller, was the only one to mess up his throw. He bounced it in the dirt. Of course, he was working with a major age disadvantage.

Seattle's starting pitcher had no such problem. The dreaded Randy Johnson was in his prime, and ready to rock.

As the Indians ran onto the thick, emerald Kentucky bluegrass wearing spotless white uniforms with red script lettering on the chest and bright-red shoes, hundreds of red, white, and blue balloons were released into the blue sky.

The scene was glorious—and, somehow, just a wee bit unsettling. It simply didn't feel like Cleveland. The 41,459 fans applauded frequently, but for most of the day there was no sign of a fan frenzy. Folks seemed almost speechless. After all those years of attending games at crumbling Cleveland Stadium, they just sat there, looking around in amazement, not quite believing what they were seeing.

Things got even odder when the game began. After only one inning, yet another ceremony broke out: the Tribe's Eddie Murray—who had been an Indian for exactly one inning—was handed a trophy for playing more games at first base (2,369) than any other person in major league history, including the immortal Lou Gehrig. The first-base bag, one inning old, was pulled out of the ground and given to Murray as another souvenir.

Seattle's pitcher was blazing some trails of his own. Through seven innings, the Big Unit had a no-hitter. Fans were beginning to wonder whether Cleveland baseball had, in fact, changed at all.

But five outs away from a no-no, Sandy Alomar singled through the right side of the infield to break the spell. He scored on a clutch double by an unknown rookie named Manny Ramirez. That tied the game at two and gave a tiring Johnson a chance to test the new showers.

Things didn't get any easier after Johnson left. In the top of the 10th, Ken Griffey, Jr., scored to give the Mariners a 3–2 lead. Again the crowd sensed defeat. But in the bottom of the inning, the Tribe came right back and tied it on a ringing double by Jim Thome. One inning later, Murray doubled, moved to third after a fly ball, and scored on a single by Wayne Kirby, who had come on earlier as a pinch-runner.

The Tribe won, 4–3. And for the first time in a long, long time,

Indians fans went home thrilled about their ballpark and equally thrilled about their team's immediate future.

Nobody loved the new park more than the players who had been in the organization for a long time. Said pitcher Charles Nagy: "If I could get a bed here, I would." Manager Mike Hargrove, a tough Texan who had been in the major leagues 15 years as a player or manager, was moved to tears the first time he saw it. Six days before the opener, as he and his wife, Sharon, looked into the park from behind left field, he choked up thinking about how far the franchise had come since his arrival in 1979.

In late June, the team began to jell. It started closing the gap on the division-leading Chicago White Sox, and, after beating Toronto on August 10—its sixth win in nine games—the Tribe was only one game out of first and actually leading in the wild-card race. But that would be the last game of 1994.

A players' strike wiped out the rest of the season, the playoffs, and the World Series. The strike carried over into the following season and sacked the first 18 games of 1995.

Talk about bad timing. When the strike came, the Tribe was leading the league in runs, hits, doubles, homers, and slugging percentage, and owned the best home record in all of baseball, 35–16. The .290 team batting average was the highest for a Tribe team since 1936. But even with the interruption of play, most fans were ecstatic—they had gotten a glimpse of their baseball future, and it was glorious.

The astonishment continued when, the following April, veteran pitcher Orel Hershiser came aboard. Hot free agents like Hershiser simply didn't settle for less money to play in Cleveland. But he did, because he loved the team and the ballpark.

Orel Hershiser had been to the mountaintop. In 1988, he won 23 games for the Dodgers, the most since the immortal Sandy Koufax, and took home the Cy Young Award in a rare unanimous vote. He pitched a complete-game victory in the deciding match-up of the National League Championship Series, a complete-game victory in the deciding match-up of the World Series, and was named MVP in both. He was absolutely dominant that year, at one point putting together a record 59 consecutive scoreless innings.

The only question mark was his health. Orel had major shoulder surgery in 1990 and battled back gamely, but he hadn't had a winning season since the injury. Plus, he was 36 years old.

In his first 12 starts with the Tribe, he was pummeled. The tall, thin righty had a 6.64 ERA, and opposing batters were hitting .341 off him—good enough to win a batting title. But he kept fighting, and, eventually, things began to click. In July, after missing several starts with a back injury, Hershiser started humming and just didn't stop. He finished the regular season with 16 victories. Even when he didn't win, he kept the team close: during his last 31 starts, the team went 22–9.

Of course, the lingering strike would delay that kind of gratification. Game after game was wiped out while the players and owners haggled.

Finally, on April 27 in Texas, the new Tribe returned to the field. Their Opening Day lineup looked like this:

Kenny Lofton, CF
Omar Vizquel, SS
Carlos Baerga, 2B
Albert Belle, LF
Eddie Murray, DH
Jim Thome, 3B
Manny Ramirez, RF
Paul Sorrento, 1B
Tony Pena, C
Dennis Martinez, P

That lineup was largely unknown outside of Northeast Ohio. But it wouldn't be long before it started gaining more national attention than any Indians lineup in decades.

By Memorial Day, the Tribe was leading the Central Division by five games. By the Fourth of July, the team was up by 11 games. By Labor Day, it was 21 games ahead. And by the last day of the season, it was an incredible, unimaginable, record-breaking 30 games ahead. That mark went all the way back to the 27½-game lead of the Pittsburgh Pirates of 1902—before the advent of flight.

Fans knew the '95 Tribe would be tough, but nobody imagined it would be *that* tough. The season was a dream. Whenever the Indians needed a key hit, they got one. Whenever they needed a key strikeout, they got one. They could make a series of dumb, fundamentally sloppy plays, then roar right back the next inning and score three or four runs to erase their mess.

The team won 27 games in its last at-bat and came from behind 48 times. Eight players hit over .300. The Tribe led the league in runs, batting average, steals, homers, ERA, and just about every other offensive and defensive category imaginable.

Almost from the start, the '95 Indians were worshipped in Cleveland, and people around the country started hopping on the bandwagon. After all, it was the classic worst-to-first story. For nearly half a century, the Indians had been the American League's version of the Chicago Cubs, the pitiful, lovable losers who couldn't win a pennant even if the Baseball Fairy gave them a five-game lead with six games to play. A full-length feature film comedy had been made about the lowly Indians only six years earlier, *Major League*, the story of a last-place team whose owner wants them to lose so she can sell the franchise. She hires a has-been manager who assembles a gang of misfits who somehow come together and make a run at the pennant. The film was so popular nationally that it spawned a sequel, *Major League II*, released in 1994.

Now, as baseball's onetime comedians marched toward a record-setting season, beating the other teams to death and setting up gargantuan expectations for the playoffs, they developed quite a following. But they also started to pick up a legion of detractors.

In fact, the farther the season progressed, the worse their press clippings became. By the end of the year, the Cleveland Indians were, in many quarters, considered the Bad Boys of Baseball. Albert Belle was consistently surly to the public and the press. Eddie Murray didn't want to be quoted, and his attitude seemed to reinforce a standoffishness in some of the younger players, including Lofton. But to most fans, that was trivia.

For every Albert Belle, smashing other people's belongings with his bat, there was an Omar Vizquel, a Wayne Kirby, a Dennis Martinez. For every Eddie Murray, lips sealed near reporters, there was Hershiser, whose gift of gab rivaled the wonderful gift attached to his right shoulder.

Besides, most of the 1995 players looked like they were having fun. One guy would stick a big, blown-up wad of bubblegum on the top of another guy's cap when he wasn't looking. Sometimes it would stay there for a long time. TV cameras would pan the dugout and catch the victim, oblivious to the wad.

On the field, one of the keys to the season was the emergence of Jose Mesa as a top-flight relief pitcher. Mesa was a starter before coming to Cleveland from Baltimore. Even after he got to the Tribe in 1992, he was used in a starting role. As late as 1993, Mesa started 33 games. But in '94 he was converted to a reliever, and in '95 he really got the hang of it.

The starting pitching was spectacular as well. The two senior citizens, Hershiser and Martinez—a combined 77 years old—rang up a combined record of 28–11.

And, of course, 1995 marked the breakout year for Belle. Every time he came to the plate, it was an event. After a while, you began to think only one of two things was going to happen: He'd hit a double or a home run. Belle did each of those 50 times during the season, the only person to accomplish that feat in a century of baseball.

The team's firepower and ability to come back were consistently astounding. In early May, the Indians scored eight runs before Kansas City could record a single out. In early June, trailing 8–0 in third inning against Toronto, they came back to win 9–8 on a ninth-inning, two-out, two-run homer by Paul Sorrento. In early August, they hit six homers in one game against their big divisional rival, the White Sox—two by Albert and one each by Murray, Sorrento, Lofton, and Baerga.

The only question was how soon the team would clinch a division title. The big moment came September 8 at home against Baltimore, after only 123 games. The drama came down to the final out in the ninth inning, with Cleveland clinging to a 3–2 lead and Mesa on the mound. Jeff Huson hit a foul popup, which third baseman Jim Thome snared easily. The crowd went ballistic.

Cleveland had its first baseball championship of any kind since 1954.

Strangers in the stands hugged each other. Drivers honked their horns throughout the city. Television stations ran bulletins, and newspapers began to assemble special editions.

The whole team ran to the center of the diamond to celebrate, then went into the locker room and donned white T-shirts reading "Central Division Champions." After about five minutes inside, they came back onto the field to share the celebration with the fans. Mark Clark, Alvaro Espinoza, Julian Tavarez, and Ramirez paraded the pennant out toward the flagpole atop the scoreboard in left-center, followed by all the others. When the flag was hooked to the clips, Murray pulled it to the top.

Clinching the division title with several weeks left in the season gave the Indians time to rest and mentally prepare for the postseason. Some observers wondered if clinching that early was bad, because the Tribe would be coasting along while other playoffs teams would be growing accustomed to playing under pressure. But the players didn't care, and they certainly didn't let up. In fact, they picked up another seven games on second-place Kansas City and finished with a record of 100–44. That's almost seven wins in every 10 games.

Northeast Ohio was on fire as the playoffs approached. Unfortunately, the atmosphere in Cleveland was in stark contrast to that in most of the rest of the baseball world. Nationally, attendance and TV ratings were way down because of fan resentment over the strike. But on the eve of the first-round series against Boston, every newscast and every conversation in Greater Cleveland seemed to center on the Tribe.

The day of the Indians' first playoff game in 41 years, the skies over Cleveland erupted in thunder and driving rain, which pummeled the city for eight hours. The only thing stirring on the field was the grounds crew messing with the tarp.

Finally, the weather broke, the tarp was removed, and the game began, 39 minutes late. Ace Roger Clemens started for Boston against Dennis Martinez. The Red Sox jumped to a 2–0 lead . . . the Tribe came back with three runs in sixth . . . and the Sox scored again to tie it. Then the skies opened up again, forcing another, 23-minute delay.

The tie lasted until the top of the 11th, when Boston scored what appeared to be a crushing blow on Tim Naehring's homer. But the Indians weren't finished. Albert came up in the bottom of the 11th and jacked a homer to tie the game yet again.

The contest went on and on. Finally, in the 13th inning—five hours after the start—backup catcher Tony Pena was at the plate with two outs. With the count 3–0, he got the "take" sign from the third-base coach. But he either missed the sign or disregarded it, because he swung and lifted a game-winning homer into the bleachers.

The clock read 2:08 a.m. And the magic was still alive.

The next night was a more traditional affair. The game lasted nine innings and was over in 90 minutes. The Indians won 4–0 behind Hershiser, and then headed off to Boston.

At Fenway Park, they got right down to business, despite facing knuckleballer Tim Wakefield, who usually gave the Indians fits.

They erupted in the second inning when Jim Thome blasted a moon-high, two-run homer into the right-field stands. The Tribe put the game away in the sixth, scoring five more runs and chasing many of the 34,211 customers toward the exits. Final score: 8–2. The Tribe's first playoff sweep in 95 years.

Next came Seattle.

The Kingdome crowd didn't have much to hoot about at the beginning of Game One. Cleveland was throwing its ace, Martinez, and poor Seattle—burned out by the Yankee series—was trotting out an unknown rookie named Bob Walcott. The first thing Walcott did was walk the bases loaded. But then he got Belle, Murray, and Thome without giving up a single run. Against all odds, Walcott went seven innings. The M's won, 3–2, wasting six solid innings by Martinez.

Cleveland returned to form in the second game. Ramirez hit two homers and got two other hits to lead a 5–2 win. Hershiser earned his second straight playoff win as an Indian—and his seventh straight dating back to his Dodger days.

In Game Three, back in Cleveland, Seattle right-fielder Jay Buhner looked like a hero when he hit an early homer. Then he looked like a bum when he dropped an easy fly ball in the eighth, allowing Cleveland to tie the game. But in the top of the 11th, he flip-flopped again, hitting a three-run homer to give the bad guys a 5–2 win.

Game Four, obviously, was crucial. And the Tribe had to play it without Belle and Alomar, both of whom were hurt. Albert showed up on crutches. He had turned his ankle the night before while trying to get out of the way of an inside pitch. He finished the game, but the ankle swelled overnight.

The game-time temperature was in the 40s—as Vizquel noted, not exactly ideal for a team with a lot of Latin players. But the Tribe jumped on starter Andy Benes. Murray ripped a three-run homer in the first inning, and the Indians went on to wipe out the M's, 7–0, and tie the series.

The only downer was the temporary demise of Slider, the big, fuzzy, purple mascot. He fell off the right-field wall late in the game and badly injured his knee. He returned the next night, on crutches, his right leg tightly wrapped, looking absolutely ridiculous. But then, so did the Indians. They played like Little Leaguers, committing four errors.

But they didn't give up, made big plays when they had to, and

Thome came through with a sixth-inning homer to lead a 3–2 win. That set the stage for the Dash in the Dome, which led, of course, to the ultimate party, the World Series.

During the postseason, even the players turn into fans. They stay up late watching other games in different time zones, partly to scout the competition but mostly just to see how things turn out. With each round of the playoffs, everything grows bigger. The media coverage. The pageantry. The fame. The money. The pressure. By the time you get all the way to the World Series, the game begins to transcend sports. Suddenly, even people who can't tell a splitter from a spittoon are riveted to their television sets.

Baseball has become such an international attraction that media from all over the world cram into the clubhouses and interview rooms. In Atlanta in 1995, two television networks and more than 400 reporters from as far away as Japan chronicled every move the Indians made.

The World Series was the third straight playoff match-up in which the Tribe suffered the home-field disadvantage. That was simply the bad luck of the draw. In those days, all the match-ups were prearranged, regardless of who had the better record. And 1995 was the National League's turn to start hosting the World Series, meaning the first two games of the seven-game war would be in Atlanta—enough to set the tone.

The Braves' ballpark, Atlanta-Fulton County Stadium (since torn down in favor of a new park next door) was nothing special. It wasn't a bad stadium; it just wasn't particularly distinctive. And the Braves' fans seemed jaded. Their team had been in the two previous Series, losing both, and when they weren't doing the moronic "Tomahawk Chop," they were mostly sitting on their hands.

The first game was a nail-biter—as would be typical for the entire series. Atlanta's ace, Greg Maddux, was virtually unhittable, giving up a grand total of two singles. Still, the Indians were able to score two runs because of Atlanta errors and more great base-running by Lofton. Hershiser pitched six marvelous innings, giving up only one run. But Atlanta manufactured two runs in the seventh off three walks and a squeeze bunt, and won 3–2.

In Game Two, Atlanta was ahead, 4–3, in the eighth inning, thanks mainly to a two-run homer by catcher Javey Lopez off Martinez, who had struggled. Manny Ramirez singled to center, putting the tying run on first. But then he wandered too far from the bag and was picked off on a snap throw from Lopez. The Braves hung on to win behind Tom Glavine, and the Tribe headed home trailing two games to none.

In spite of that deficit, the city was exploding with enthusiasm. Game Three, played on Tuesday, October 24, marked the first World Series game in Cleveland in 41 years.

Everybody wanted to be part of it. Five hours before the game, hundreds of fans were walking around the outside of the park, without tickets, just to look inside the gates at the empty field, just so they could say they were there. Some took pictures; most simply stared. As game time neared, fans honked their horns on the way into the parking decks. Nobody seemed especially bothered by the wind-chill factor of 29 degrees.

During pregame introductions, 43,584 patrons stood screaming the entire time—even cheering lustily for trainer Jimmy Warfield. When a 73-year-old fan named Sam Danze attempted to throw a strike into a net and win $1 million in a promotional gimmick, they chanted, "Sammy, Sammy, Sammy . . . " And when Akron's Chrissie Hynde, internationally known as the lead singer of the Pretenders, sashayed onto the field to sing the national anthem, they roared.

As if anyone could possibly forget the identity of the event, the players were wearing a specially designed blue-and-gold World Series logo just below their right shoulders.

Al Michaels, Jim Palmer, and Tim McCarver were in front of the ABC microphones, raving about the city, the ballpark, and the team.

The pregame noise was subtle compared to the sound that erupted when Albert Belle ripped a single to give the Tribe a 4–1 lead in the third inning.

A couple of hours later, the noise grew even louder. Atlanta had staged a rally and tied the game. Lose this one and the ugly memory of the 1954 sweep would be looming large. But in the bottom of the 11th, Eddie Murray came through with a single, scoring Carlos Baerga, to give the Indians a dramatic 7–6 win.

It was the first World Series victory for a Cleveland team since 1948.

Unfortunately, much of the media was being converted to the opinion that the Cleveland Indians were a royal pain in the butt. Immediately before Game Three, Belle erupted in his infamous tirade against NBC reporter Hannah Storm, who was sitting in the Indians dugout, waiting to interview Lofton. Although Storm didn't file a formal complaint and the incident wasn't much more than a minor distraction to the players, it pushed plenty more people onto the anti-Cleveland bandwagon.

Sports Illustrated called the Tribe "not the kind of team you'd want to take home to mom. Hanging in their clubhouse is a framed and matted essay called *The Art of Getting Along* by Wilfred Peterson. Now, if they would only read it."

So when the Indians lost Game Four, 5–2, press row wasn't exactly suicidal. It was the only game in the entire series decided by more than one run. More important, it left the Indians only one game away from a long winter vacation.

The situation certainly wasn't hopeless. Six teams had been down 3–1 in a World Series and ended up wearing championship rings. In 1985, Kansas City rallied to beat St. Louis. In 1979, the Pirates did the same against the Orioles.

Still, to survive the next game, the Tribe would have to get past the amazing Maddux, who usually mowed down Indians like paper targets.

In the bottom of the first, Albert lit up Maddux for an opposite-field, two-run homer. Cleveland got two more runs off him before Thome knocked him out in the eighth with a homer.

Hershiser was superb again, going eight tough innings, and the Tribe hung on to win, 5–4, sending everybody back to Atlanta.

Meanwhile, the Braves were dealing with a small media problem of their own. Midway through the Series, one of their players, David Justice, ripped the Atlanta fans for being so laid back. He said the Cleveland fans were louder and that the Braves fans were spoiled from seeing three World Series in five years.

He backpedaled a bit before Game Six, telling reporters that, although he didn't deny making the comments, he didn't mean them to be a strong as they were.

The first two times he came up to hit, he was booed. But it's amazing how quickly people forget. In the sixth inning, he led off with a homer against reliever Jim Poole—a stroke that would become the lone run in the deciding game—and the cheers were thunderous.

Cleveland's offense went with barely a whimper: one hit, a bloop single. Even though shortstop Omar Vizquel turned in the defensive play of the series—a flip from his glove to Baerga's hand to Murray's mitt—a team just can't win a game without scoring any runs.

Suddenly, the miraculous season of 1995 was over. Although the loss stung, given the fans' high expectations, their pain passed relatively quickly. Just getting to the World Series was enough for most folks. That spirit came through two days later during a big rally at Public Square in downtown Cleveland.

Although the weather was cold and drizzly, an estimated 40,000 people turned out to cheer—probably 30,000 of them skipping school or work. One police official said it was the biggest crowd for a downtown event he had seen since joining the force in 1969.

Confetti and streamers fell to the ground as balloons soared into the sky. High school marching bands paraded ahead of the team bus as it crept west from Euclid Avenue and East 22nd Street to the square. Bells on the landmark Old Stone Church played "Take Me Out to the Ballgame." Governor George Voinovich, Mayor Mike White, team owner Dick Jacobs, and a bunch of other dignitaries were on hand.

White took delight in reciting the Justice quote about Cleveland fans being more enthusiastic than Atlanta fans. "He was right," said the mayor. "But, David . . . we've got the best team, too."

Manager Mike Hargrove thanked the crowd and praised the fans who showed up at the airport in the wee hours of Sunday morning to welcome the team back the night of the loss. "I have never been so excited in my entire life to see you people at the airport for us," he said.

That airport scene really was amazing. At 2:40 a.m., in a cold rain, people were standing five deep along a 550-foot fence at the I-X Jet Center. Authorities estimated the crowd at 6,000. Over and over the fans chanted, "Thank you, Tribe. Thank you, Tribe." Instead of getting right off the plane and onto the buses as usual, the players went over to chat and touch hands through the fence.

Now, at the noontime rally two days later, about 20 players were on hand, including all of the regulars except Belle and Ramirez. They sat on a grandstand in the heart of the city and took turns in front of the microphone.

The biggest surprise was the lighthearted banter of shortstop Vizquel. Although he had been talkative to the media all year, this was the first time his personality really came through to the public.

When two parachutists dropped into the square to deliver an

American flag and an Indians flag, Vizquel said: "We're still waiting for Julian Tavarez and Manny Ramirez. They were supposed to jump from the airplane. They're probably in Lake Erie somewhere."

He told some anecdotes about the "glory" of playing in a World Series, including this one: "I was in a store in Atlanta buying a shirt. A sales lady asked me if I was a ballplayer. I said that I was. She said, 'Oh, I love how you play!' I thanked her and bought the shirt. On the way out, I heard another sales lady say, 'Who was that man you were talking to?' The first lady said, 'Oh, that's Mark Lemke, the second baseman for the Braves.'"

The crowd ate it up. Vizquel was having so much fun that Hargrove started to make slashing motions across the throat, urging Vizquel to cut off his monologue. Finally, Wayne Kirby, who was carrying an umbrella with a curved handle, grabbed him by the neck and started to pull him away from the microphone, just like the guys with "the hook" during the old vaudeville days.

The Indians had certainly hooked their fans. During the next six years, the team would set an all-time major league record for consecutive sell-outs: 455.

That may well be the most amazing baseball statistic of all time.

THE MOVE

MONDAY, NOVEMBER 6, 1995

The Cleveland Browns were one of the most successful franchises in football history. Even during bad years, fans flocked to the horseshoe on the lakefront to cheer the guys in orange helmets. But after a quarter-century of unwavering fan support, owner Art Modell shocked the city and the nation by moving the Browns to Baltimore.

THE DEMISE OF THE ORIGINAL Cleveland Browns may have begun in earnest on an otherwise nondescript weekday afternoon in Berea.

The year: 1993. The setting: a practice field at the team's $14 million training complex.

Coach Bill Belichick, frustrated by the Browns' offensive performance in the "red zone" the previous Sunday, had devoted the entire week to working on plays inside the enemy's 20-yard line. Play after play, day after day, the offensive unit was drilled on ways to punch the ball the last few yards into the end zone.

Belichick gathered around his offensive troops and said he expected much better results in the upcoming game. "Any questions?" Belichick asked, almost rhetorically.

"Yeah," replied veteran quarterback Bernie Kosar. "How do we get here?"

Not long after that exchange, the phrase "diminishing skills" would come into the local lexicon.

Belichick was supposed to be the smart-ass, not his players. To question the coach's practice philosophy in front of the entire offense was the ultimate insult, and Belichick was not about to put up with it. Even if it had some validity.

Kosar and Belichick were already at war. In the second game of the season, in a *Monday Night Football* home game against San Francisco, the Browns had upset the 49ers thanks in large measure to a 30-yard touchdown pass from Kosar to wide receiver Michael Jackson. It capped a long drive with the clock running down on the first half, and gave the Browns a seven-point halftime lead. But when Kosar arrived at the bench after the pass, he and Belichick got into a screaming match. The problem: Kosar had changed the play. Bad Bernie. Never mind that his improvisation had created a crucial TD.

Kosar's crack on the practice field pushed Belichick over the brink. He put together a "lowlight" reel of Kosar's worst plays, screened it for owner Art Modell, and eventually convinced Modell that the Browns would be better off without their native son, a player Modell once compared to his own son.

When Modell bought Belichick's argument, the team was 5–3 and in first place. They would finish the season 7–9.

After cutting one of the most popular players in Cleveland history, the Browns tried to sell Northeast Ohio on the notion that Todd Philcox was more qualified to lead the offense than Kosar. But the fans weren't nearly as gullible as the owner.

History will show that Belichick—even more than issues involving luxury boxes or big-city politics or foolish player contracts—was the catalyst for the departure of the original Cleveland Browns.

Never in a half-century of football had the fans encountered a more surly, smug, abrasive coach than Bill Belichick. Although he had never been a head coach before, he rode into town acting as if he owned the combined record of Vince Lombardi and Tom Landry. His social skills were on the order of Idi Amin's.

Belichick didn't merely blow off reporters. He blew off the fans as well. An innocent "Hi, Coach" in a hotel lobby would more often than not be returned with a wordless sneer.

The players became a reflection of their coach. On October 7, 1995, former center Mike Baab, speaking with Mike Snyder on radio station WWWE (1100 AM), bemoaned the change he had witnessed in the character of the team. Baab said the modern Browns were showing "disdain" toward the fans.

When Baab first joined the Browns, he said, teammate Doug

Dieken approached him and the other newcomers and ordered them to do charity work. For example, Baab continued, the entire team would show up every year for a Christmas party at Rainbow Babies and Children's Hospital. "You know how many players were there last year?" he asked. "Three."

The players' detachment from the community was not lost on the public. And it certainly didn't go unnoticed by the media. In early December of 1994, with the Browns in first place but attendance sluggish—at least by Cleveland standards—I attempted to explain the discrepancy in a column in the *Akron Beacon Journal*:

> Northeast Ohio sports fans are bright enough to with-hold their affection for a coach who shows outright con-tempt for them and for their liaisons in the media. The team has been molded by Belichick in his own image. You can't root for the team without rooting for him.
>
> I don't blame the fans for refusing to lend their hearts to the worst group of trash-talking thugs this side of Lu-casville. . . .
>
> Granted, pro football is a tough game, a weekly war. And it attracts tough people. But the average fan was more than willing to fall in love with stand-up guys such as Mike Johnson, Clay Matthews, Bob Golic, Ozzie Newsome, and Al "Bubba" Baker. They played hard but clean. And off the field they were funny, talkative, multi-dimensional human beings.
>
> Maybe this isn't entirely the players' fault. Maybe we're not seeing their real personalities because Belichick has made clear he doesn't take kindly to candor. But at this point, the 1994 Cleveland Browns are not the kind of folks we're going to stay up nights worrying about.
>
> I'm proud of Northeast Ohio's sports fans [who have] re-fused to make a major personal or financial investment in a team [they] simply don't like.

To be sure, a sports team does not need a transcendent personal-ity—a Brian Sipe, a Rocky Colavito, an Omar Vizquel—to sell tick-ets. But a team simply can't sustain a relationship if its most promi-nent figure is an obnoxious ass.

For longtime Browns watchers, the situation was even more

shocking because owner Art Modell was letting Belichick get away with it.

A former New York City advertising and TV-production executive, Modell knew full well how important the goodwill of the public could be. Since arriving in Cleveland three decades earlier, Modell and his wife, Pat, generally had enjoyed a good reputation. They were active in charity work. He was open and quotable. In later years he poured plenty of his own money into trying to fix the ancient stadium.

If there was a major knock against Art Modell, it was that he was too hands-on. He would second-guess good coaches and scouts and sometimes pull rank on them to the detriment of the overall program. Football experts wished he would take one step back and let the head football guy run the football side. Now, after 30 years, Modell finally seemed to have latched on to that concept.

Right idea, wrong guy.

Almost from Day One, Belichick seemed to go out of his way to alienate people—including the players. In his dealings with underlings, Belichick made Paul Brown look absolutely warm and fuzzy. Almost every player ripped Belichick on the way out of the revolving door.

Even winning wasn't enough to negate the bad vibes. In 1994, the Browns reached the postseason for first time in five years, and then won a first-round playoff game. But well into that season, while sporting a 9–3 record, the front office found itself with 10,000 unsold tickets the day before a key home game. That was unheard of—as was the steady decline in the rental of loges.

In the late 1970s, a waiting list for loges contained 180 names. Loge sales dropped 40 percent after the Indians left for Gateway—at least partly because Modell was offering a very modest decrease in price despite the loss of 82 events. But now, coming off a 12–6 year (including playoffs), eight more companies declined to renew. When 1995 kicked off, 24 of the 102 loges remained unsold.

From 1991 on, overall attendance had dropped each year. Apparently failing completely to detect the mood of the public, in 1995 the team jacked up its $37 tickets to $55. Now *there's* a great way to win back the masses.

Still, for all the abuse hurled Modell's way, he certainly had some legitimate beefs.

The Indians were virtually handed a new, $169 million baseball-only palace. The Cavs were handed their own $150 million gem. And Art, the big cheese in town for three decades, was still saddled with Cleveland Stadium, into which he had sunk $28 million by the time the Indians started talking about moving in 1989.

The city of Cleveland was doing nothing to compensate him for taking away his major tenant. And the city had stolen virtually all of his main parking area, the 3,000-car lot to the east, which had been gobbled up by the Great Lakes Science Center and the Rock and Roll Hall of Fame. The western lot was soon to be raided as well, for warehouses. Compared to the Indians and Cavs, Modell also was getting hosed on property taxes.

When Modell said he might be forced to move, he was branded an extortionist. When he stopped making public threats, declaring a "moratorium" on public discussion and instead dealing directly with Mayor Mike White's administration, he was ripped for not letting the public know how bad things had become.

But one cold fact remained: a huge tax hike was the only real solution.

Fans who are alienated don't vote for tax increases for new stadiums. And the fans detested Belichick.

Money simply wasn't available. The city was facing a large deficit, the county was broke because of an investment scandal, and Governor George Voinovich wasn't exactly knocking himself out to rustle up state funding for Modell. Moreover, the Gateway project had rocketed into debt and had to be propped up with $28 million more in public money. Everybody was tapped out—including Modell. *Especially* Modell.

Figures made public because of a lawsuit showed that the Browns lost money every year but one from 1982 to 1989. During all of the 1980s, they dropped a total of $12 million—at the same time the Cincinnati Bengals were netting $38 million.

In a book about the move to Baltimore, Modell's longtime controller, Michael Poplar, wrote that by 1995 Modell owed the banks $60 million.

How do you lose that kind of money when 71,000 fans show up no matter how bad the team is? Well, offering ridiculous contracts to the wrong free agents certainly helps.

Modell's worst all-time signing came at the worst possible time. The addition of cantankerous underachiever Andre Rison not only cost the team even more popularity, but put a huge dent in Modell's pocketbook when he coughed up an absurd $5 million signing bonus. Among the new wide receiver's more memorable quotes: "[Bleep] the fans." Rison was cut after one year. Nice investment.

Sports Illustrated, a non-provincial judge if ever there was one, wrote: "Modell's own misguided business decisions are largely responsible for the mountain of debt he now faces." The magazine focused on his 1973 acquisition of the stadium itself and a shady land deal that came back to bite him. (Minority owner Robert Gries won a lengthy lawsuit accusing Modell of inflating the price of a piece of property in Strongsville that Modell had bought as a possible site for a new stadium, then later sold to the debt-ridden Stadium Corporation, which he then tried to fold into the Browns.)

The move to Baltimore was not exactly the best-kept secret in town. As early as April 1995, people in the Browns' front office believed a move was inevitable. Almost as soon as the lease was signed on October 27, 1995—on buddy Al Lerner's private jet in a darkened corner of Baltimore-Washington Airport—word began to leak out.

Things really heated up the first weekend in November, when, during an early-morning radio interview with Mike Snyder, Modell conceded that he was leaving. Even then, plenty of people thought he might be bluffing.

Two days later, at noon on a Monday, Northeast Ohio went into a state of shock. The official, unqualified, no-turning-back announcement was made at a Maryland news conference: after 50 seasons in Cleveland, the Browns were moving to Baltimore.

On that sunny Monday, virtually every TV and radio in Northeast Ohio was tuned to a live news conference originating from the parking lot in front of Camden Yards. The dais was arranged so that cameras would show, in the background, the exact spot where the city would build a $200 million, football-only stadium within three years. Meanwhile, the Baltimore Browns, as they were being called, would play at renovated Memorial Stadium.

Modell is sitting on the dais, looking vaguely uncomfortable, perhaps even embarrassed. Another of the speakers has no such qualms. Maryland Governor Parris Glendening is downright giddy. He jokes about secret knocks and passwords. "I'm sure all of us involved will never forget the early-morning calls, the late-evening calls, and the weekend visits. It was fun, no question about it." The longer Glendening talks, the more he sounds like a little kid who has figured out

---

a way to steal another little kid's most prized baseball card—and not feel one whiff of guilt.

Modell sheepishly approaches the microphone. He looks horrid, like he hasn't slept in a month. "Frankly," he says, "it came down to a simple proposition: I had no choice."

Say what?

Here was a franchise that was considered among the best in all of professional sports, tied to the most rabid fans in the NFL and based in the heartland of football, a mere 50 miles from the Pro Football Hall of Fame in Canton.

You're protected by a salary cap of $37 million, you're getting $38 million from television rights before you sell a single ticket or hot dog, and you're up to your ruddy cheeks in debt?

Not enough fan support? Surely you jest. In 1990, the Browns finished a horrendous 3–13—and *still* averaged 71,012 fans per home game. During the previous decade, the *worst* average attendance was 69,948. Where's his beef?

The reaction of fans was instant, vehement, and relentless. Death threats poured in, as he had anticipated. (He told his family to leave their longtime home in Waite Hill before the announcement was made; they did, and never came back.) The more civilized fans flooded the local courts with lawsuits.

Local writers instantly mauled Modell, identifying him not only as "pathetic" and "greedy," but "a spoiled child with a paunch and several chins."

Even the national media jumped down Modell's throat. "What does the NFL stand for?" asked *Time* magazine. "Could it be—greed? . . . How else do you explain Art Modell betraying the most loyal fans in pro football by taking his Browns from Cleveland to Baltimore?"

Sports Illustrated was even more vehement. The powerful weekly printed a rare cartoon on its cover showing a big-nosed Modell sucker-punching a Dawg-helmeted fan in the stomach. The magazine sold out instantly in Northeast Ohio, and *SI* cranked up a second printing. In the end, 86,000 newsstand copies were sold in Cleveland, compared to the normal 50,000, and 10,000 more were sold in Akron, compared to the usual 1,000.

The news was very much national, though. Unlike the situations in other cities that teams had fled, Northeast Ohio's love affair with the Browns seemed almost impossible to ruin. If it could happen in Cleveland, people realized, it could happen anywhere.

During the decade following World War II, the Browns won seven titles. That lit a football fire under the populace, and that fire was passed down to the baby boomers. Every baby-boomer boy in Northeast Ohio at one time or another pictured himself as Jim Brown—unstoppable . . . uncatchable . . . unbelievable . . . running and running and running . . . flashing down the sidelines with Number 32 on his back as a cosmic roar rained down from 80,000 hysterical fans. The 100-yard-long patch of grass on the lakefront was ground zero for excitement.

Over the years, the heroes changed but the fantasies didn't. Little kids wanted to play like Otto Graham or Jim Brown or Brian Sipe or Bernie Kosar. Didn't matter exactly when you were born, because the players were all connected, all linked directly to a glorious heritage.

Even when the team slumped in the 1970s, it was still *our* team. We hung in there, taking a sort of perverse pride in riding out the storm. A popular T-shirt at the time read, "Cleveland: You Gotta Be Tough." And nobody ever accused Cleveland football fans of lacking toughness. Merely surviving a full season in the grandstands was an accomplishment. Early in the schedule, September sunlight would sparkle off the shiny orange helmets, which, along with the brown jerseys and white pants, would contrast gloriously with the rich emerald field. But as the schedule wound down, the grass turned beige, the blue skies were obliterated by a permanent smear of gray, and the arrogant winds of Lake Erie thundered around inside the big horseshoe, making everyone miserable.

The late-season weather always seemed oddly fitting. Football is a physical test, a competition of wills. *You gotta be tough.* Think it's easy living in a Dawg Pound?

But suddenly, after the arrival of Belichick, it was no longer *us* against *them*. It became *us* against *us*. Among the companies that failed to renew a loge after years of occupancy was a manufacturing firm owned by retired Cleveland Brown Gene Hickerson. The former All-Pro guard said flatly that he was leaving because he hated Belichick's offense.

The average fan appropriately defined that offense as "Metcalf up the middle." No one—players included—could understand why the head coach had developed such a fetish for running a five-foot-ten,

185-pound scatback into the heart of the line, time after no-gain time.

Another popular slam was a reference to Belichick's imported quarterback as "Vinnie Intercept-averde." Point well taken. A good quarterback generally throws twice as many touchdown passes as interceptions. In 1994, Vinnie's INTs outnumbered his TDs.

As early as 1992, star players such as Metcalf, Webster Slaughter, and Michael Dean Perry were either demanding to be traded or speaking out publicly against Belichick. But Art never wavered. Belichick was his man. Belichick would stay. On December 30, 1992, Modell went all the way out to the end of the Belichick limb.

"I'm so positive of Bill Belichick's future here, and that of the Cleveland Browns' organization," said Modell, "that if we don't get the job done by the end of his contract [in 1995], I will get out of football and leave Cleveland. . . . He's the last coach I hired. I will not hire another coach."

That stance would cost him dearly, even among his most long-standing customers.

But perhaps, in retrospect, Modell's move to Baltimore should have been anything but a shock. He was, after all, the same man who fired Paul Brown.

In business, when your name is on the front of the building, you tend to call the shots. Paul Brown's name was on the football team. Who was going to mess with him?

Granted, he didn't actually own the team. Art Modell owned it, having put together a group that paid $4 million—most of it borrowed—in March 1961.

But Brown was the de facto king, a living legend whose 17 percent ownership stake yielded a nice return and was replaced by a guaranteed contract would pay him $82,500 for each of the next eight years. (In modern dollars, that's $498,750 annually, paid at a time when football was so lightly regarded by our society that even a Browns championship didn't necessarily make the front page.)

Paul Brown revolutionized the sport. When he began his tenure by winning seven titles in 10 years in two different leagues, it was not just a matter of finding the right bodies. He was the first guy to develop a playbook, the first to give written tests to the players, the first to use film to grade player performances, the first to chart opponents using film, the first to lay out detailed pass routes, the first to create a "taxi squad," the first to employ assistant coaches year round, the first to attach face masks to helmets, the first to call plays via a system of rotating "messenger guards," and the first to use a little CB radio transmitter to send his plays to his quarterback.

Brown had cut a wide swath at Massillon High School, upgrading the program so dramatically that the grandstands were expanded from 5,000 seats to 21,000 seats. He moved on to Ohio State and kicked butt there, too, coming home with a national championship in 1942.

When wealthy Cleveland businessman Mickey McBride signed Brown as his first head coach in the new All-American Football Conference, that signing drew more publicity than the awarding of the franchise had—and far more publicity than anything given to the existing pro team, the Cleveland Rams.

In addition to being a lifelong winner, Brown was a micromanager. He called the shots on everything from halftime entertainment to advertising to travel arrangements.

Unfortunately, Art Modell was a micromanager, too. He was a hands-on, backslapping, big-city mover-and-shaker who wanted to be involved with everything. Brown didn't want him involved with anything. Brown didn't respect Modell and largely ignored him. The fact that they managed to coexist for 22 months is something of a miracle.

One of their biggest conflicts involved one of the saddest episodes in Browns history. The Browns gave up a future Hall of Famer when they traded Bobby Mitchell to the Redskins for the rights to Ernie Davis, a running back who had broken many of Jim Brown's records at Syracuse.

Immediately after that, Davis was diagnosed with leukemia. Although his days were numbered to not more than a year, he remained strong for a while, and Modell wanted to put him into a game. *Just one play. Let him run back a kick or something.* Paul Brown refused. He thought it would be nothing more than a PR stunt, and his definition of football did not include PR stunts.

On Monday, January 7, 1963, Modell called Brown into his office at Cleveland Stadium and told him he was through.

Fortunately for Modell, both of the city's big newspapers, the *Plain Dealer* and the *Press*, were shut down by a strike. You had to go to Akron to read any second-guessing. On January 10, *Beacon Journal* sports editor Jim Schlemmer painted the move as an issue of personality rather than football:

> Paul Brown is out! Arthur Modell, ex-advertising ex-
> ecutive with much guts and gold, has taken over the role
> of god in the Cleveland Browns football extravaganza.
> It is the role Brown played with such marked success
> since the birth of the Browns in 1945—and earlier at
> Ohio State, Great Lakes, Severn Prep, and Massillon
> High—that he is both an institution and a legend.
> Model coveted the role.
> Model is a 39-year-old New Yorker with only a fan's
> background in football. . . . Reminiscent of Frank Lane,
> who guided the ruination of the Indians from an office in
> Tower A in the lakefront stadium, Modell walked into his
> Tower B office late Wednesday afternoon and ordered
> the minions on his publicity staff to broadcast forthwith
> the following: "Paul E. Brown, head coach and general
> manager of the Cleveland Browns, will no longer serve
> the team in those capacities."

Other Cleveland teams had been named after coaches or owners—
among them, the Cleveland Naps baseball team, after star player-
manager Napoleon Lajoie, and the Cleveland Rosenblums basketball
team, after department-store honcho Max Rosenblum—but the
names always changed when the legend went away. Only the Cleveland Browns endured, simply because no team in the history of Cleveland sports—maybe *any* town's sports—had ever been so dominant.

The early years of pro football were not precisely as they have
been portrayed. Contrary to our image of football's gritty roots—
Canton steelworkers taking out their frustrations on rock-strewn
fields—the sport was anything but a blue-collar game. In the early
days, it was played most often, and watched most enthusiastically, at
institutions of higher learning.

The first hotbed of football was the Ivy League. Early practition-
ers in our area included the Case School of Applied Science and
Adelbert College (Western Reserve University). The formation of
the Ohio Athletic Conference in 1902 to better organize the sport
and weed out ringers predates even the formation of the NCAA.
Collegiate football was so popular locally that pro football had a hard
time gaining a foothold.

Paul Brown continued in that upscale tradition. He demanded that his players dress in coats and ties. He forbade them to smoke or drink in public. On game days, he prowled the sideline in a suit, tie, overcoat, and hat. For a long, long time, nobody questioned him. How can you complain about a guy who goes 105–17–4 during his first decade on the job?

By the time he was fired, his team was no longer dominant, and society was beginning to loosen up. Society was still tight in 1963; that the same day Schlemmer wrote about Brown's firing, his newspaper printed a story headlined, "Sunday Car-Wash Business Ruled Legal." In Ohio, it was against the law to operate a business on the Sabbath unless the business was "a work of necessity" or "incidental to travel." Pro football, apparently, was a work of necessity.

Anyway, Modell saw Brown as far too rigid for the changing times. Clearly, the players had a great deal to do with creating that belief. According to longtime Cleveland wire service reporter Bill Levy, at least seven top players went to Modell and said they would quit or ask to be traded if Brown wasn't fired.

One of them was the best player in football. In Jim Brown's autobiography, *Off My Chest*, Brown admitted going directly to Modell and threatening to walk away unless Paul Brown was fired. When JB talks, people listen.

Quite a contrast to the efforts of the "Cleveland Crybabies" in 1940. When the Indians tried to oust manager Ossie Vitt, owner Alva Bradley told them to pound salt. Word got out, and everywhere they went for the rest of the season they were taunted as "crybabies."

Guess there's no crying in football.

It's impossible to know how many fans were thinking about Paul Brown as they filed into Cleveland Stadium for the last time on Sunday, December 17, 1995. But his era seemed 500 light-years away.

Fittingly, the final home game pitted the Browns against the Cincinnati Bengals—the team Brown formed after leaving Cleveland.

Regardless of the result, or the result of a game the following week in Jacksonville, there would be no postseason for the 1995 Browns. A team that had been picked by *Sports Illustrated* and the *Sporting News* to reach the Super Bowl wasn't even close to the playoff hunt, having collapsed to 4–10.

Little wonder. The '95 season had turned into an absolute circus. What took place out on the field ran a distant second to everything else.

On the final Sunday, the big scoreboard that doubled as an advertising billboard had more wasted space than the Mojave Desert. All the ads had been taken down at the insistence of their sponsors. The only thing remaining on a scoreboard that Modell had paid $1.6 million to rebuild in 1978 was the main stat board, the game clock, and the time of day. All around the stadium, advertisements had been removed or blacked out. Sponsors pulled their ads from the game programs, too, and yanked their spots from radio and TV. Nobody wanted to be associated with a traitor.

The lame-duck team drew 55,875 fans. Historically speaking, that was a poor crowd. Given the circumstances, it was an amazing crowd. Clearly, many fans' affection for their sporting heritage was even greater than their dislike of Belichick and Modell.

Still, the fans were conflicted. They seemed unsure whether to boo in protest or cheer the players in the name of loyalty. Management didn't give them an option during the pregame introductions; for the second straight week, individual introductions were dispensed with.

When Cleveland came out hitting on all cylinders—Testaverde throwing crisply, Earnest Byner racking up rushing yards, the defense clamping down—the fans gradually, almost reluctantly, began to pull for the team. The notable exception was Andre Rison, who was booed lustily even after making a first-down catch.

Chants of "Modell sucks" boomed out from various parts of the stadium all the livelong day. The chant got so loud with five minutes left in the game that officials began to play "Jingle Bell Rock" to try to drown it out.

Plenty of venom was left over from rallies held earlier in the day. That morning, in the plaza at Lakeside and West Third Street, Mayor White had urged a crowd of several thousand to keep the pressure on the NFL as it prepared to vote on Modell's move. Not far away, radio talk host Mike Trivisonno staged a mock execution. About 500 people turned out to join him in singing a popular new ditty, "Go to Hell, Art Modell," and revel in the mistreatment of three effigies. First, Belichick's effigy was put in a noose, and a trap door was released. Next, an effigy of Modell's son, David, was hung and tossed into the crowd, where it was dismembered. For the crowning moment, a remarkably lifelike effigy of Art Modell was brought out.

Trivisonno to the fake Modell: "Do you have any last words?"

Modell's recorded voice: "I'm deeply, deeply sorry from the bottom of my heart."

After "Modell" swung from the noose, Trivisonno declared that he wasn't quite dead. So the effigy was placed in an electric chair. When Trivisonno flipped the switch, the dummy shook and smoke rose. Trivisonno then donned a stethoscope and announced that he was going to check Modell's heart. He walked to the effigy and placed the device on the dummy's rear end. The crowd roared.

Hours later, as the game was ending, all that rage began to give way to despair. At least 15 players (Rison not among them) ran to the Dawg Pound for a final good-bye. As the players mingled with the crowd, exchanging hugs and high-fives, they could see tears in the eyes of many.

The Dawg Pound had been like a family. Meeting only on Sundays (and an occasional Monday), total strangers had gotten to know each other, gone to each other's houses, gone on vacations together. People of different colors and ages, people with totally different backgrounds and jobs, became one for three hours a week, often with the aid of smuggled-in beverages.

During that final farewell, players threw wristbands and hats to their admirers. Wide receiver Michael Jackson heaved three footballs into the upper reaches of the Pound. Earnest Byner, long since forgiven for his last-minute fumble in the AFC title game in Denver, worked his way from one end of the Pound to the other, high-fiving his way along the railing. Tony Jones grabbed 385-pound John Thompson, "Big Dawg," in a bear hug, and thanked him for his unwavering support.

Jones, a veteran offensive lineman who had led the farewell trek to the Pound, then returned to midfield and knelt down in prayer. He wanted to give thanks. He thanked the Lord for his nine years at Cleveland Stadium. "The old stadium, the dirt painted green—this is the NFL right here," he said later. "I never wanted the day to be over."

The game was blacked out in Cleveland. Because it was meaningless in terms of the standings, few areas outside of central and southern Ohio picked it up. But the halftime show aired from coast to coast, and Cleveland fans would have loved it. Bob Costas, the biggest gun at NBC Sports, drilled Modell with both barrels.

Uprooting the Browns "shapes up as one of the outrages of the century in the world of sports," said Costas. Noting that Modell grew up in Brooklyn, he compared the exiled owner to the man who devastated Brooklyn by moving baseball's Dodgers to Los Angeles. "He has become his sport's—and his generation's—Walter O'Malley." Commentator Mike Ditka said Modell had "destroyed" his reputation "in one greedy move."

Only analyst Will McDonough defended Modell, saying there was no solid evidence that the city of Cleveland had a workable financial plan for a stadium upgrade.

Although the network's cameras understandably avoided certain banners, such as the huge "[Bleep] Modell" sign that appeared in the Dawg Pound in the third quarter, NBC did show plenty of negative signs, such as "Good luck, Baltimore, you'll need it."

Late in the game, the cameras lingered as whole rows of seats were torn from their moorings and passed down to the field. Quipped analyst Randy Cross, "A mob can come in handy. You don't need a saw if you have a mob. They can break up boards."

For the record, many fans did bring saw blades, hidden inside their pant legs, and early on began to systematically set about freeing souvenirs while their friends covered for them. Gradually, the subtle sawing gave way to the blatant ripping out of entire rows. Some fans were so eager for mementos that they tried to rip out sinks, paper towel dispensers, and even turnstiles. The cops, no doubt miffed at Modell themselves, mostly turned a blind eye, hoping the anger would burn itself out in vandalism rather than fighting.

As the NBC cameras displayed a mangled row of seats that had been thrown onto the closed end of the field, Cross got in a nice dig at the "personal seats licenses" that supposedly were going to help make Modell rich in Baltimore. "Let's see . . . there's about 20 seats right there. That's about $80,000 worth of PSLs."

Somehow, when fans started ripping out the seats with their bare hands, their actions did not seem wholly inappropriate. Arthur B. Modell had wrecked the franchise. He had wrecked a half-century tradition. And now it was time to wreck his stadium.

GAME SEVEN

The Indians were two outs away from winning their first World Series in 49 years. Their ace relief pitcher was on the mound. But instead of finishing the job, the 1997 team sent home one of the most heartbreaking moments in Cleveland sports history.

OF ALL THE MARVELOUS Cleveland Indians teams that graced Jacobs Field during the six beautiful summers from 1994 through 1999, the 1997 version was the weakest. It also may have been the most lovable.

On paper, the Class of '97 simply wasn't up to the standards of the newly buff Chief Wahoo. The team's earned-run average, 4.73, was the worst of any year except 1999—and the '99 team scored 141 more runs. The team batting average, .286, was also the second-worst of the era. And the winning percentage, .534, was dead last.

The Tribe plodded along during the regular season, staying ahead in their weak division but doing little that was spectacular. Comebacks just didn't happen. This team won exactly one regular-season game after trailing in the eighth inning.

The Indians captured the Central Division title by only six games over the White Sox—the closest of any race after the strike season of '94. Even the third-place Brewers were only eight games back, closer to the Indians than any other opponent in the second half of the decade.

Cleveland's preseason roster looked like it had been switched with the roster for an old-timers' game. One of the Tribe's big free-agent signings was designated hitter Kevin Mitchell, who proved to be a 35-year-old burnout. He was hitting .153 when he was cut in June.

Julio Franco—true age unknown—lasted a bit longer. He was cut in August after striking out 75 times in 78 games.

Former Cy Young Award–winner Jack McDowell was age 31, going on 71. He appeared in only eight games.

Orel Hershiser was nearing the end of a marvelous career. His ERA had plumped to nearly 4.5.

And Kevin Seitzer, acquired from Milwaukee for Jeromy Burnitz in late 1996, was coming off four consecutive seasons of hitting .311 or better. But, at 36, his bat was now shot and his legs were even worse. Seitzer's speed from home to first began to mirror the movement of tectonic plates.

But Hershiser and Seitzer were two of the most likable people you'd ever want to meet. It's no coincidence that, when the Top 100 Indians of all time were recognized at a game during the 2001 season, Hershiser received the loudest ovation.

And Seitzer was the kind of guy who, during the sunset of an All-Star career, with his average plummeting and his playing time sparse, was so enthusiastic that, in key situations, he'd climb off his seat on the bench, stand on the top step of the dugout and wave a towel to try to get the home fans riled up.

New centerfielder Marquis Grissom, obtained in a preseason trade that sent Kenny Lofton to Atlanta, was a borderline saint. Nobody knew it at the time, but throughout the season, on off days, he would travel to Atlanta, where his sister was in a hospital, battling AIDS. She died the day after Game Seven of the World Series.

Grissom had 14 siblings, and when he starting making big-league money, he bought a house for every one of them. Bought his parents a house too. If you're part of the family, he believed, you shared both the good and the bad.

Even with all that pressure on his smallish shoulders, Grissom never whined. He never threw a clubhouse temper tantrum. He just went out every day and played the game as hard as he could.

Gone from the team was Albert Belle, the great slugger and insufferable boor. Gone was Eddie Murray, the 3,000-hit star who would sooner talk to a concrete block than a guy with a microphone. Gone too was Lofton, who would mellow as his career progressed but in his first go-round with the Tribe took his hints from Murray and Belle.

The fans knew the '97 team couldn't field an All-World lineup like the '95 team. But this team was fun. The Indians were the antithesis of the feuding Oakland A's of the Reggie Jackson years. In fact, the '97 Tribe was the kind of team that fans always want the home team to be but rarely is: a bunch of decent guys pulling together for the common cause. That unity manifested itself in the season's least-expected development: the Saga of the Big Socks.

The story begins on August 27, which not so coincidentally coincides with the birthday of Jim Thome. Thome was a throwback—not to the previous era, but to the era before that. One era back, players wore their pant legs just below their knees, but wore high stirrups that revealed much of the white sock underneath the colored stirrup. Thome went back even further, to a time when the players' pants stopped just below the knee but the lower leg was virtually all colored sock.

Thome wasn't the only player in the league to dress that way. A few players did it in honor of pioneer Jackie Robinson. Not Thome. He did it that way just because he had always done it that way. And if was good enough for Peoria, Illinois, then, by gosh, it was good enough for Cleveland, Ohio.

Anyway, on Thome's 27th birthday, several of his teammates decided to honor him by folding under their long pant legs and exposing their colored socks. They beat Anaheim 10–4 that night and, unwilling to risk alienating the baseball gods, repeated the tribute the next game. They won that one, too, beating the Cubs. The fashion statement was now carved in stone.

That, sad to say, may have been the highlight of the regular season. Not that 86 wins was anything to sneer at, especially given Cleveland's baseball history. But this was the fourth straight year of high expectations. We already knew the melody.

Truth be told, the single best Tribe game from late March to late September was an exhibition game.

The 68th Major League All-Star Game came to town on July 8. It had been awarded in 1994 as a reward for coming up with a new ballpark.

During the intervening years, Cleveland had acquired quite a taste for the national spotlight. The focus was no longer on burning rivers. The word "revitalization" had been escaping from the mouths of network announcers so often that we were beginning to shake off our half-century of touchiness.

When an out-of-town broadcaster like ESPN's Karl Ravech made fun of our river, jokingly referring to it as the "Cuya-WHO-ga," we laughed. It's considerably easier to laugh when the cameras are displaying a parade of fancy yachts flowing up and down the river in question.

The city was on the crest of its best PR roll in four decades. Earlier in the year, the nation had visited for the NBA All-Star Game. And not just *any* NBA All-Star game. This one was the 50th and the biggest, capped by a halftime presentation of the top 50 NBA players of all time.

Two months after that, the Rock and Roll Hall of Fame induction was held, at long last, in the city that built the museum. People like Michael Jackson and Prince were running around town as the national media genuflected.

Now came baseball's All-Star Game, Cleveland's fifth—a major league record—and easily its best. Never before had a hometown hero won the game and been declared the Most Valuable Player.

That was the glorious fate awaiting catcher Sandy Alomar on a night that began with a tornado watch and ended with the thunder of fireworks celebrating his two-run homer that powered the American League to a 3–1 victory.

The crowd of 44,945 let its emotions fly all night. The fans gave a huge pregame ovation to Lofton, surprising the former Indian, who was standing on the foul line in an Atlanta Braves uniform. And they offered up a warm greeting to the Phillies' Curt Schilling, who, according to the rumor mill, might be interested in pitching in Cleveland in the near future.

Of course, one member of the All-Star team, the Chicago White Sox's Albert Belle, received a somewhat different reception. He was booed so quickly and so loudly when he was introduced before the game that his name was indistinguishable over the public address system.

Belle was Mr. Charming from start to finish. On his way to the ballpark, as he strolled past the Gateway parking garage wearing a maroon golf shirt, beige shorts, and white sneakers, an excited security guard with a walkie-talkie asked politely for an autograph. Belle shot him a look of utter disdain, then shook his head, as if he couldn't believe the audacity of the man. Belle kept right on truckin'—without uttering a single word of response.

Alomar's climactic shot was especially sweet, coming with two outs and a tie score in the seventh inning. As the 430-foot blast soared into the bleachers, a World Series–caliber roar greeted his jaunt around the bases.

Otherwise, the summer of '97 did not specialize in drama.

The story of 1997 is really the story of two totally different seasons. After the mundane regular season, the postseason turned into a magical mystery tour. Everything that normally happens to Cleveland sports teams happened to Cleveland's opponents.

Your top pitcher blows out his arm.

A game-winning hit squeaks through your infield.

Close calls by umpires go against you.

An opponent fails to connect on a suicide squeeze and the runner *still* scores.

A guy who started the season in Double-A ball turns into the reincarnation of Cy Young.

Add them all together, and a string of certain victories evaporates into the cruel night sky. Take that, bad guys.

None of this was in keeping with Cleveland's baseball history. Even the weather was glorious for most of October.

Maybe it *was* the socks.

In any event, as the Tribe prepared to play Game Seven of the 1997 World Series in balmy South Florida, something besides humidity was hanging in the warm, tropical air. It was a feeling of destiny.

This was finally The Year. This would take its place next to 1920 and 1948 in the exceedingly tiny pantheon of Cleveland baseball championships. Surely the baseball gods were ready to smile. After all, they had frowned in 1995, apparently on the basis that winning it all in '95 would have been too easy. The '97 team had struggled, escaping spectacularly exciting playoffs with the Yankees and Orioles. They had overachieved. And now, finally, they would be rewarded.

The baseball gods were displaying a real sense of humor, though. Why, they were making us wait until the very last game.

The World Series usually doesn't go a full seven games. The Series was played 96 times during the 20th century, and only 34 of those times did it go the distance. So this was going to be *extreee* special.

Baseball purists may have cringed at the very notion of the Marlins in the World Series, a team that had been in existence only five years and had been assembled not through a careful nurturing of the farm system but with megabucks spent on free agents by a wealthy owner. And the team's uniforms were *teal,* for heaven's sake. Worse yet, the Marlins frequently took batting practice at home games wearing shorts! No self-respecting high school team would wear shorts in batting practice.

Still, if a win over the Marlins wouldn't bring the traditional charm of, say, a win over the Dodgers or Cardinals or Braves, few Indians fans were going to quibble.

The stadium itself was odd. From the outside, at night, it resembled the old Coliseum in Richfield. It sat all by itself on 160 acres, halfway between downtown Miami and Fort Lauderdale, surrounded by a gargantuan parking lot. Unlike the Coliseum, it was open to the sky, so at night it looked like a huge spaceship that had been looking for a wide-open landing area and found one on the scruffy plains of Dade County.

Although Pro Player Stadium lacked the ambiance of Jacobs Field, it did have its unique charms. The grounds had held a two-part, week-long festival with an international flavor that was lacking in Cleveland. Forty-nine percent of the population of Dade County was Hispanic, a statistic that was reflected in the language, music, and dress. Half the people were talking about *beisbol,* and all of the people were inundated by blaring Latin rhythms, ranging from a radio station's gigantic fake boom box in the parking lot to salsa bands performing on the stadium's club level.

The parking lot also contained a 30-foot shark. Because the site was not far from the Universal Studios tourist trap in Orlando, employees of the theme park had driven a 7½-ton "Land Shark" to the game to drum up attention. And attention it got. Rolling along on four five-foot, seven-inch Goodyear tires, the Land Shark was powered by a 550-horsepower engine and packed a boatload of special effects, including flames that shot from the side tailpipes and smoke that belched from the great white's nostrils and tail. Big gull-wing doors opened hydraulically, revealing an interior that could be used as a radio studio.

The inside of Pro Player was even odder. The place was designed as a football stadium—in fact, a Dolphins–Bears game had been scheduled for the same day and had to be bumped to Monday night—and in its full baseball configuration, thousands of the seats were miles from home plate.

The regular-season configuration contained 42,000 seats. Everything in the upper deck of the outfield between the foul poles was covered with tarps. But for the World Series, the whole place was opened up. Some of the new seats were literally 600 feet from home plate and 128 feet in the air.

Although plenty of contemporary ballparks were criticized for excessive advertising, the Marlins went where other teams feared to tread: they even sold advertisements on their foul poles. An office-supply chain was touted in big black letters on both of the bright yellow poles.

Hey, why worry about commercial excess when your ballpark is named after underwear? Pro Player was the brand name of sports apparel made by Fruit of the Loom, which bought the naming rights in 1996.

The team's entertainment offerings were over the top as well. The semiofficial team mascot was "Muscle Boy," a preadolescent kid who could have been the prototype for the 98-pound weakling. He was shown on the Jumbotron every game, shirt off, flexing his nonexistent muscles.

The official mascot, "Billy the Marlin," made Slider look shy. Billy was not the warm-and-cuddly type favored by mascot creators worldwide. He was a big, pointy, shiny, plastic fish head with a wobbly plastic fin on top.

Between the top and bottom half of the fifth inning, the Marlins always played a music video on the Jumbotron called *Do the Fish*. It contained such scintillating lyrics as "Everyone's doing the fish, yeah, yeah, yeah." Even worse, the fans actually got up and danced the Fish.

They'd put one hand on top of their head with their elbow pointing forward. The elbow was supposed to look like the bill of a Marlin. With their other arm, they would do a swimmer's crawl eight times. After swimming, they'd wiggle. That was followed by the backstroke, again for eight repetitions. And they'd wind up exactly where they started. Which is to say, looking like buffoons. Believe me, after four games of this, Slider was beginning to look like Baryshnikov.

Nearly 900 media credentials had been issued to organizations from all over the world. During batting practice, when members of the media were allowed to roam the sidelines, the field was a zoo. At any World Series, you see all kinds of people who don't usually request media credentials to sports events—like Larry "Bud" Melman from the David Letterman show.

Letterman's Biff Henderson was making waves too, especially before Game Six when he interviewed Bip Roberts. Biff, meet Bip. Bip, Biff.

"Will you hit a home run for me tonight?" Biff asked Bip.

"You're asking the wrong man, dude. My job is just to get on base."

"How about an autograph?" At which point the player reached out for Biff's pen—and Biff kept the pen, signed his own name, and handed it to the player.

The player howled. He looked down at the signature and immediately fired back: "You a doctor or something?"

Earlier, Henderson had posed a dicey theoretical question to Indians manager Mike Hargrove. "What happens if the Series is tied after seven games?"

Hargrove, laughing: "We're all in deep trouble."

Virtually all of the fans and many in the media were wearing shorts for Game Seven. Quite a contrast to the weather in Cleveland, where during Game Four the temperature was 38 degrees, the wind chill was 18, and everybody in the park was wearing heavy gloves and parkas. What are the odds of setting the record for the coldest game in World Series history—followed four days later by one of the warmest games in World Series history?

It certainly didn't feel like October. It didn't feel like a Sunday, either. For that matter, it didn't feel like *any* previous day. The Indians in Game Seven of the World Series? You must be joking.

About mid-afternoon, the players boarded buses at their hotel, the Sheraton Bal Harbour. Actually, the place was considerably more than a hotel. It was a high-priced resort, right on the Atlantic Ocean, with a 10-acre swimming pool that wound around through tropical gardens. Across the street was an ultra-upscale mall.

Owner Dick Jacobs was picking up the tab not only for the players but for their wives and fiancées. During the season, that happened on only a couple of designated road trips. But the playoffs were special; spouses had been welcome on every road game in every series. It was a reward for reaching the playoffs, as well as an attempt to make the players feel at home. Several Indians brought their children and parents, too.

The day of the game, Florida's fans turned out early. Salsa music was booming throughout the ballpark again, the temperature was 80 degrees, and the site became a world-class party. At least for the fans. By contrast, the Indians pregame locker room reflected the competitive tension.

During most of the previous eight months, the clubhouse had been a relaxed, easygoing place, with guys constantly cracking jokes and playing music. But on October 26, as the 1997 Cleveland Indians pulled on their blue jerseys and gray pants for the last time—win or lose—nobody said much of anything. Nobody cranked up the volume on the CD player. Everyone was lost in quiet anticipation.

The blue tops were a bit of a departure. For most of the postseason, the Tribe had dressed for road games in gray. But before Game Six, outfielder David Justice asked Hargrove whether the blue would be okay. Hargrove agreed and the Indians won, once again solidifying a fashion statement.

At 7:35 p.m., lefty Al Leiter took the hill for the Florida Marlins.

Batting first and playing shortstop, Number 13, Omar Vizquel.

Vizquel never liked to lead off. He thought he was better suited to the second spot, and, for much of his career, that's where he hit. But the Indians' leadoff hitter during the first six games, Bip Roberts, told the manager he couldn't play because of a sore throat. Seriously. He took a powder in Game Seven of the World Series. So Vizquel moved up.

He was actually a pretty good leadoff hitter—a guy who took a lot of pitches, a guy who could steal a base, a good bunter.

The 1993 trade that brought Vizquel to Cleveland was not only one of the best by John Hart but one of the best of any era. The Tribe got a perennial Gold Glove shortstop for a run-of-the-mill shortstop (Felix Fermin) and a run-of-the-mill first baseman (Reggie Jefferson). Even though Vizquel was forced to deal with a cast of thousands at second base, his defense never suffered.

Vizquel became a fan favorite after the 1995 season when he delivered a hilarious, rambling monologue at the welcome-home rally at Public Square.

He endeared himself to Tribe fans even more with a huge defensive stop in Game Six of this series, diving to his right to stop a shot by the Marlins' Charles Johnson and throwing him out at first.

Vizquel also had built a reputation as a clutch hitter, an affinity he displayed in Game Five of the '97 divisional series when his single won the game and sent the New York Yankees packing.

However, Vizquel's most noteworthy offensive play of the '97 playoffs was a near disaster. After splitting the first two games of the ACLS in Baltimore, the Tribe returned to Cleveland and staged a five-hour marathon. In the bottom of the 12th, with the score tied, Vizquel was at the plate with Marquis Grissom on third. On a 2–1 count, the Tribe called for a suicide squeeze. Vizquel squared around . . . and whiffed. Fortunately, the Orioles' catcher, Lenny Webster, made an even worse play. He dropped the ball. It rolled just far enough away that Grissom was able to score.

On this night, in his first at-bat, Vizquel grounds out to third baseman Bobby Bonilla.

BATTING SECOND AND PLAYING SECOND BASE,
NUMBER 1, TONY FERNANDEZ.

Second base had been a trouble spot all year. The team got only 60 RBI from Franco, Fernandez, and Roberts. Now Roberts was sidelined and Franco was long gone.

But in the playoffs, Fernandez had made huge contributions. He was the hero of Game Six in Baltimore, when the Tribe clinched the pennant. The game was a pitchers' duel, scoreless for 10 innings and two outs, until Fernandez smacked a 2–0 slider from Armando Benitez over the centerfield fence.

(Fortunately for radio announcer Herb Score, the Indians were able to retire Baltimore in the bottom of the inning, saving him from the radio equivalent of "Dewey Beats Truman." When Fernandez's ball cleared the fence, Score exclaimed: "The Indians are going to the World Series!" He sheepishly acknowledged the need for three more outs a few moments later.)

Fernandez was born in Puerto Rico, but he had seen more of North America during his baseball career than most North Americans. Before arriving in Cleveland, he had toiled for Toronto, San Diego, the Mets, Toronto again, Cincinnati, and the Yankees.

He was only 34, but it was an old 34. He had missed all of the 1996 season with a broken bone in his right elbow. He also had lost a step after 13 big-league seasons.

In Fernandez's first at-bat of Game Seven, he lines out to centerfielder Devon White.

Batting third and playing right field, Number 24, Manny Ramirez.

Manny had turned in a typical Manny season. At times he appeared to be absolutely clueless; at times he appeared to be the greatest player in the history of the game.

Most of the latter times came when he had a bat in his hands. Didn't matter whose bat. He'd use his own bats, other people's bats, whatever. He'd hit a homer with one bat and then switch to another bat.

Nobody knew what was rattling around inside his noggin, but nobody doubted his prowess at the plate. During the season he hit .328, with 26 home runs, 40 doubles, and 88 RBIs. At 26 years of age, in his fourth full year in the bigs, he had firmly established himself as a consistently fine hitter, averaging .320 with 27 homers.

Except for two homers in the ALCS, his bat had been largely AWOL during the playoffs. Still, pitchers wisely continued to treat him as one of Cleveland's biggest threats.

Manny had a strong throwing arm, but his attention in the outfield tended to wander. Same thing on the bases—decent speed, but not always the best judgment.

Born in the Dominican Republic, Ramirez was raised in a Spanish ghetto in New York City. He was shy around strangers to begin with, and his problems with the language didn't help. After a while he quit talking to reporters.

He was liked by his teammates, even though he tended to do weird things, such as wearing their clothes.

Ramirez was a product of the Indians' farm system, but he wasn't in it long. He was wearing a big-league uniform before his third summer was out.

In his first at-bat, Manny grounds out to Marlins shortstop Edgar Renteria. Three up, three down.

Batting fourth and playing left field, Number 23, David Justice.

One thing the 1997 Indians could do as well as any previous team was hit homers. They tagged 220 in 1997, a Cleveland record (until the 2000 team upped that total by one). Five guys hit more than 20 homers. Everybody was hitting them—old guys, young guys, little guys, steroid guys, guys married to movie stars.

David Justice, known almost as much for his relationship with his former spouse, actress Halle Berry, as his baseball exploits, had cranked 33 taters, second best in his eight-year career.

Two years earlier, a Justice homer in Game Six of the World Series won the championship. Unfortunately, Justice was wearing a Braves uniform at the time.

Now, in his first year in Cleveland, he had reached career highs in homers and batting average, with a glittery .329. He even finished fifth in the MVP vote, and the *Sporting News* named him the American League's Comeback Player of the Year.

Justice had come through in the playoffs as well, hitting .300 during the first two rounds.

He was not the warmest-and-fuzziest guy in the clubhouse, but he didn't cause major problems, either. He was probably the best-known Indian outside of Northeast Ohio, and not just because of the Halle Berry connection. During the off-season his own handsome mug had been pictured on the cover of Chex cereal boxes and Crispy Wheaties 'n' Raisins.

In the second inning, Justice leads off by grounding out to first baseman Darren Daulton.

BATTING FIFTH AND PLAYING THIRD BASE,
NUMBER 9, MATT WILLIAMS.

When the former San Francisco Giant became an Indian during the off-season—in exchange for future National League MVP Jeff Kent, pitchers Julian Tavarez and Joe Roa, and infielder Jose Vizcaino—he was billed as a good-natured humanitarian who would be highly involved in his community and provide a level head in the locker room. The first thing he did after the trade was donate $50,000 to Cleveland charities.

But Cleveland fans came to know him as a head case.

Every time Williams came to the plate, he looked like a guy facing a fight to the death with Darth Vader. He squeezed the bat so hard you half expected sawdust to come out the bottom of the handle. He looked not so much like a man who had moved from the National League to the American League as a man who had moved from Earth to Mars.

At third base, he looked far better. Even if he was gnashing his molars into powder, he did resemble the guy who had three Gold Gloves in his trophy case.

The problem, or at least part of it, turned out to be marital woes.

His wife and three children stayed at the family home in Arizona when Williams moved to Cleveland, and his emotional distress poked its way into his play. Trouble on the home front can tie anyone into knots, even someone who is six-foot-two and 216 pounds.

He did hit 32 homers, but only a late splurge at the plate got his batting average (.263) into the realm of respectability.

Williams was not exactly a proven postseason commodity, either. In his only previous World Series, in 1989, he hit .125.

In his first at-bat in Game Seven, he is fanned by Leiter.

BATTING SIXTH AND CATCHING, No. 15, SANDY ALOMAR, JR.

For Sandy Alomar, 1997 was the most charmed year in a charmed life. Everything he touched turned into a smiley face.

Sometime between 1996 and 1997, Alomar had been transformed into a hitting machine. His game-winning homer in the All-Star Game was only part of it. All year, when the chips were down, he seemed to be the guy coming through. In fact, he was responsible for one of the most dramatic homers in Cleveland history, in Game Four of the Division Series against the dreaded New York Yankees.

The Yankees were four outs away from sending Cleveland home for the winter. And the guy out on the mound, Mariano Rivera, was the most feared relief pitcher in the American League.

Alomar didn't blink. He lashed at a Rivera fastball and sent it flying toward the right-field seats. As it cleared the green wall, the previously solemn crowd of 45,231 erupted in an explosion of joyous noise that may have made it all the way across the lake and bounced off the skyscrapers in Toronto. The Tribe catcher hit .316 in that series and would hit .367 in the World Series.

It wasn't simply a matter of good timing. All year long he knocked the cover off the ball, posting a regular-season average of .320. That was his career best, as were his 21 homers, 83 RBIs, and 37 doubles. Heck, he never hit .320 in seven years in the *minors*.

From late May to early July, Alomar went on a 30-game hitting streak, tying the longest streak in the major leagues all year.

After the 1997 season, he would be voted the Tribe's Man of the Year.

Just one year after his brother, Roberto, was crucified (appropriately) by fans and media for spitting at an umpire, Sandy had become a huge fan favorite, a five-time All-Star, a big, friendly guy whom trainer Jimmy Warfield once called the toughest player he had ever worked with. Sure, Alomar missed a lot of playing time with injuries. This was only the second time in his eight-year career that he managed back-to-back 100-game seasons. But most players with his injuries would have been sidelined far longer.

Alomar arrived in 1990 in another great John Hart trade. The Tribe got both Alomar and Carlos Baerga from San Diego for an aging Joe Carter.

In this first plate appearance in Game Seven, Alomar flies out to centerfield to end the second inning.

BATTING SEVENTH AND PLAYING FIRST BASE, NUMBER 25, JIM THOME.

Thome was a homegrown guy who in the early '90s bounced up and down repeatedly between the majors and the minors. He kept working, had a breakout season in 1995, and in 1997 turned into a full-fledged star. He was chosen for the Midsummer Classic in Cleveland on his way to 40 homers. That was the most by an Indians lefty since Hal Trosky hit 42 six decades earlier.

Thome was getting bigger physically every year, and hitting more homers every year. Since '94, he had hit 20, 25, 38, and now a heavy-duty 40.

Unfortunately, he looked like a different guy in the postseason. A lousy guy. A guy with terrible timing and no confidence. By Game Six of the ALCS, he had been moved from the cleanup spot to sixth.

No matter how things went on the field, Thome was always a star in the clubhouse. During an era when a player would complain if another player had more souvenir T-shirts in the team shop, Thome didn't make a peep when he was asked during the off-season to switch from his lifelong position, third base, to first base to accommodate the arrival of Williams. If it would help the team, he told the manager, he would be happy to give it a try.

Thome made the adjustment relatively smoothly, although he would tend to make great plays (like his diving stop of a Paul O'Neil shot late in the final game of the ALCS) and butcher some easy ones.

He also turned into one of the most-walked players in baseball. He had an excellent eye for the strike zone, but it's not beyond reason to think that his Big Socks made his knees look higher to umpires. Thome walked 123 times in 1996, and 120 times in 1997.

Leading off the third inning, he walks.

Batting eighth and playing center field, Number 17, Marquis Grissom.

The man who replaced Kenny Lofton in center was not as flashy, not as fast, not as tall, not as good a hitter. But he was rock solid in the field.

Four straight times Grissom had been handed a Gold Glove, symbolizing his standing as the best centerfielder in the National League. He was still only 30 years old.

He seemed like the perfect candidate to take over for Lofton as the leadoff hitter, but he went into the tank early in the season and was eventually moved way down in the order. With less pressure, or more American League experience, or maybe both, he began to hit again, but never got fully back up to speed and wound up the season with a watery .262 average and about half as many homers (12) as he had had the previous year.

Grissom came through when he was needed the most, though, by smacking his way to MVP of the ALCS. With Cleveland down one game to none, and losing by two runs in the eighth inning of Game Two, Grissom stepped to the plate and drilled a three-run homer off Armando Benitez to win the game and change the momentum of the entire series.

When he comes up in the third inning of Game Seven with Thome on first, he works the count to 3–2, then singles to left.

Batting ninth and pitching, Number 27, Jaret Wright.

This can't be. The roster says Number 27 is a rookie, a lad of 21, a mere infant in professional baseball. And this is the Seventh Game of the World Series.

True enough. This is the same Jaret Wright who began the season wearing a purple uniform with "Aeros" written across the front. His first win of 1997 came against the Bowie Baysox. Now, mind you, the home of the Aeros, Canal Park, was a gorgeous ballpark, a $32 million facility that was reminiscent of Jacobs Field. But it was two leagues away from Jacobs Field. It was Double-A ball. It was a level where three-quarters of the players are only a year or two from a job selling insurance.

Despite going only 3–3 for Akron, Wright was called up to AAA

Buffalo, where he quickly found his groove, winning four of five decisions on a 1.80 ERA.

He was called up to the Tribe on June 24, won his first game, and finished the regular season at 8–3.

During the playoffs, Wright had been on fire. The stocky Californian was 3–0, his first win coming in the biggest pressure-cooker in baseball, Yankee Stadium. After being shelled for three runs in the first inning of Game Two, with the crowd all over him, he hung tough and shut down the Yankees for the next five innings while the Indians rallied to win.

In Game Five of the ALCS, he took the mound at Jacobs Field and held off the hard-hitting Yankees long enough to collect another win.

Then, in Game Four of the World Series, he went six innings, giving up five hits and striking out five, becoming one of only half a dozen rookie pitchers in history to win three games in a single postseason.

Good thing, because Hershiser had completely run out of gas. In 10 innings of World Series work, his ERA was 11.70. By 1998, he would be gone.

The only thing Wright had *not* done to raves was swing a bat. In his second big-league start, in Houston, he attempted to bunt and put his hand in the way. The resulting cuts and bruises kept him out of action for two weeks.

Now, in another National League park, he has to pick up the lumber again, this time in a crucial situation.

With guys on first and second, he tries another bunt. It works. He pulls off the sacrifice, moving Thome to third and Grissom to second.

Now Vizquel stands in for the second time. He pops out to the shortstop.

With two outs and two runners in scoring position, the pressure falls on Fernandez. The Tribe second baseman works the count to 2–1, then hits a soft liner to center, giving the Indians a 2–0 lead in a game that has all the makings of a low-scoring contest.

That has certainly not been the case for most of the series. In the first five contests, the winning team scored 7, 6, 14, 10, and 8 runs. The third game, won by Cleveland 14–11, was the second-highest-scoring game in World Series history.

But Game Seven will remain low-scoring, and part of the credit must go to Cleveland's manager.

MANAGING THE INDIANS,
NUMBER 21, MIKE HARGROVE.

Hargrove was a tough Texan, an all-state high school football player. In the winter he played on the high school basketball team. In the spring, he played not on the baseball team, but the golf team. He jumped into baseball only after enrolling at Northwest Oklahoma State University—but reached the bigs just two years after college, hooking up with the Rangers in 1974.

By 1997, though, Hargrove was more of a Clevelander than most Clevelanders. He was here in the early 1980s, playing first base in front of 4,000 or 5,000 fans in the dead zone known as Cleveland Stadium. He here for Len Barker's perfect game. He was here for the Dime Beer Night Riot (albeit in the uniform of the Texas Rangers). He was wearing the Cleveland manager's cap when two players died in a boating accident in spring training in 1993. He was here for the last game ever played at Cleveland Stadium.

When Hargrove first laid eyes on the new park, Jacobs Field, those eyes filled with tears. He was thinking about how far the franchise had come, and how proud he was to be associated with it. Even after things went sour in Cleveland and he took a job in Baltimore in 2000, his family home remained in Richfield, just south of the city.

He has experienced an Indians World Series, too. But even Hargrove has never seen a Game Seven.

When filling in the last line on his lineup card, he weighed experience—Charles Nagy, a guy who has 201 big-league starts but was miserable throughout October—against a hot hand. The hot hand won, even though it was Nagy's turn in the rotation and Wright would have to go on short rest.

When Wright takes the mound, he immediately begins to make Hargrove look like a genius. He's consistently staying ahead of the hitters and mows down the Marlins with incredible ease, inning after inning. Through six frames, he hasn't surrendered a run.

In the seventh, Wright begins to tire. No wonder. In high school and the minor leagues, he never pitched more than 129 innings in a season. As he warms up for the seventh, he is starting his 216th inning of the year.

Bobby Bonilla leads off. Bonilla has been a World Series washout. The fans have been riding him because he's hitting .167 with no homers. His two RBIs are no better than the record of an Indians pitcher, Chad Ogea, who hit and pitched his way to his second World Series win on Saturday night. Bonilla is going so badly that he has been bumped from his customary cleanup spot to sixth.

Naturally, he jumps on the first pitch, a changeup, and hits it into the seats, pulling the Marlins to within one run.

Wright fans the next Marlin, weak-hitting catcher Charles Johnson, but walks the eighth batter, Craig Counsell.

Hargrove goes to the bullpen, and reliable lefty Paul Assenmacher gets his team out of the inning.

Mike Jackson gets the call in the eighth, and retires the first two batters. Lefty Brian Anderson takes care of the third.

Meanwhile, Cleveland's bats are making less noise than a falling Kleenex. Since the two-run third, the Tribe has managed only two hits, singles by Alomar and Vizquel.

In the top of the ninth, though, the Tribe is beginning to make some offensive noise. Williams walks. Alomar forces him, but Thome singles to right field, sending Alomar to third.

Relief ace Rob Nen comes on to face Grissom. On a 2–1 pitch, Grissom hits the ball to short. Unaccountably, Alomar takes off for home and is gunned down by Renteria. The threat ends when Brian Giles flies out.

But Cleveland still has the lead. The Indians need three more outs, just three, to win their first World Series in 49 years.

After 35 spring training games, 162 regular-season games, and 17 playoff games, it has all come down to this. One inning that can make or break a 215-game season.

NOW PITCHING FOR CLEVELAND,
NUMBER 49, JOSE MESA.

Mesa seems to be the right man for the job.

He saved the deciding game of the Division Series against the Yankees. He saved the deciding game of the Championship Series against the Orioles. Why shouldn't he save the World Series?

But on Mesa's third delivery, Moises Alou strokes a single to center. Mesa keeps him on first temporarily by fanning Bonilla, but then Johnson pops a single to right, putting runners on the corners with only one out.

Counsell rips a liner to right field. It's caught by Ramirez, but Alou scores easily from third to tie the game.

Mesa gets the next batter to ground out. But Cleveland's story-book ending has already been defaced.

The Tribe goes meekly in the top of the 10th. Vizquel, Ramirez, and Justice all strike out against Nen, with a harmless Fernandez single filtered in.

In the Marlin 10th, Mesa retires the first hitter but gives up singles to Renteria and Sheffield before striking out John Cangelosi. Hargrove waves to the bullpen for Charles Nagy.

This is the fourth time Nagy has warmed up tonight. The UConn T-shirt he's wearing under his blue jersey is already soaked with perspiration, and he hasn't set foot on the field.

Nagy is not exactly a fixture in the bullpen. This will mark the second relief appearance of his entire career. He hasn't done it in seven years, since coming out of the pen in Toronto. But in a game like this, all bets are off.

Nagy has been a solid starter for years. He has been in the Cleveland system since turning pro in 1989. He jumped to the big leagues in 1990. And since 1994, the only pitchers in either league to win more games than Nagy are Greg Maddux and Mike Mussina.

Nagy personifies the recent Cleveland Indians. He suffered through the lean years at the stadium, rolled with the psychological sucker punch of the 1993 spring training tragedy in which two players were killed in a boating accident, and rode the team's big wave of success in 1995. Now he is looking to put an exclamation point on his career, looking to shut down the Mariners for as long as it takes, looking to grab himself a World Series ring.

He preserves the tie, inducing Alou to fly out to Ramirez.

And the game goes on.

The most uncomfortable people—outside of the men in uniform—may be the men and women in the press box. Of the 900 people with media credentials, about 899 of them are fighting a deadline. Their customers are expecting to read all about the biggest baseball game of the year in the morning. But that's simply not going to happen if the game keeps going.

Cleveland's half of the 11th inning starts well, as Williams walks. But Thome kills the rally, grounding into his second double play of the night.

Now it's the bottom of the 11th. Bonilla is up again. He's the guy with the game's only homer. Nagy gets him into an 0–2 hole, but Bonilla smacks a single to center.

Greg Zaun tries to move him over with a bunt, but pops it up to Nagy.

Next up is Counsell, hitless in two at-bats. Nagy gets ahead of him 1–2, then Counsell hits a routine grounder toward second base. It looks like Cleveland will get out of the jam on this perfect double-play ball. But Fernandez boots it. He looks just like a Little Leaguer. The ball rolls directly under his glove and on into right field. Bonilla steams around to third and stops 90 feet from a championship.

Pro Player Stadium is on the brink of exploding.

Fernandez is a great fielder. He owns four Gold Gloves, given annually to the best defender at each position. He earned those at shortstop, where he toiled for years before making a concession to age and sliding over to second base. He works hard. He is selfless. He has been a clutch player throughout October. But he couldn't come up with this routine grounder.

Hargrove orders an intentional walk to set up a force. The strategy pays off when White hits a grounder to Fernandez, who fires to the plate to get Bonilla. The bases are still loaded, but now the Tribe can get out of the inning with an out. Any kind of out.

Renteria walks to the right-hand batters' box and digs in. The thin, dark-skinned shortstop, a product of Colombia, is a solid but not spectacular hitter. He batted .277 during the regular season, but has struggled during the playoffs, hitting a mere .154 in the divisional series and .227 in the championship series. As he comes to the plate to face Nagy, he is hitting .267 in the World Series.

Strike one.

After four hours and 10 minutes of baseball, Nagy looks in to Alomar for the next sign. Alomar calls for a slider. Renteria swings and hits it right up the middle, a soft line drive that barely eludes Nagy's raised glove. Vizquel and Fernandez have no chance, as the ball floats high between them and lands gently in short centerfield.

The fiesta to end all fiestas erupts inside Pro Player Stadium. The Marlins are sprinting around on the diamond, piling up, hugging each other, throwing their fists into the air. Queen's "We Are the Champions" booms from the P.A. system as the fans roar and shower the field with confetti. The Marlins' manager, Jim Leyland, runs a victory lap.

Cuban defector and ace pitcher Livan Hernandez, whose mother got special permission from Castro to attend the World Series, holds the MVP trophy above his head and declares: "I love you, Miami."

Nobody but a bitter Indians fan would point out his bulbous 5.27 ERA.

The Indians are zombies. Vizquel makes a point to hug Fernandez, the unlikeliest and cruelest of goats. Then he sits in the dugout, jealously watching the celebration to which he was not invited. The other Indians file back into the clubhouse to stare blankly for a long, long time.

Up in the visiting team's radio booth behind home plate, high above the celebration, Tribe play-by-play announcer Herb Score, calling the last game of his 34-year broadcasting career, signs off with this: "In 11 innings tonight, the Florida Marlins are the world champions of baseball, as they beat the Indians in 11 innings. The final score: Florida 3, Cleveland 2."

It is as simple as that, and as painful as that.

Many of the Indians cry on the bus back to the hotel. And the hotel has become just another stop, another temporary residence in the long, strange path of glory and disappointment.

Someone once compared a baseball season to a person's life. The spring is short, exciting, and filled with youthful promise. The losses are few, and insignificant. Before you know it, spring gives way to the long summer, the workaday grind, a numbing routine that seems to stretch out indefinitely. Then, toward the end, there's the crisp, desperately short autumn—a time of keen awareness that things are drawing to a close, that you have one final opportunity to make things right.

The World Series is a baseball team's last stand. That's when a particular group of players either soars into sports immortality or slips quietly into the long, dark night.

Halloween was nigh, and the frost was on the pumpkin.

ACKNOWLEDGMENTS

I'm PARTICULARLY GRATEFUL to Terry Pluto, not only for his solid reporting but his personal guidance. I'm thankful for David Gray's steady hand at the wheel, and for the boundless enthusiasm of publicist Jane Lassar.

Special thanks as well to the best play-by-play man in the universe, Joe Tait, who was extremely generous with his memories, insights, and audiotapes. (Can you believe the guy still owns a reel-to-reel tape recorder?)

Akron Beacon Journal sports editor Larry Pantages has never been my boss, but for more than a decade he has helped me at every turn, and he made some key suggestions for this book.

The work of *Akron Beacon Journal* writers past and present provided crucial background information. They include David Adams, Mary Ethridge, Bart Hubbuch, Ron Kirksey, Bill Lilley, Steve Love, Patrick McManamon, Tom Melody, Ed Meyer, Bob Nold, Bill O'-Connor, Sheldon Ocker, Pantages (a proud member of Ted Stepien's Enemies List), Jim Quinn, Ralph Paulk, Pluto, Roland Queen, Marla Ridenour, Arnie Rosenberg, Jim Schlemmer, Michael Weinreb, and Ray Yannucci. Also helpful were stories by Tom Withers, a top-quality sportswriter for the Associated Press.

Thanks also to two guys named Mark Price—the basketball player and the *Beacon Journal* staffer. Both contributed to this book.

An array of columnists and reporters from the *Plain Dealer*, the late *Cleveland Press*, and the even-later *Cleveland News* were unwitting but important partners in the project.

This volume would not have been possible without the Western Reserve Historical Society's superb local history collection, nor Cleveland State University's marvelous archives from the *Cleveland Press*, nor CSU's massive microfilm collection of *Plain Dealer* editions going all the way back to the 1800s.

A half-century's worth of media guides from the Browns, Cavaliers, and Indians: priceless.

Joe Horrigan and Pete Fierle at the Pro Football Hall of Fame in Canton were nice enough to crack open their archives.

One Internet site offered an incredible collection of meticulously compiled baseball statistics, including game-by-game results and box scores dating to 1871. The site, www.retrosheet.org, was a lifesaver for several chapters. (Per the group's request: "The play-by-play information used here was obtained free of charge from and is copyrighted by Retrosheet. Interested parties may contact Retrosheet at 20 Sunset Road, Newark, DE 19711.") Additional online sources included BaseballLibrary.com and ESPN.com.

The following books also were valuable resources:

Cavs: From Fitch to Fratello, by Joe Menzer and Burt Graeff
Cleveland, The Best Kept Secret, by George E. Condon
Cleveland's Greatest Fighters of All Time, by Jerry Fitch
Covering All the Bases, by Lou Boudreau and Russell Schneider
Don't Knock the Rock, by Gordon Cobbledick
Fumble! The Browns, Modell and the Move, by Michael G. Poplar and James A. Toman
Off My Chest, by Jim Brown and Myron Cope
Sam, Sipe, & Company, by Bill Levy
Sports in Cleveland: An Illustrated History, by John J. Grabowski
The Ballparks, by Bill Shannon and George Kalinsky
The Official NBA Encyclopedia, edited by Zander Hollander and Alex Sachare
The Killer in the Attic, by John Stark Bellamy II
Unguarded and *The Curse of Rocky Colavito*, by Terry Pluto

A story by Jack DeVries in a 1993 *Game Face* magazine helped fill some gaps in Indians history of the mid-20th century. So did an excellent videotape, a WVIZ (Channel 25) special called *Indian Summers: Cleveland Baseball Memories*.

Past and present colleagues at the *Beacon Journal* gave me the psychological and bureaucratic support I needed to take on this project. Chief among them were Jim Crutchfield, Thom Fladung, Jan Leach, Mitch McKenney, John Murphy, Debra Adams Simmons, Mariedna Taylor, Scott Thomas, Phil Trexler, and Craig Webb. Help with the newspaper's photo archives came from Linda Golz, Norma Hill, Diane Leeders, Susan Kirkman, Phil Masturzo, Lindsay Semple and Ed Suba, Jr..

Chris Andrikanich, Clarence D. Meriweather, and the rest of the gang at Gray & Company were right on top of things again.

And, as usual, the Indians' media folks were awesome, especially Curtis Danburg, Bob DiBiasio, Susie Giuliano, and Bart Swain. I'm also grateful for the long-ago services of Kevin Byrne and Nate Wallack of the old Browns, Bob "Bingo" Price of the Cavs, and Dino Lucarelli of the 1970s Indians and, later, the now-defunct Cleveland Stadium Corporation.

Past and present broadcasting mavens Nick Anthony, Les Levine, Larry Morrow, Bill Needle, Jeff Phelps, Denny Schreiner, and Bob Stevens offered help and/or encouragement for this project.

Still more information was gathered through firsthand interviews over the years with the players themselves, including Sandy Alomar, Mike Baab, Lenny Barker, Buddy Bell, Bobby Bonds, Austin Carr, Jim Chones, Dennis Eckersley, Bob Feller, Travis Fryman, Bob Golic, Mel Harder, Mike Hargrove, George Hendrick (really! he talked to me when he wasn't talking to anyone—I still don't know why), Orel Hershiser, Willis Hudlin, Mike Johnson, Duane Kuiper, Rick Manning, Clay Matthews, Sam McDowell, Larry Nance, Dave Logan, Reggie Rucker, Brian Sipe, Paul Shuey, Jim Thome, Nate Thurmond, Jaret Wright, and my little buddy, Omar Vizquel.

In the name of full disclosure, small portions of this book have already seen print. To wit:

Much of the information about Brian Sipe that appears in the chapter called "Red Right 88" is based on a story by the author that appeared in the *Akron Beacon Journal*'s Sunday magazine on August 21, 1988.

Much of the chapter called "Last Dance with a Great Lady" first appeared under the author's byline in a special section of the *Akron Beacon Journal* published December 1, 1996. Other parts of that chapter were adapted from a *Beacon Journal* story by the author that ran on April 1, 2001.

Portions of this book's chapters on the 1995 and 1997 Indians were imported from the author's book *Omar!*, written in 2001 with Tribe shortstop Omar Vizquel. Part of the 1995 chapter was drawn from an article by the author that appeared in the March 27, 1994, edition of *Beacon Magazine*. Parts of the 1997 chapter were drawn from his articles that appeared that season in the *Beacon Journal*.

Some paragraphs in the chapter about Earnest Byner's fumble were taken from *Akron Beacon Journal* stories written by the author during a 10-day assignment in Denver in 1988.

Some of the information about Nate Thurmond in the "Miracle

of Richfield" chapter was taken from an article by the author printed in the *Sunday Beacon Magazine* on November 26, 1989.

Some descriptions in the chapter about the Browns' last game at Cleveland Stadium were taken from the author's reporting on December 18, 1995.

Part of the chapter about the 1920 Indians was lifted from a story about League Park written by the author for the April 1, 2001, edition of the *Beacon Journal*.

Large portions of the chapter on the National Air Races were adapted from stories by the author that appeared in the *Beacon Journal* on August 29, 1993, and February 7, 1999. Valuable background information for that chapter was gleaned from Bellamy's book *The Killer in the Attic*.

Most of the information for the actual play-by-play description of Johnny Kilbane's championship fight was drawn from a *Plain Dealer* report published February 23, 1912.